HOW TO WIN AT OTHELLO ®

HOW TO WIN AT Othello®

GORO HASEGAWA with Maxine Brady

A HARVEST/HBJ BOOK

First Harvest/HBJ edition published September 1977

ISBN 0-15-642215-8
Library of Congress Catalog Card Number 77-5259
Printed in the United States of America

JOVE PUBLICATIONS, INC.
(Harcourt Brace Jovanovich)
757 Third Avenue, New York, N.Y. 10017

Acknowledgments

The authors wish to express their appreciation to the following for their help in the preparation of this book:

Yoko Macnow, for her invaluable editorial assistance on the original manuscript.

Gabriel Industries, Inc. manufacturers of Othello in the United States, for their enthusiastic cooperation.

CONTENTS

Foreword 9
Introduction 10

I. Learning to Play 12
Setting up the board; some general rules to keep in mind; how to move, outflank, and flip discs; a bit about strategy and scoring; how to use the diagrams in this book.

II. The Opening Stage 27
Strategy and tactics for the first to the 20th move; the all-important Basic Diagram with the key to square values; advantages and dangers of the various positions on the board; some problems for you to solve.

III. The Middle Stage 100
Tactical alternatives for the 21st to the 40th move; the question of keeping a balanced number of discs; how to avoid a forced move or trap your opponent into one; the devious 17-disc strategy.

IV. The Final Stage 188
The 41st move to the 60th move, where the board can change dramatically; how strategy differs here from other stages of the game; how to make the "great reversal" work in your favor.

FOREWORD

I am delighted to welcome new players to the fun and challenge of Othello. All you need to play Othello is a few minutes of study and your own natural intelligence.

Some people play Othello just for fun, while others take the game very seriously. In Japan we have annual championship matches, with thousands of players, and I understand that tournaments are now being held in the United States. Should you play Othello in competition or just for fun, good luck!

Let me say a few words to those of you who want to learn to improve your play. The best Othello players enjoy the challenge of using their common sense to outwit their opponents. They are good at creating plans and strategies, and then throwing them away and creating new plans when the old ones no longer work. There are no dice or "lucky cards" in Othello. To win you need judgment, wit, and finesse. Naturally, it also helps if your opponent makes an occasional mistake.

A game of Othello usually takes from fifteen to thirty minutes. It is easy to learn, yet very profound. It is also a game of infinite possibilities: Often it isn't possible to tell who's winning until the last few moves.

So happy reading, and happy playing.

Goro Hasegawa
Tokyo, Japan

INTRODUCTION

Othello is a paradox. You can learn the basic rules in only a few minutes, yet experts spend years perfecting their technique. Beginners have fun playing their very first game, while experienced players often go for hours in a series of games without stopping. And unlike many games, it's even fun for an advanced player to play against a beginner.

Othello? No, you may not know much about it. It hasn't been around very long, but in its short life it's made quite an impression on those who've tried it. Perfected in 1971 in Tokyo by Mr. Goro Hasegawa, the game quickly became a national craze in Japan, where it seems to be played anywhere and everywhere: in small factories between co-workers or in giant sports stadiums with ten thousand eager contestants. Or wherever two players get together.

Exported to the United States and then to Europe, Othello tournaments are springing up everywhere, and the game is quickly joining such popular pastimes as chess, bridge, and backgammon as one of the most exciting games around—in the tournament hall, the living room, or the college dorm.

Action and Suspense

No matter how much experience you have, once a game of Othello gets under way, whether with rank beginners, national champions, or anyone in between, the tension begins to mount. White seems to be winning. Black moves. White solidifies his position. Then Black innocently puts down a disc—and the whole board goes crazy!

Suddenly a large section of the board now belongs to Black! White moves desperately, trying to stem the tide. Black smugly puts down another disc—

and it's an error! Black wins a disc but loses the whole offensive. White sees the advantage, and a whole group of discs flips over, this time to White's color. Back and forth, each player strives for that final advantage, the key play that will decide the winner.

You can play Othello for fun, looking at each move as it comes, just enjoying the excitement. Or you can take it seriously, planning advance strategies, foreseeing possibilities, scheming and plotting to outwit your opponent. Either way, this book will help.

Here's How

How to Win at Othello is written for players of different strengths and abilities. It begins with a section on the basic rules of the game, with examples of legal and illegal moves. If you're a beginner, learn this section and you're ready to play your first games. If you're an experienced player, glance at the rules. You may find some fine points you aren't sure of!

The rest of the book discusses strategies to improve your play. Othello games can be divided into three stages: the opening, the middle, and the final stage. For each stage you'll find a full chapter, explaining the key points to watch out for, what to do—and what *not* to do—during that part of the game, and discussions of how to achieve your goals.

Hundreds of diagrams illustrate the positions being discussed, and many of the examples come from actual tournament games, with annotations by Othello's inventor and by many of the world's finest players.

To learn the game most effectively, set up your board and follow the diagrams and discussions. Then apply what you've learned, and watch your game improve. But remember to stop, once in a while. Othello can be habit-forming.

Maxine Brady
New York, New York

LEARNING TO PLAY

Contents

Each Othello set comes with a 64-square board and a set of special discs. Each disc is black on one side and white on the other. The squares of the board are all the same color, and they are separated by lines. There are four dots on the board, too. They are there to help you keep track of locations on the board.

When you put down each disc, it's important to keep in mind how close it is to the edge of the board or to a corner. It's also important to keep track of where your opponent is putting his discs. The dots help you keep track of locations. They also make it easier to find a square when you're studying a game in this book or playing it for yourself. Finally, the dots help you see which moves were good and which were not!

The Object of the Game

To win a game of Othello, the majority of the discs on the board must be your color. After each move, many discs may be flipped to the opposite color. Sometimes it's very difficult to tell who the winner will be until the last move has been made. But it doesn't matter how many discs a player has in the beginning or the middle of the game; all that counts is what the board looks like after the last move. The player who has the largest number of discs showing his color is the winner.

How to Begin

Choose either black or white as your color. (Flip a coin if you prefer. If you play more than one game, switch colors for each game.) Then each player takes 32 discs.

Set up the board. Black places two black discs diagonally in the center of the board; White places two white discs near them to form the pattern shown in Diagram 1. Every game begins with this same setup.

Black always moves first.

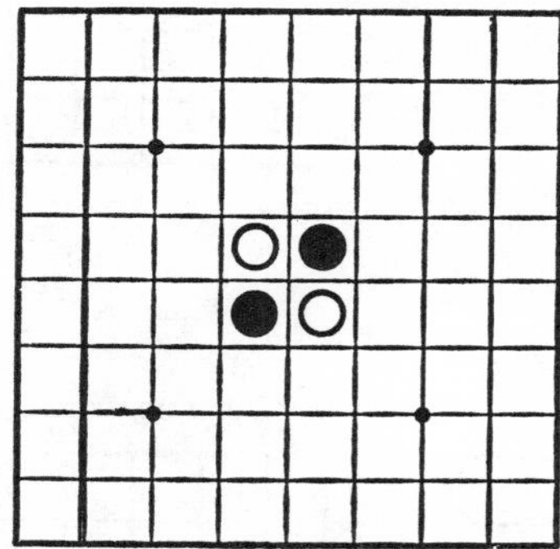

Diagram 1

How to Move

Every time you move, you must *outflank* one or more of your opponent's discs, and then turn that disc or discs over to your color. Turning a disc is called *flipping*.

To outflank a disc, place your disc on a square so that your opponent's disc is in between your new disc and another disc of your color.

Suppose you're White:

Disc A was already on the board with a black disc next to it.

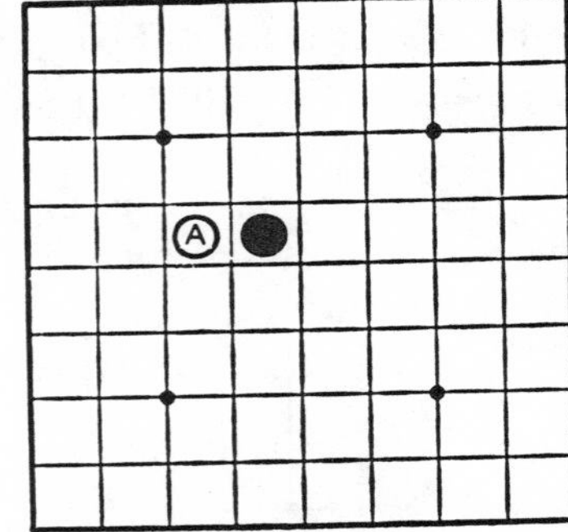

Diagram 2

Diagram 3

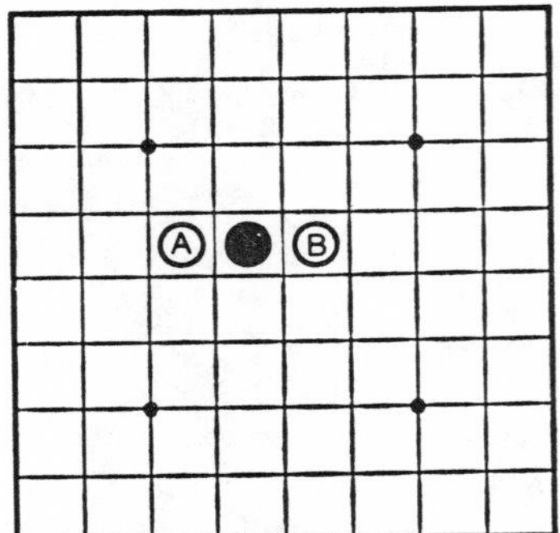

Now you put down disc B and outflank Black.

Diagram 4

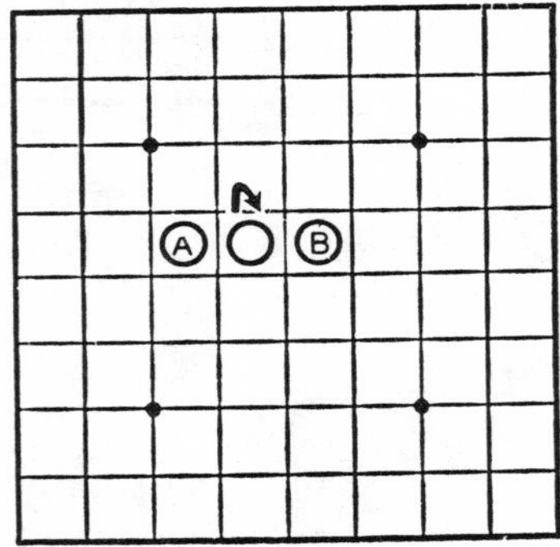

Don't stop yet! Remember to flip over the black disc to your color.

All About Outflanking

1. A disc may outflank any number of discs in one or more *rows*. A row is one or more discs in a *continuous* straight line. There cannot be any spaces or any discs of the opposite color breaking the continuity of the line.

LEGAL
Black can put down disc B and outflank the three white discs between A and B. The three white discs can now be flipped to black.

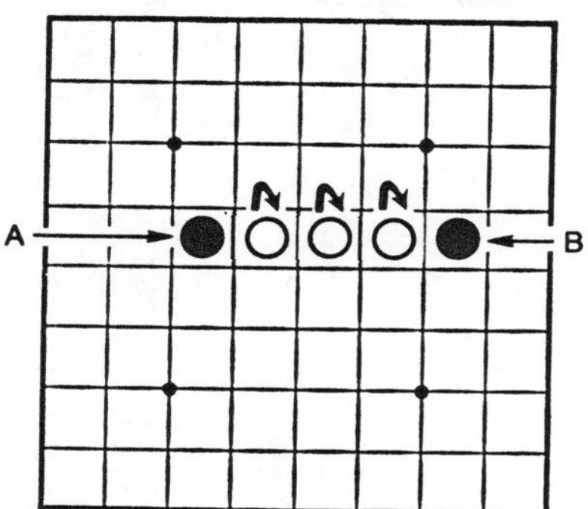

Diagram 5

ILLEGAL
Black *cannot* put disc B here. There is not a continuous line between A and B. The space gets in the way.

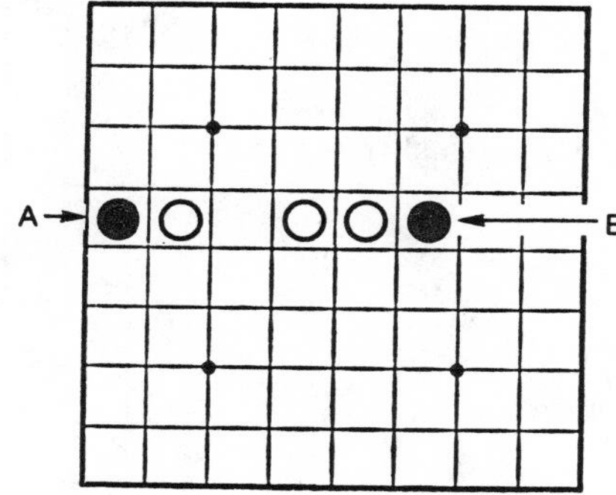

Diagram 6

2. A disc may not outflank other discs that are nearby but are not in the continuous row.

Diagram 7

Here's the position. It's White's turn.

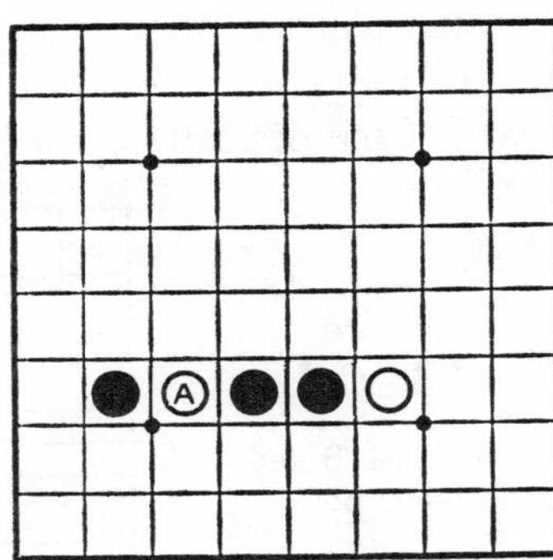

Diagram 8

White puts down disc B. It outflanks only *one* black disc—the disc between White's A and B.

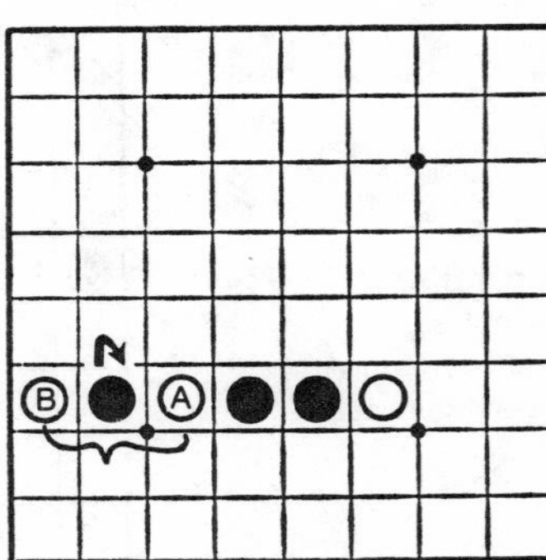

3. A disc may outflank any number of discs in any direction: horizontally, vertically, or diagonally.

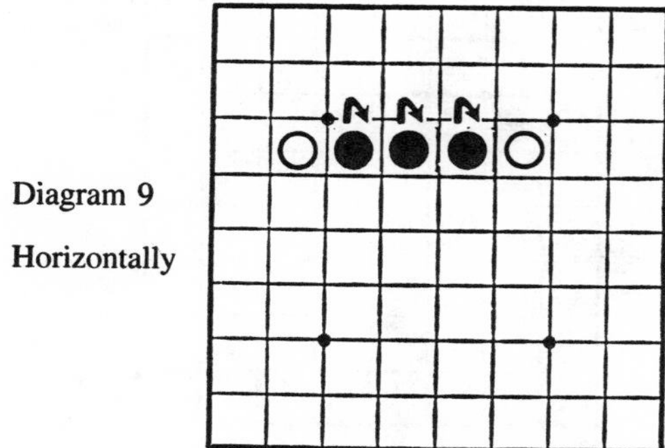

Diagram 9

Horizontally

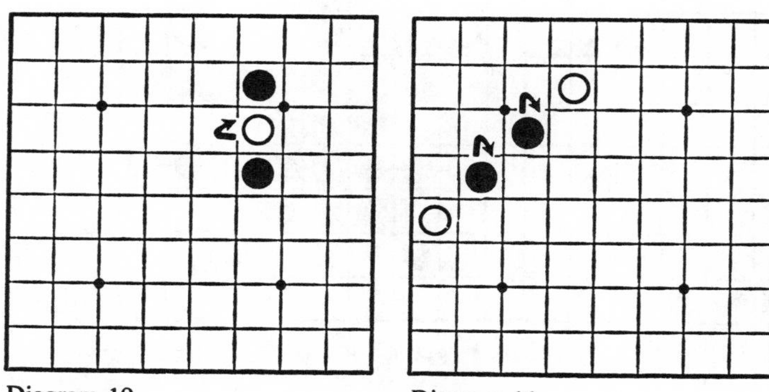

Diagram 10

Vertically

Diagram 11

Diagonally

A disc may outflank in any number of directions at the same time.

Diagram 12

White's C outflanks the black discs between B and C, and between A and C.

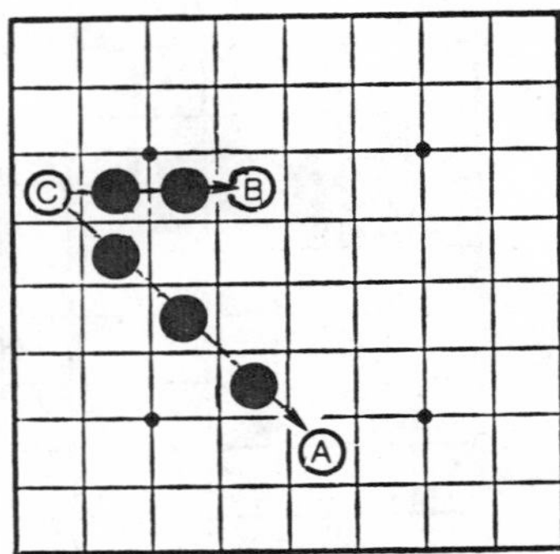

Diagram 13

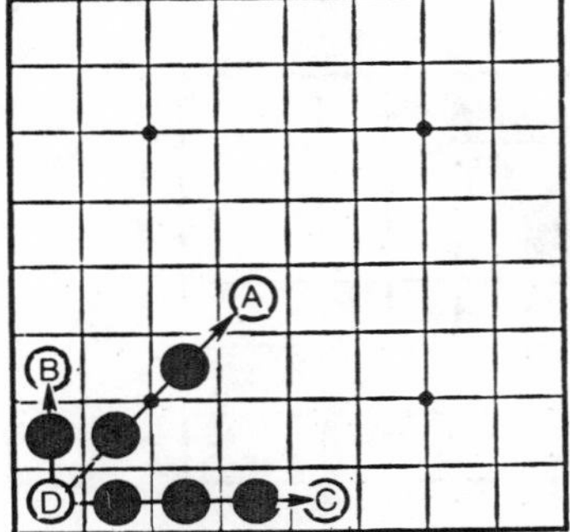

D outflanks the black discs between B and D, between A and D, and between C and D.

Diagram 14

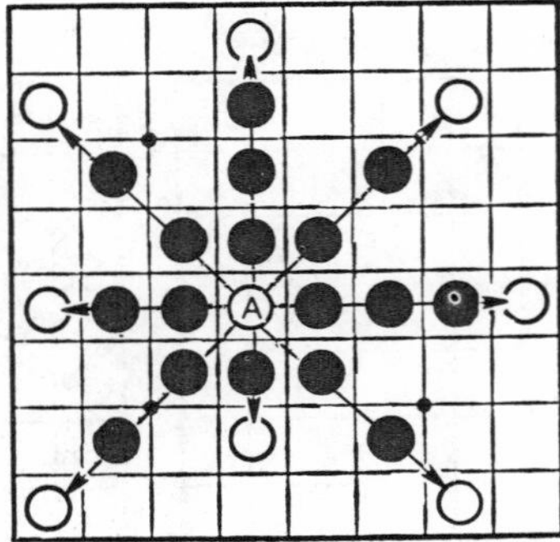

By putting down disc A, White outflanks Black's discs in eight directions.

But remember, a disc may only be outflanked as a *direct result of a move*, and it must be in the direct line of the disc placed down. (See Diagrams 7 and 8, also.)

Diagram 15

Black just put down disc A. Only the two white discs between A and B are outflanked by this move. They will be flipped.

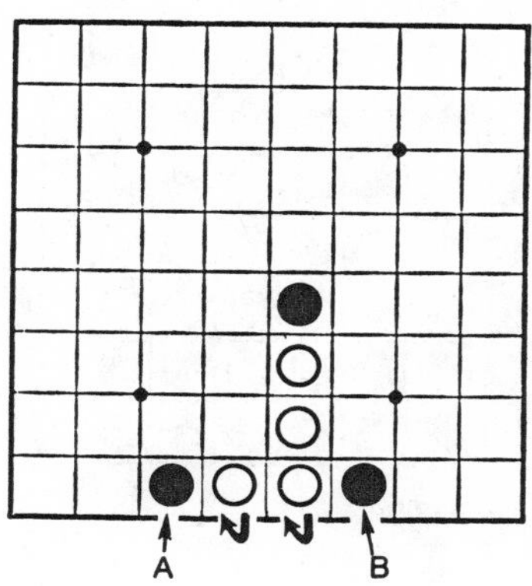

Diagram 16

But the other white discs would *not* be flipped, even though they look as though they're outflanked. They are not in a direct line of Black's disc A.

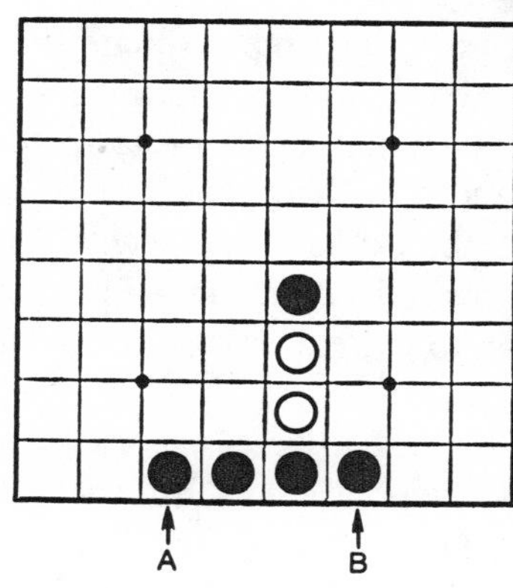

Here's an example of how three-way flanking can win a game that seems lost.

Diagram 17

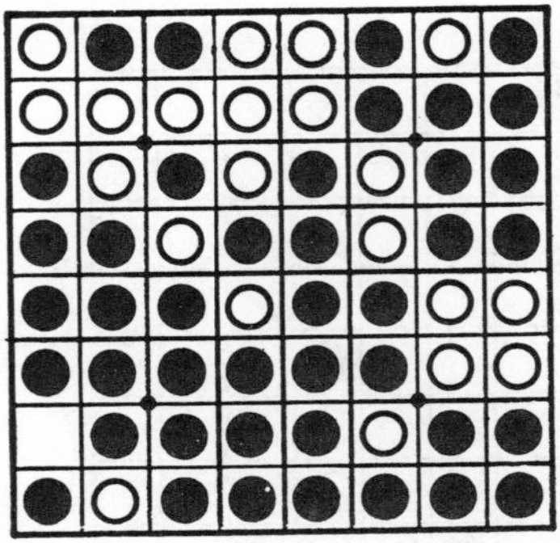

Black is winning with 42 discs. White has only 21 discs. But. . .

Diagram 18

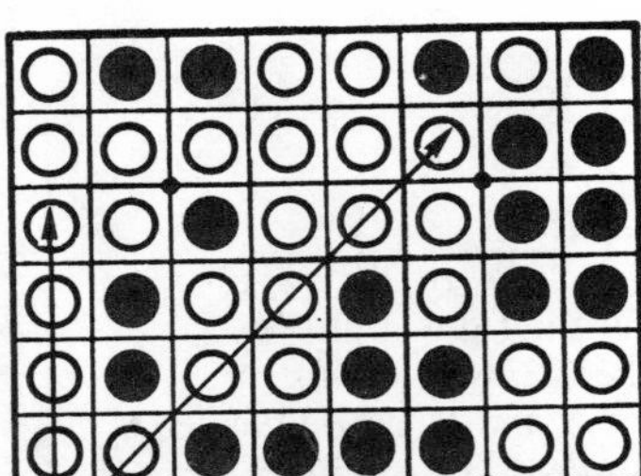

now Black has only 29 discs! White is the winner, with 35 discs.

In Diagram 17 there are 42 black discs against 21 white, with one more space left. Do you think Black has won? It certainly looks that way. But wait! Black cannot go to the empty square because he cannot outflank any white discs. He must pass. So White takes the square and captures 13 black discs (4 vertically, 5 diagonally, and 4 horizontally). White now has 35 discs to Black's 29, and it is White's victory.

Note that the black disc at the lower left-hand corner remains unturned. It is good to remember that discs in the four corners can never be captured. There's simply no way to place a disc on the outside of a corner. The corner is as far out as you can go.

Because of this, if a player captures a corner, he keeps it for the rest of the game. That's fine, if it's you. But try to prevent your opponent from gaining possession of the corners. These valuable squares assume more and more importance as the game progresses, and taking a corner near the end of the game can mean the difference between winning and losing.

Some General Rules

If you can't outflank and flip at least one opposing disc, you can't move. You forfeit your turn, and the other player moves again. This can happen several turns in a row, but each time your opponent moves, the board changes. As soon as you can outflank one or more discs again, you can make another move.

If a player runs out of discs, but still has an opportunity to outflank an opposing disc, the opponent must give the player a disc to use. This can happen as many times as the player needs and can use a disc.

Once a disc is placed on a square, it can never be moved to another square. Its color may change as it is flipped back and forth, but its position may not change until the game is over.

You *must* flip all discs that were outflanked in a move, even if it is to your advantage not to flip some of them.

If a player flips a disc which should not have been flipped, he must correct the mistake immediately, before his opponent moves. Once the other player moves, the mistake cannot be corrected, and the discs must remain as they are.

End of the Game

A game is over when it is impossible for either player to move. Sometimes this happens when the discs are used up and the board is completely full. But it can happen when many squares are empty, if there are just no discs that can be outflanked by either player.

Scoring

To find the winner of a game, count the number of discs each player has on the board after the game is over. The player with the most discs wins.

To find the winner's score, subtract the smaller number of discs from the larger number. For example, suppose:

Black has 44 discs
White has 20 discs

44 black
-20 white

Black wins with a score of 24 points.

(For more advanced ways of scoring, see Appendix A.)

Strategy

A game of Othello usually goes through three stages:

the opening stage—the first move to the 20th move.
the middle stage—the 21st move to the 40th move.
the final stage—the 41st move to the 60th move.

During each stage of the game, different parts of the board become more or less important. At the beginning, for example, much of the play will be located around the center squares. As more squares become filled with discs, the focus moves outward, to the edges and the corners. As you play, always keep two things in mind: which squares should you try to control (by outflanking your opponent and flipping the discs to your color) and which squares should you try to keep your opponent from controlling? When you have several possible moves, remember these two questions before you decide where to go.

Plan Ahead

Decide on a plan at the very beginning of the game, and work toward it. Often you will have several possible moves. Whenever you can, choose the move that will help you gain control of key squares or important areas of the board. The last few moves of Othello can dramatically change the balance of power and change large areas of the board from one color to the other. But what you do in the opening and middle stages of the game is very important. The moves you make then can give you control of key positions and increase your chances of winning in the final stage.

Be Flexible

When the game does not go the way you planned, be ready to switch to different tactics. The more you play and study Othello, the more you will be able to depend, to a certain degree, on your intuition. And the more you learn to look ahead ("If I move here and flip this disc, then he'll probably move there. . ."), the more you can anticipate your opponent's moves. But unexpected moves will happen, and when they do, stop for a moment to reconsider your original plan. Is it still a good plan? Maybe it is. Maybe you should continue to make moves with that original plan in mind. Or maybe the situation on the board has changed things, so that you should make a new plan and make your moves with that new goal in mind.

How to Use the Diagrams

You'll find several different kinds of diagrams of the Othello board in this book.

Diagram 19

This kind of diagram shows an actual position during a game. It shows where every disc is, and whether each disc is white or black at the time of the move that is being discussed. For example, this diagram shows what the board looked like after the 12th move. (Note: There are 16 discs on the board. The four center discs were used to set up the game. Only 12 moves have been made.)

Diagram 20

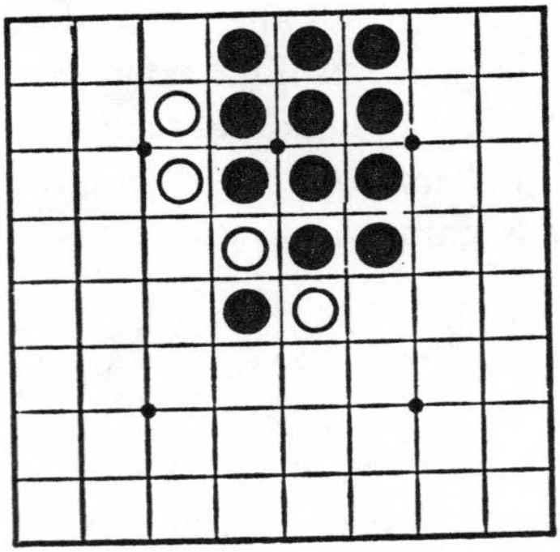

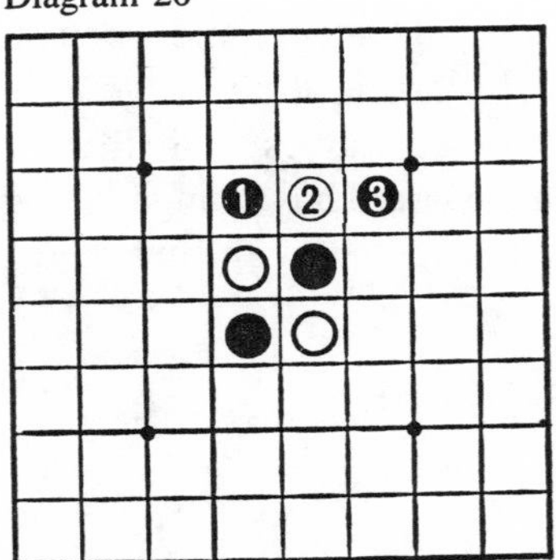

This kind of diagram shows what moves were made by each player. It does *not* show you what the board looked like after each move. In this example, there are 7 discs on the board. The four center discs, of course, were put down before the game began, so they are not numbered. Then Black moved first —the black disc with the number 1 in it shows you where he moved. The white disc with the number 2 in it was White's move, and then Black made the third move, shown by a black disc numbered 3.

To see what the board looked like after each move, you can follow the moves on your own Othello board. Or sometimes there will be several diagrams in a row, showing the way the board changed after each move. The three moves indicated in Diagram 20 would be shown like this:

Diagram 21

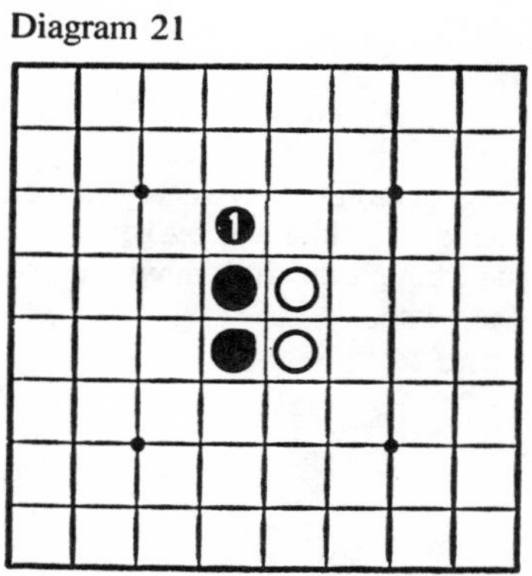

Position after Black made move 1.

Diagram 22

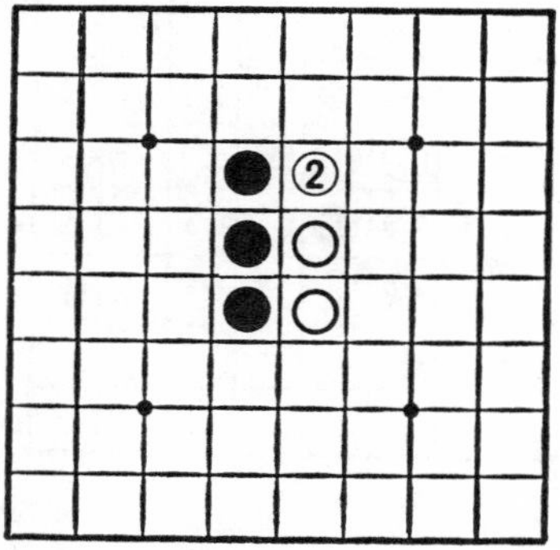

Position after White made move 2.

Diagram 23

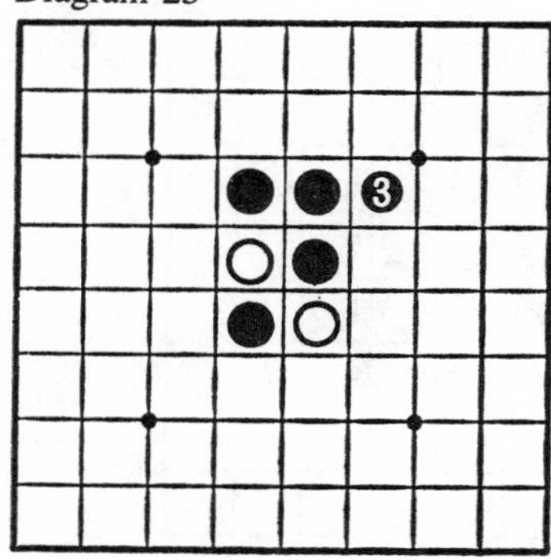

Position after Black made move 3.

Many times two diagrams will be shown. The first, like Diagram 20, will show you all of the moves made up to a certain point in a game. And the second diagram will show you what the board looks like at that point.

		15					
		10	14				
		3	13	12	11	18	
		4			2		
		5			1		
	6	7	8		9	16	17
		19					
			20				

Diagram 24

This diagram shows every move made by White and by Black up through the 20th move of the game.

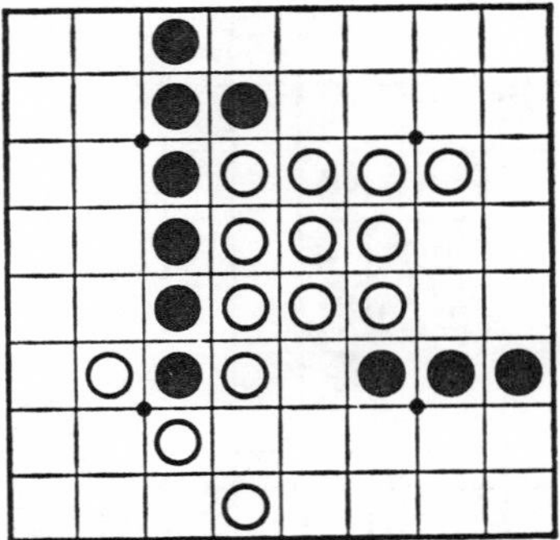

Diagram 25

And this diagram shows what the board looked like after the 20th move.

THE OPENING STAGE: THE FIRST MOVE TO THE 20TH MOVE

Now is the time to make your plan, to map out which areas of the board you're going to try to control. But how do you make a plan? And which squares should you try to fill with your color discs?

The Basic Diagram of Othello

Diagram 26 shows the Othello board with various symbols in the squares. This diagram allows you to consider the importance of each square of the board, so that you can plan your playing strategy, and so that you can figure out your opponent's plan. Throughout this book we'll refer back to this diagram, as we discuss which squares are important to capture, or to avoid, during the three stages of the game. But right now, let's apply the Basic Diagram to the first stage of the game.

Diagram 26

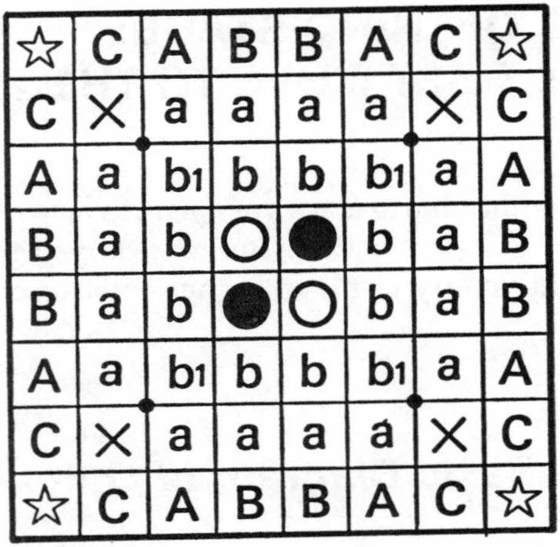

☆	C	A	B	B	A	C	☆
C	X	a	a	a	a	X	C
A	a	b1	b	b	b1	a	A
B	a	b	○	●	b	a	B
B	a	b	●	○	b	a	B
A	a	b1	b	b	b1	a	A
C	X	a	a	a	a	X	C
☆	C	A	B	B	A	C	☆

Key to Square Values in the Opening Stage

☆ Absolutely advantageous position.

X Position you must avoid.

A Good position (that is, a good base to operate from).

B Good position (comparable to **A**, depending on how the situation develops).

C Risky (danger, 70%; success, 30%).

a Position to be taken as a preliminary step toward a good position, such as **A** or **B**.

b The 12 squares within the four small dots on the board. There is no direct danger in any of the **b** positions, but they may limit your choice of moves and lead to the loss of strategic positions. In the opening stage moves to **b** must be made cautiously, while **b1** positions are key points.

Aim for ☆

Always aim for the corner positions because once you take a corner, your disc can never be captured by your opponent. See Diagrams 27 and 28. Black took a corner position as early as the 7th move of the game. This gives him an excellent chance of winning.

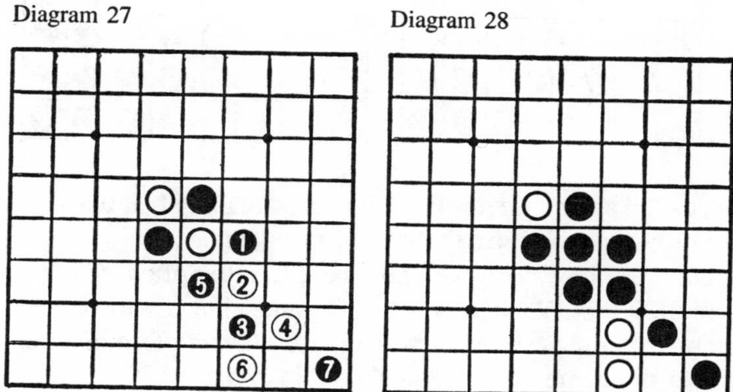
Diagram 27 Diagram 28

White had made the mistake of going to an **X** position. This is not just a bad move—it can be strategically fatal. In the opening stage, *never* move to an **X** square. Once the mistake was made, White's following move, going to the **A** position, could not save the situation.

Actually, an experienced player would not have made such a blunder. Unless you are playing with a real beginner, you cannot capture a corner so easily.

Diagrams 29 and 30 show how Black can eliminate White by operating from his corner base. Look at moves 9, 11, 13, and 15. Black is capturing White steadily, as if he were flaking away the white discs with a file. Such an

Diagram 29

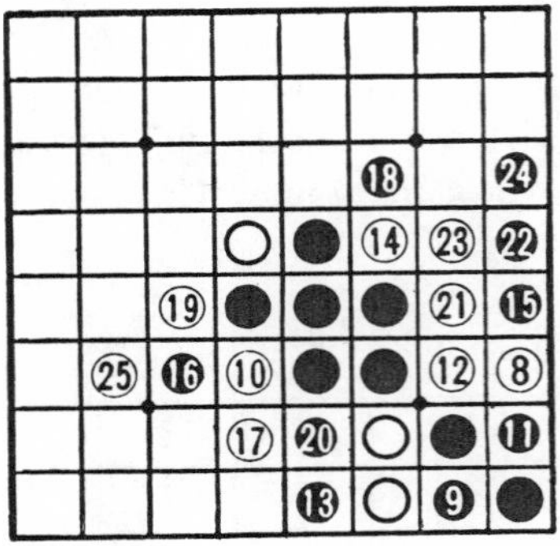

Diagram 30

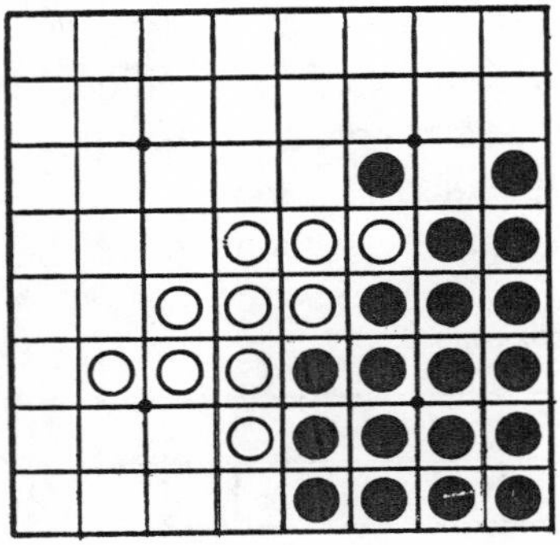

operation is called a *filing tactic*. If White keeps making bad moves, he could have virtually no discs left by the end of the game.

Such a total loss, however, does not take place too often. It is easy to see from Diagram 29 that Black will win this game, but it will be difficult for Black to capture all the white discs. Suppose players of equal strength and skill took over the game at the point shown in Diagram 29. Black probably would win, but the best he could do would be to win by a margin of 30 points.

Why not set up the board at the stage of Diagram 29 and see how it works out for you and your opponent?

Avoid X

In the opening stage of the game, your primary concern should be to take corner positions as quickly as possible. Ownership of a corner can help you gain permanent control of many squares. Obviously, then, try to prevent your opponent from capturing a corner. In most cases you give a corner position to your opponent when you move to an **X** position. Once you move to an **X** position, your opponent will concentrate on taking a corner, and you can rarely prevent it.

Therefore, the **X** position is taboo. But your opponent will not want to go there either. So while you're avoiding this pitfall, plan your strategy so that your opponent has nowhere but an **X** position to move to.

Below is an example of what happens when a player is forced into an **X** position.

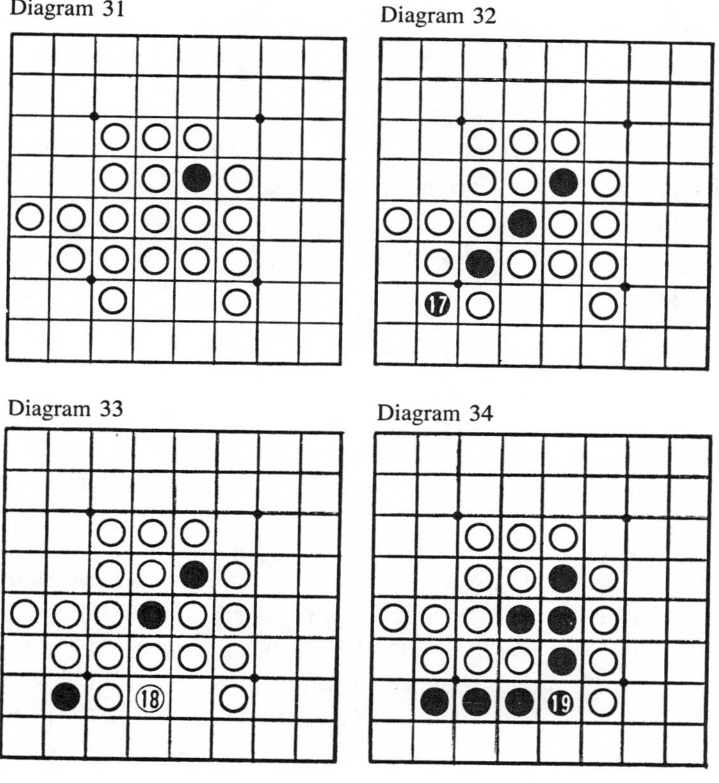

Diagram 35

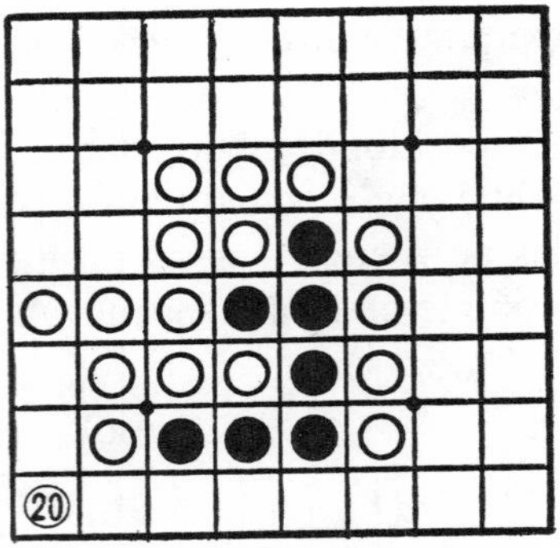

Diagram 31 is an example taken from an exhibition game. Black has the next move, and he has seven possible positions to move to. However, all except one position will lead to immediate defeat. The one position open is **X** (17 in Diagram 32).

The game proceeded as shown in Diagrams 32 through 35. Eventually Black suffered a complete defeat, and the reason is that he lost too many discs in the opening stage. He lost flexibility and was forced to move to the forbidden position **X**. This is called a *forced move*.

Go to A

How did Black get into the predicament of Diagram 31? He neglected to establish flexible bases of operation in the early stage of the game. Such bases are shown as **A**'s and **B**'s in the Basic Diagram.

The value of **A**'s and **B**'s depends on the situation, and you cannot favor one exclusively over the other. However, an early move to any of the **A** positions will not hurt you later on, whereas **B**'s have more delicate implications. Sometimes **B** moves are more advantageous than **A** moves, but occasionally **B**'s can prove to be harmful. You will have to weigh the possibilities, and only experience will give you the necessary insight.

A combination of the two positions can be strategically sound. Look at Black **A** in Diagram 36. If White moves to **C**, Black can go to the corner position. If White moves to **B2**, Black can move to **B1**, a strategic position. White will find it difficult to attack Black **A**, while for Black this is a flexible base.

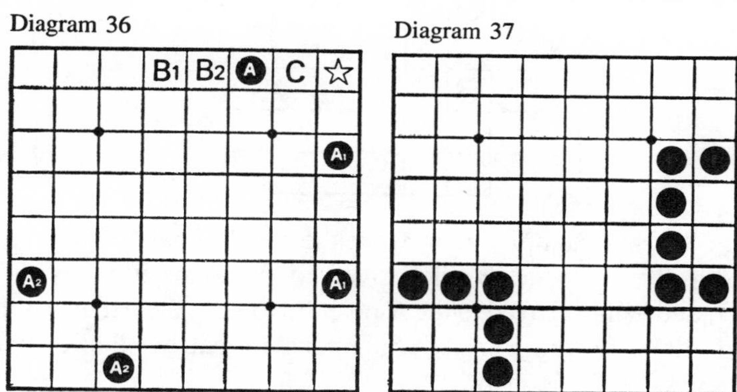

Diagram 36

Diagram 37

A combination of two **A**'s is particularly formidable. See the pair of **A1**'s and **A2**'s in Diagram 36. The ideal developments from these **A** positions are shown in Diagram 37.

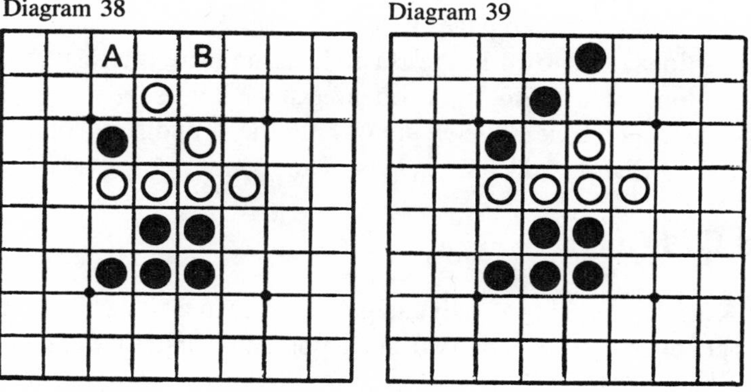

Diagram 38

Diagram 39

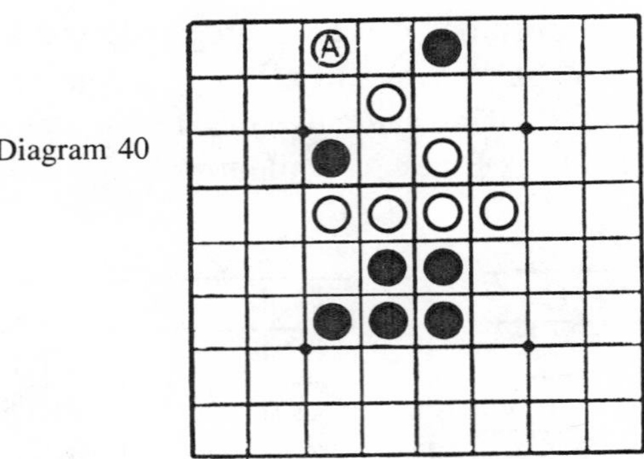

Diagram 40

Diagram 38 is an example taken from the men's finals of the All-Japan Championship Tournament. Black moved to the **B** position as shown in Diagram 39, and White moved to the **A** position to keep the balance of power.

See pages 42-47 for diagrams of championship matches that demonstrate the effectiveness of Position **A**.

The Advantage of the B Position

For a study of the timing of a move to the **B** position and a comparison of the values of **A** and **B** spots, see pages 61-83.

The **B** positions, as shown in the Basic Diagram, are interesting and you can do many things with them. In the opening stage it is usually a good idea to take a **B** position as a base. Ownership of both the **A** and **B** positions is very important in the middle and final stages of the game.

Position C is Risky

Although **A** and **B** positions are advantageous bases to take early in the game, if your opponent takes one or two such positions first, it does not mean immediate danger for you. But watch out for the moves he makes from his **A** or **B** bases; those following moves (which usually occur in the middle stage of the game) can be dangerous for you.

The **C** position is very different from the **A** or **B** positions. If you make an isolated move to a **C** position in the opening stage of the game, you are inviting disaster. No, it's not as bad as the **X** position, and in some operations the **C** position can be useful. But do not go to **C** without a plan. An isolated entry to the **C** position is very risky.

Diagram 41 illustrates the danger of this move. White made his 6th move to **C** and followed it up with thoughtless 8th and 10th moves. Black's skillful move 11 completed White's defeat.

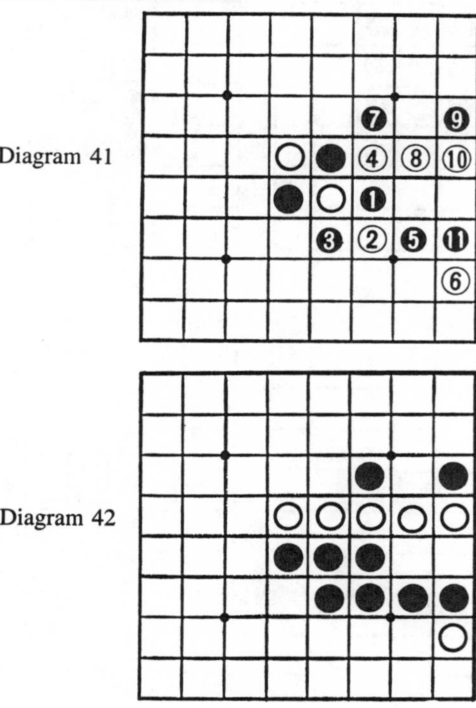

Diagram 41

Diagram 42

Another example is shown in Diagram 43. White took two **C** positions (14 and 16). Black's 17 was a lure, and White was taken easily because he was too eager to go to the **A** position (18). White could not see through Black's intention behind his 19th move, either, and White's 20th was a mediocre move. Black's 21 was a fatal blow to White (Diagram 46).

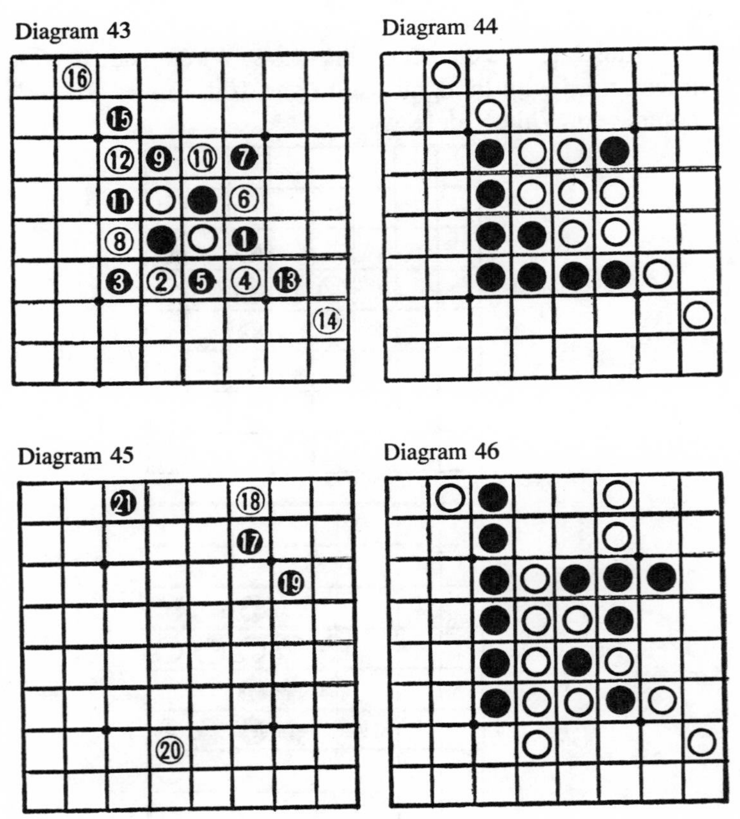

The diagrams below show how this game ended.

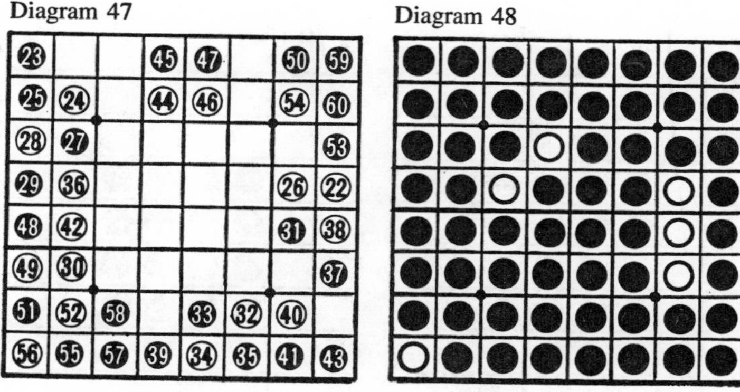

Diagram 47

Diagram 48

(Black's win, 52 points)

See page 84 for other examples of the dangers of a **C** move.

The a and b Positions as Stepping Stones

Look at the Basic Diagram again. We have studied the implications of the **A**, **B**, **C**, **X**, and corner positions. However, as you know, you cannot jump to these positions as you please. The rule says you must outflank your opponent's discs each time you make a move. The game of Othello starts in the middle of the board and spreads to the outer edges and corners through **a** and **b** positions; therefore the **a** and **b** positions are stepping stones, foundations for your operational plans.

Don't go to **a** and **b** positions at random. Try to think ahead: "If I move here, where will my opponent move?" Incidentally, this is a time when greediness can defeat you. Don't choose a move just because it outflanks the greatest number of discs. Make sure to leave yourself options, or a game can be finished within the **a** and **b** rows (Diagrams 49 and 50).

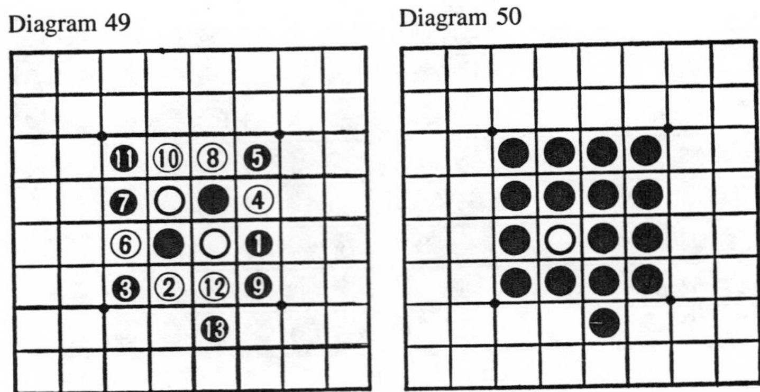

Diagram 49

Diagram 50

(Whichever way White goes, he will lose)

The See-Saw Stratagem

In the opening stage try to keep the board fairly balanced between black and white discs. Don't let yourself control too many discs: the more you own the more you can lose. And don't let your opponent control too many discs; you won't be able to move freely.

The Importance of the Opening Stage

To prove a point about the importance of the opening stage in Othello, a match was arranged between a Japanese businessman and Ms. Sachiko Shinozaki,

All-Japan Women's Champion. Mr. X, the businessman, was a competent player, but he doubted the need for concentrating on the opening stage.

"Even if you are at a disadvantage earlier, you can always turn the tide in the final stage of the game," he said. "I am very good in final-stage tactics. Concentrating on that alone, I have won twenty-four matches in a row in my company's Othello contests."

Beginners tend to think that way, but not usually someone as expert as Mr. X. In fact, many veteran players think the opening stage is the most important. Moves to **a** and **b** positions decide the future course of the game.

In the first game Mr. X (Black) made a strong move at the beginning. The opening stage was an even game. Since Mr. X had previously boasted of his strength in the final stage, we expected to see an interesting game throughout, but as early as the 26th move he had to make a forced move. After that he was powerless. At the end of the game there were only two black discs on the board.

"I didn't think I made particularly bad moves, but by the beginning of the middle stage I was against the wall," Mr. X said. "I was almost annihilated."

Although a game of Othello can be turned around with one move, if you keep making reckless moves against a skillful opponent in the opening stage, you won't be able to switch the situation in the middle stage. A second game between Mr. X (White) and Ms. Shinozaki (Black) simply proved again the theory that the opening stage is the most important in many ways. (For a step-by-step analysis see pages 42-47.)

Problems

Now that you have been introduced to some of the strategies of the opening stage of Othello, see if you are ready for middle-stage play. Test your skill with these problems and study the diagramed games that follow. Then you will be ready to move on.

Problem 1: This is a phase of a very intense battle in its middle stage. White has the next move. There is one very good move White can make which will assure his victory. What is it? (The solution follows Problem 2.)

Diagram 51

Problem 1
What is White's next move?

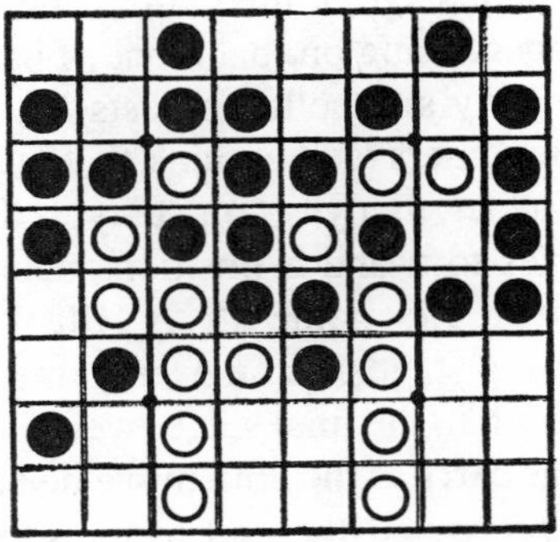

Problem 2: White has a somewhat unguarded formation. If Black made a clever attack, he would certainly win. Plan Black's strategy. What is the first move Black should make in order to carry out his strategy?

Diagram 52

Problem 2
What is Black's strategy?

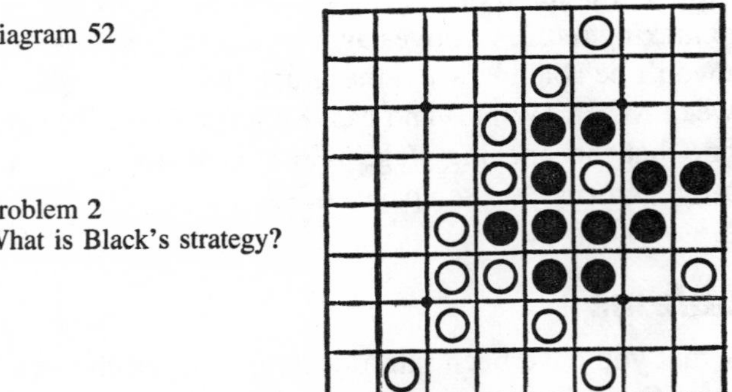

Solution to Problem 1: White should go to position 1 in Diagram 53. Black cannot prevent White from taking the corner position. If Black goes to the **B1**

position and captures White's 1, White can go to **B2**, then to the corner. (If you can assess a situation like this at a glance and make the right move, you are an advanced Othello player!)

Diagram 53

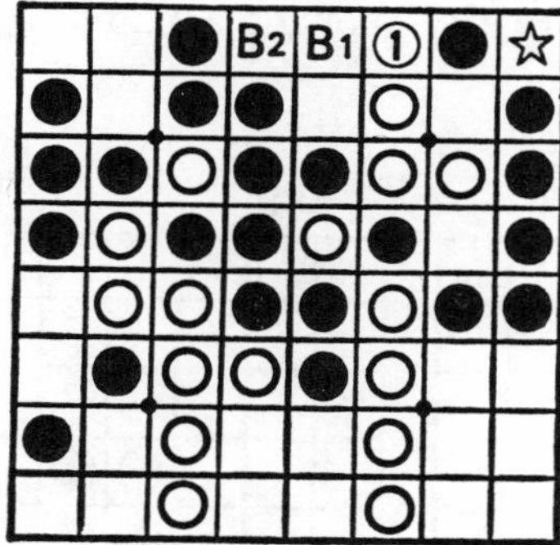

Solution to Problem 2: White has three empty squares between his **C** and **A**. This is a weak front, and Black should attack there and go to the **A1** position. Even if White captures it by moving to the **B2** position, Black can go to **B1** and capture the corner. At the point shown in Diagram 52, Black cannot go to **A1**. Therefore, prepare for the move by going to the 1 position in Diagram 54.

Diagram 54

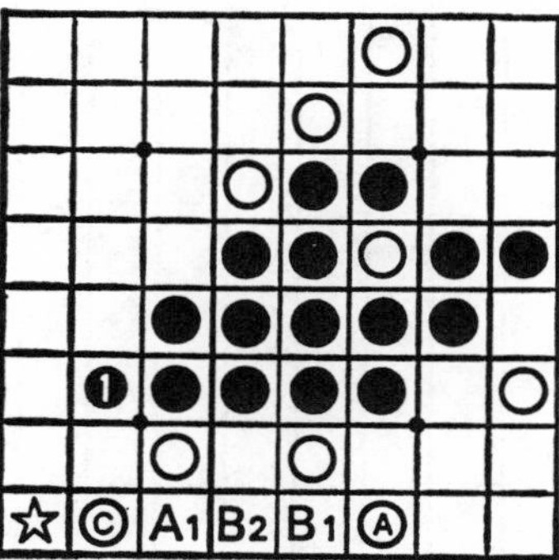

The Advantages of Position A

Diagrams 55 to 55-26 show the game played by Sachiko Shinozaki, the Japanese women's champion (Black), showing a masterful grasp of position **A** tactics.

Diagram 55: Game moves 1–26. How Black moved to **A** positions.

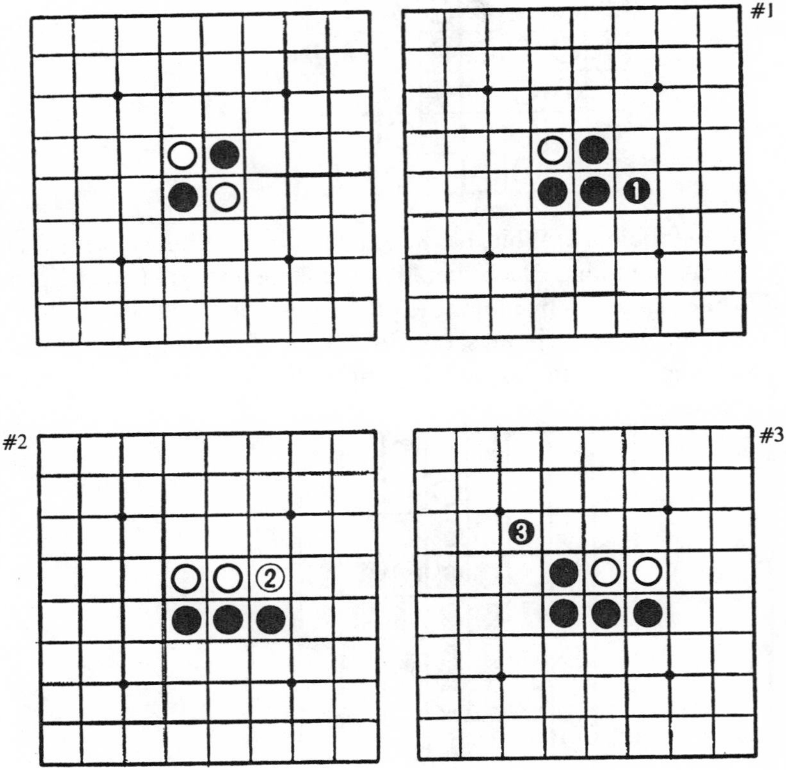

#1

#2

#3

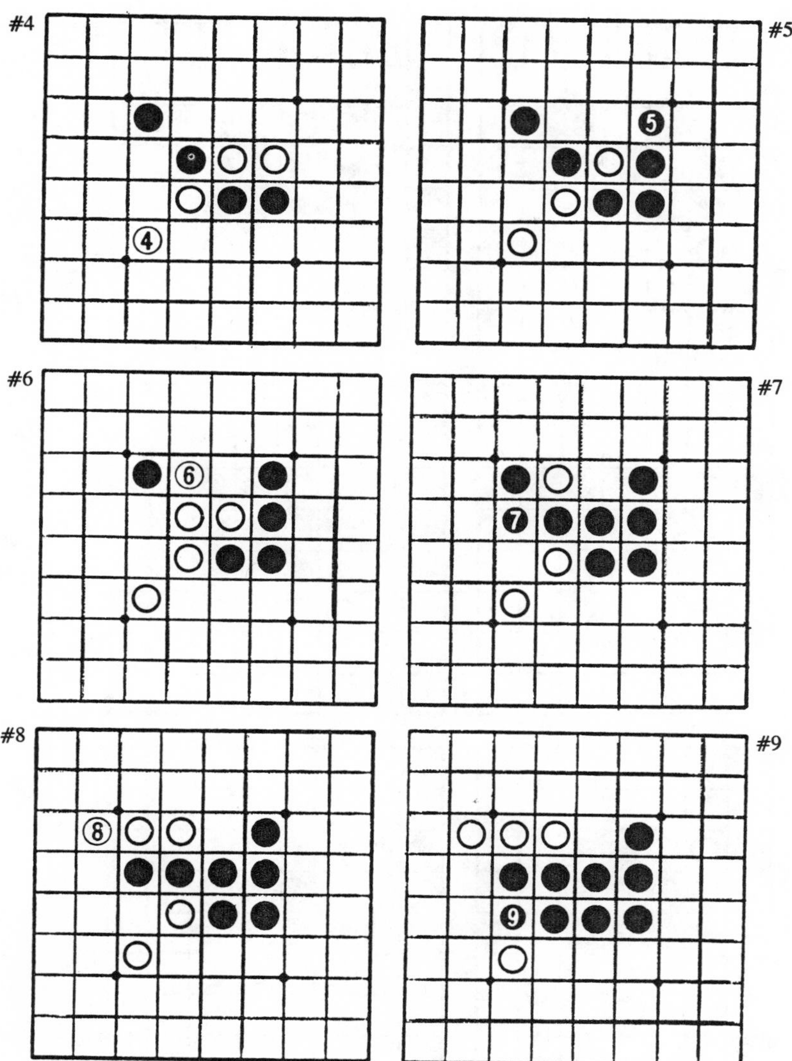
#4
4
#5
5
#6
6
#7
7
#8
8
#9
9

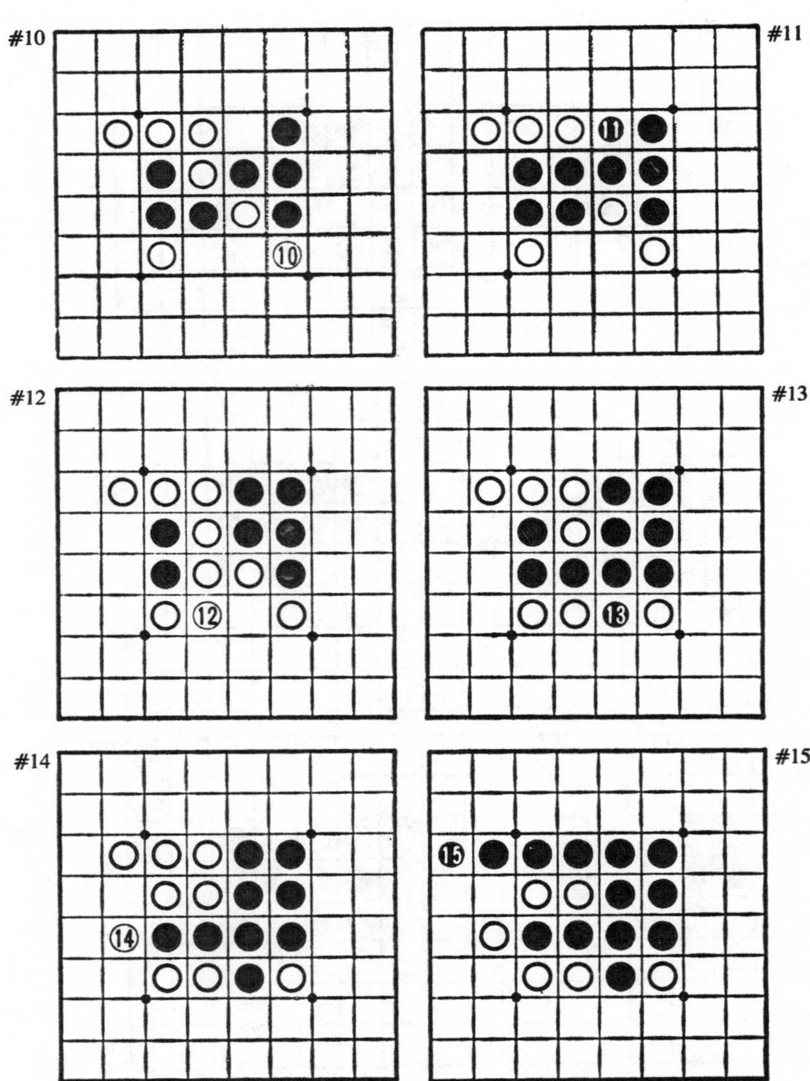
#10
10
#11
11
#12
12
#13
13
#14
14
#15
15

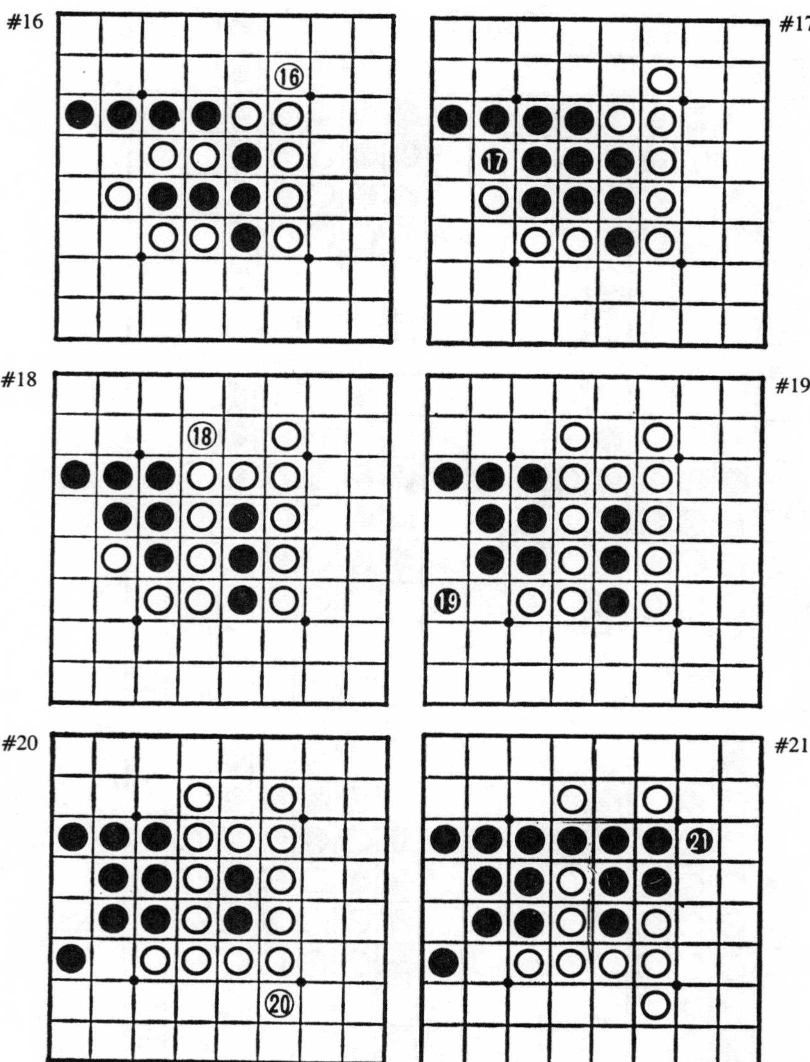
#16
16
#17
17
#18
18
#19
19
#20
20
#21
21

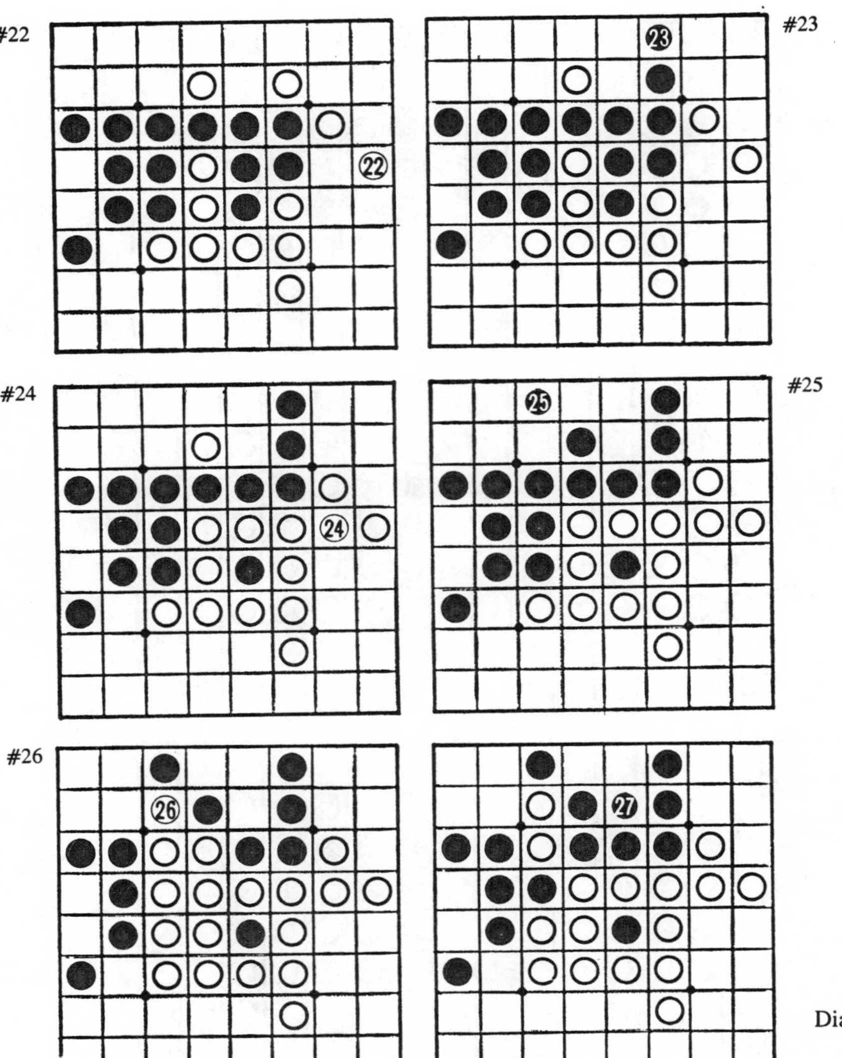

Diagram 56

Black quickly moved to key points, **b1**'s (3 and 5), then to 7, forcing White to an **a** position (8). Black's moves 9, 11, and 13 are skillful and speedy offensives, enabling her to reach an **A** position (15). Then her 17th move prevented White from getting a foothold, and 19 took another **A**, completing an ideal formation. By moving to 21 Black gave White a chance to go to a **B** position (22) but quickly retaliated in the 23rd and 25th moves, capturing two more strategic **A** positions. Black's victory is firmly assured at this point.

In Diagram 56 the game is already decided. Diagrams 57 and 58 show how it was fought and ended: Black wins by 59 discs.

Diagram 57

45	34		35	36		38	41
43	37					28	42
							47
30							
31						52	48
	29					56	53
33	32	40	39	54		58	57
46	49	50	44	51	55	60	59

Diagram 58

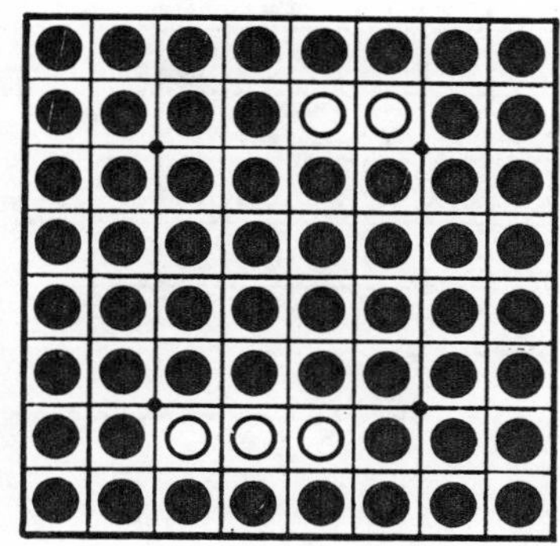

Ms. Shinozaki's forte is not only the position **A** tactics described above. In other games she allows her opponents to take **A** and **B** positions, only to upset their entire game plan later on. (For this she uses the famous 17-disc tactic, explained in the final chapter of this book.)

In order to go to **A** positions, you must make your opponent go to **a** positions first. One way to induce him to do so is to occupy all four **b1** positions, because in order to capture discs in **b1** positions your opponent must go to either **X** or **a**.

An X-cellent Example

In this tournament game title-holder Kaichiro Tsuji, playing White, forced his opponent into moving to an **X** square. Watch how White takes away all of Black's options until finally, on move 33, Black has no choice: he is forced to take the **X** position.

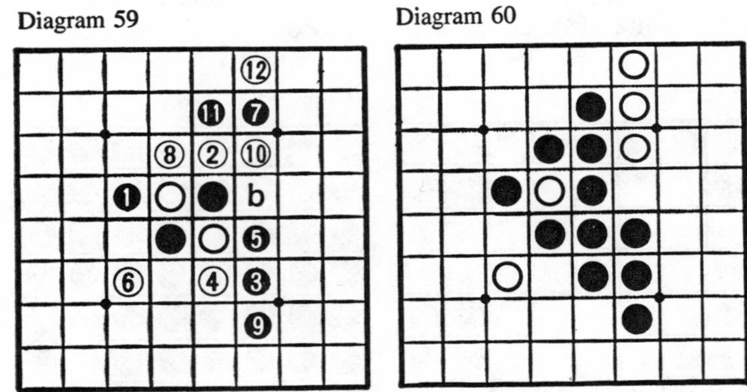

Diagram 59 Diagram 60

Black moves to 3, taking advantage of his lead, and the game progresses as follows:

- 4—a thoughtful move by White.
- 6—White takes a key position.
- 7—Black dares to go to an **a** position.
- 8, 10—the only moves possible if White wants the **b** positions.
- 11—a dubious move. The 11th move should have been made to a **b** position to keep up with the positive moves of 7 and 9. It is obvious that White will go to the **A** position (12), making 11 ineffective.

After Diagram 60 the game develops into a close battle, both players trying to establish good base points, capturing and recapturing discs to keep the balance of power. But White is constantly in the lead because he has a strategic base in position **A** which he captured quickly in the beginning, and eventually he ends the game in a victory.

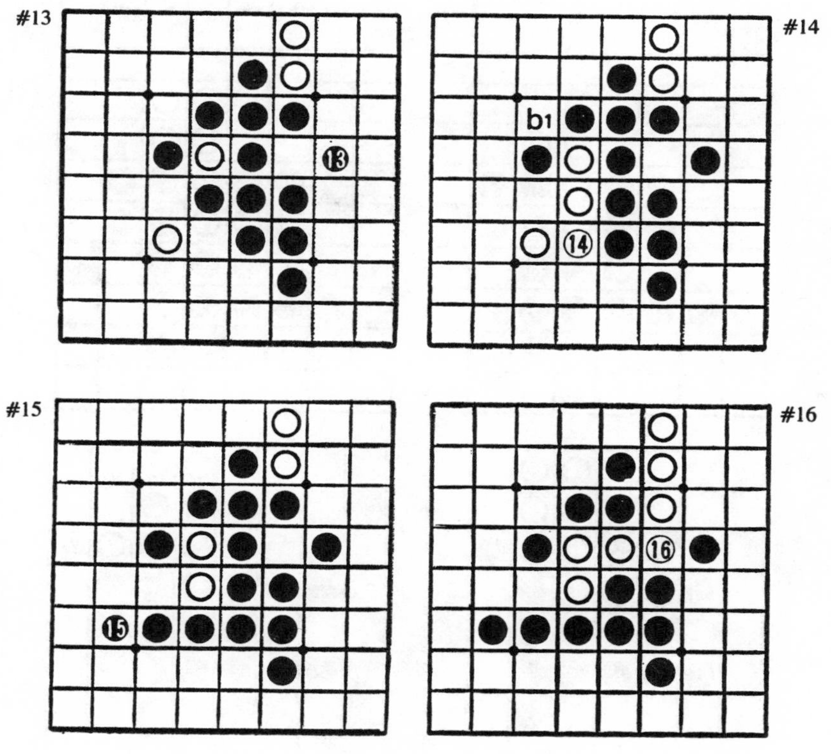

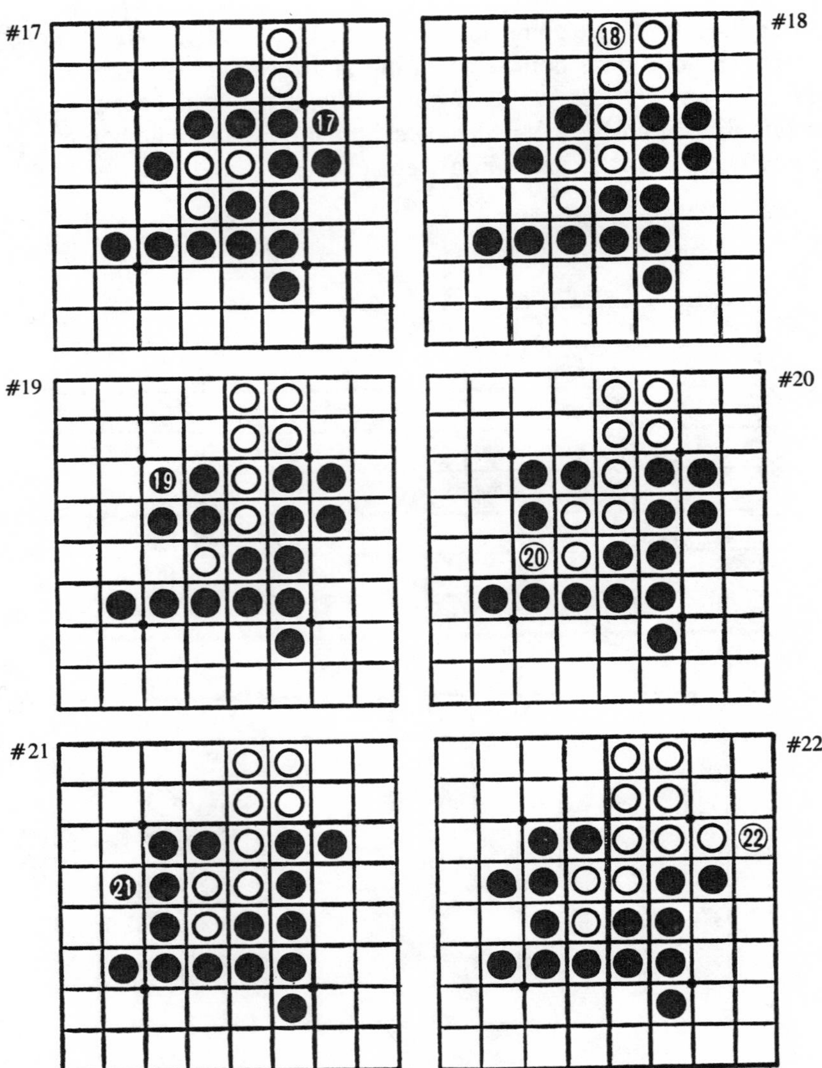
#17
17
#18
18
#19
19
#20
20
#21
21
#22
22

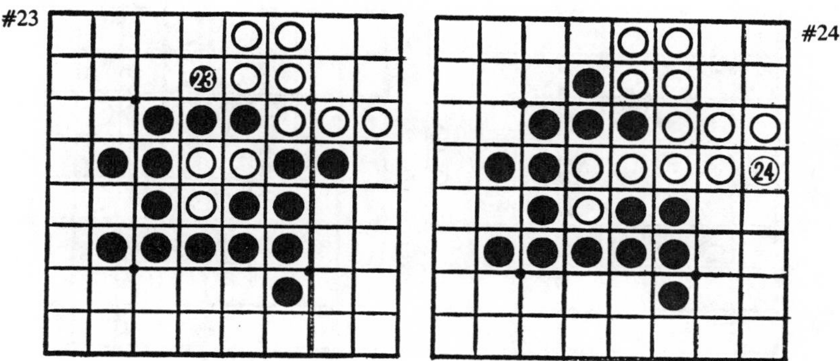

The 15th move upsets the balance of power. Black should have gone to a **b1** position. White's 20 is a good move. It will give him a definite lead. Black tries desperate resistance with 21 and 23, but White is unperturbed and makes move 24, closing in on Black.

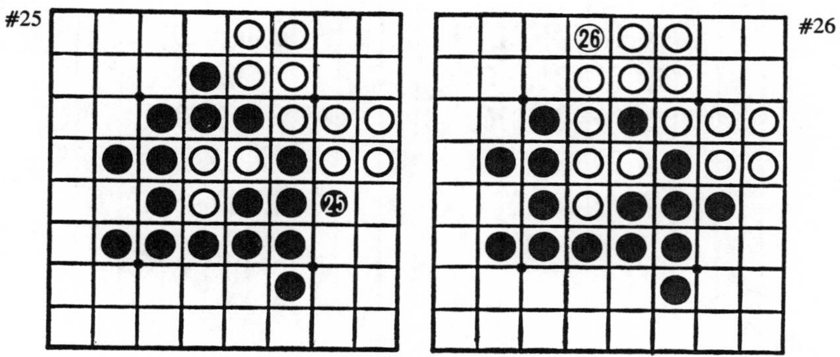

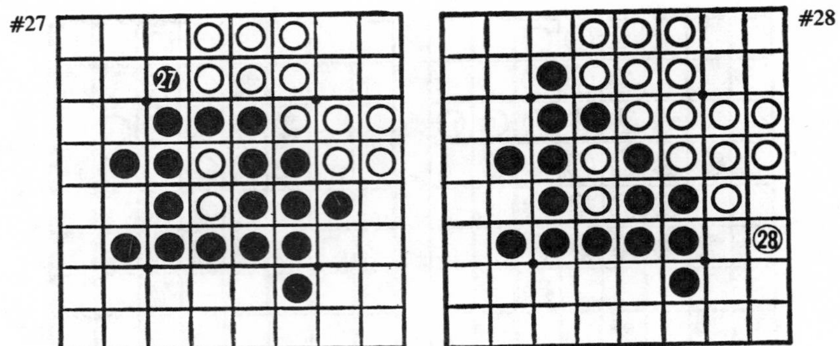

Moves 25 and 27 are Black's tenacious last stand. They may frustrate White a bit. . . .

But no! Move 28 is the champion's miraculous feat! It lures Black to 29—and *Pow!* 30! Black is indeed in a fine fix now.

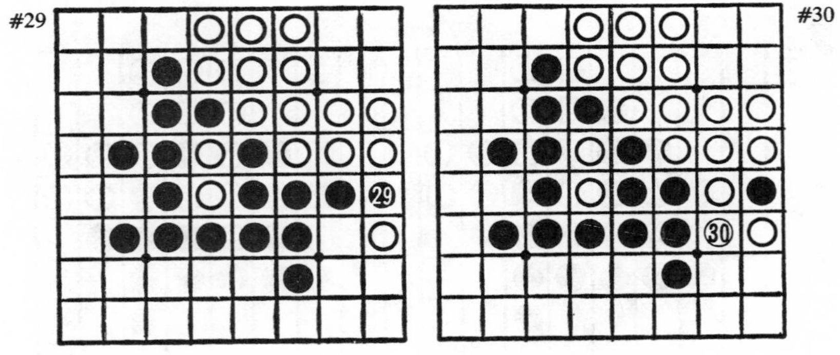

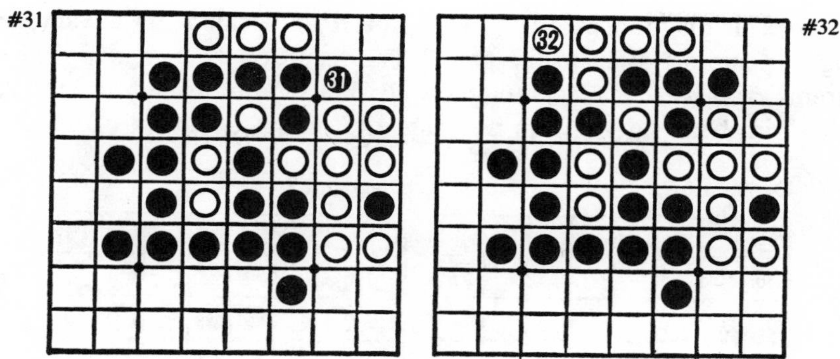

After Black's 31st move White goes to 32, pushing Black into 33 (a forced move into an **X** square). White's 34 does not help Black at all. Whether he moves to **C1** or **C2**, the coveted corner position is White's. White has definitely won this game.

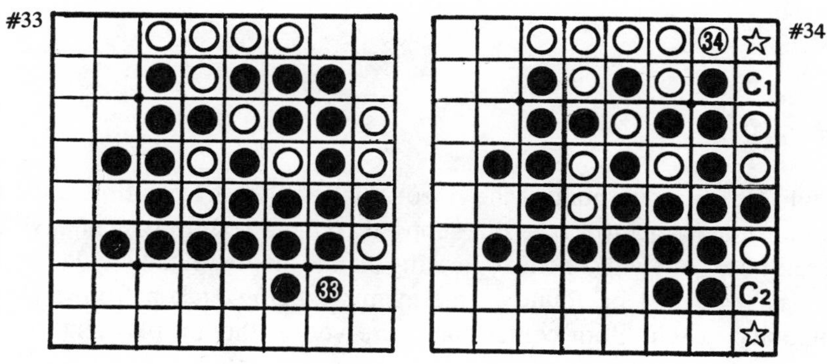

Study each diagram carefully; then you'll understand the advantage of taking **A** positions early in the game. The result of the game is shown in Diagrams 61 and 62. Black fought well, but White's steady moves kept pushing him back, giving him no chance to mount an attack of his own.

Diagram 61

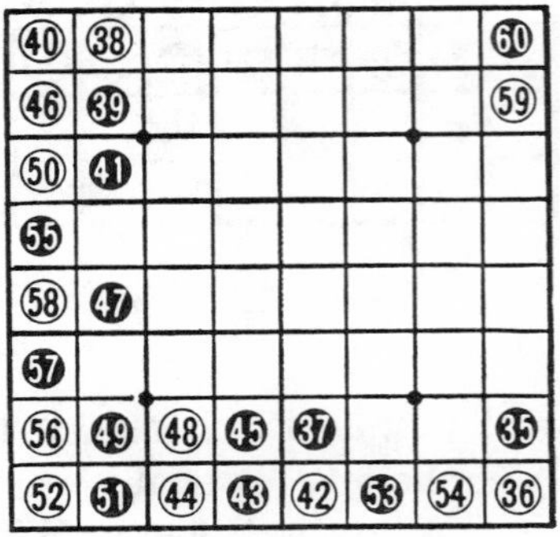

40	38						60
46	39						59
50	41						
55							
58	47						
57							
56	49	48	45	37			35
52	51	44	43	42	53	54	36

Diagram 62

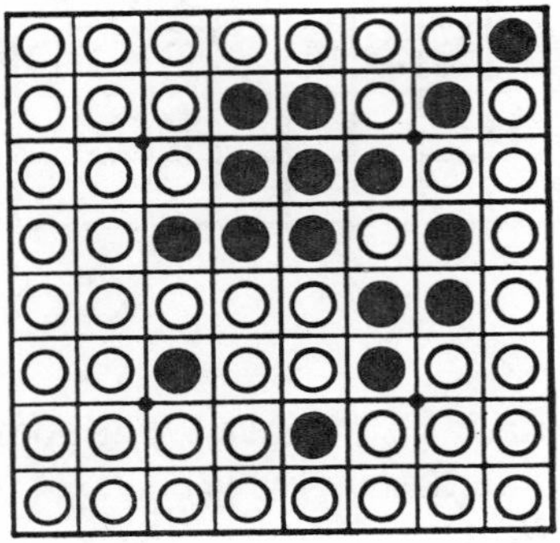

(White—48-disc victory)

The Big A

All right. It's great to control the **A** position, and the **b1** position is the best stepping stone to get to an **A**. But suppose you and your opponent have both read this book, and you're both operating on this theory. What would happen?

The answer may be found in the example below, taken from a district preliminary match. Both contestants were very orthodox players.

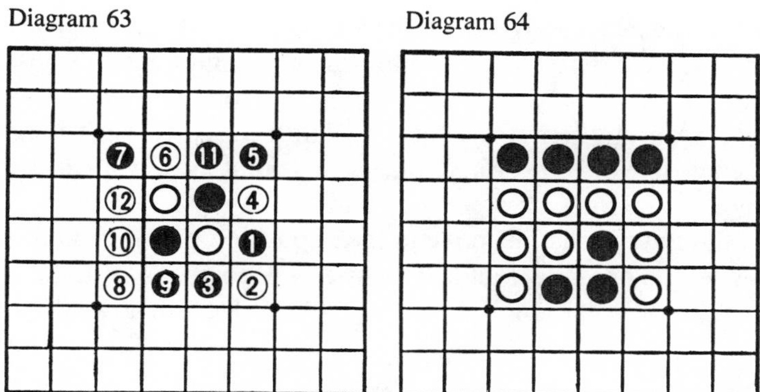

Diagram 63 Diagram 64

Diagrams 63 and 64 show that both Black and White gained good positions in the opening stage, such as 2, 5, 7, and 8. At the time of the 12th move they were facing off, confronting each other squarely.

Both Black (15) and White (20) gained **A** positions. Black's 17 is an interesting move. White's 20 and Black's 21 keep them well matched in power. Now they are going into the middle stage of the game (Diagrams 65 and 66).

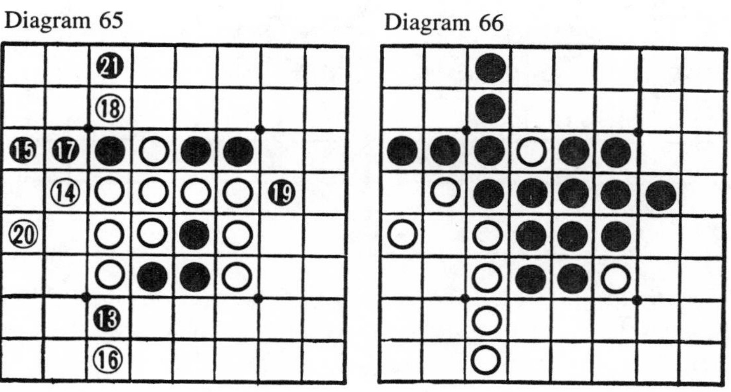

Diagram 65 Diagram 66

Both White and Black moved to **A** positions again (24, 25). White's 26 is a calm move. In a traditional game like this it's important to consider the choices before making any move.

Black had several alternatives for the 27th move, and each would have turned the game in a different direction. At this point the move Black actually made cannot be judged either good or bad.

White could have made his move to the **A** position on the right as early as the 28th move. He chose to wait and moved to **A** positions with the 30th and 32nd moves. The situation looks slightly favorable for him now (Diagrams 67 and 68).

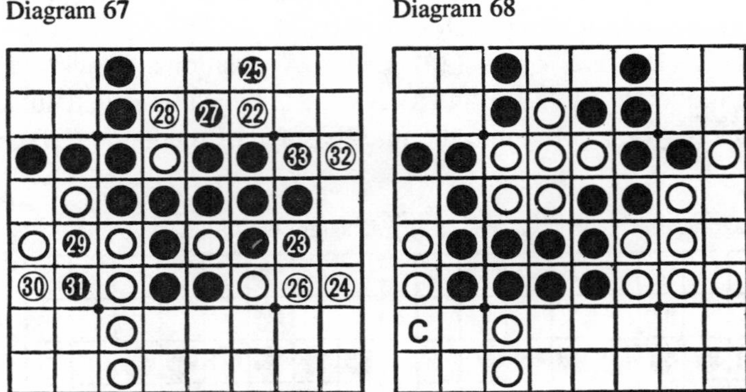

White's 34 is questionable. A move to **C** (Diagram 68) would have been better. After White's 34 Black would naturally advance to 35 (Diagram 69). Subsequently, 36 and 38 are natural moves.

If both players try to get **A** and **B** positions and avoid **C**'s and **X**'s, somewhere around the middle stage the board is likely to show a cross-shaped formation of discs like the one shown in Diagram 70. An interesting thing about this formation is that no one can tell for sure who has the upper hand. When the game analyzed here developed to the point of Diagram 70, none of the observers could tell who was winning, and each of the players was confident of his victory.

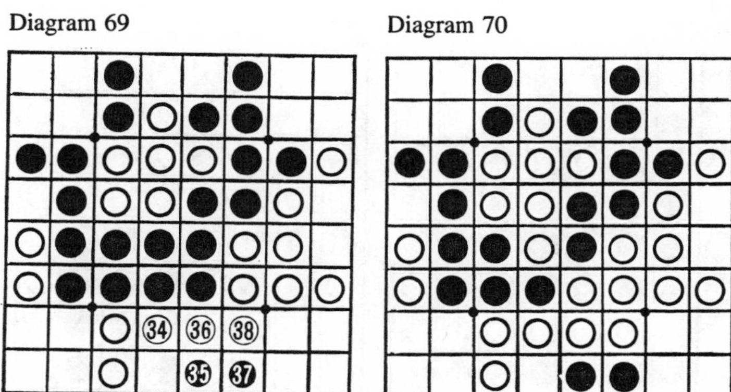
Diagram 69 Diagram 70

Avoid a Cross Formation

A cross formation usually occurs as the result of one player's lack of insight. He has probably played into his opponent's hand.

In the game we've been discussing the opening stage was a confrontation of equal power and the middle stage was a repetition of advance and retreat, like a see-saw, with White holding a slight edge over Black. But in the final stage White made a few mistakes, whereas Black played skillfully, turning the situation in his favor.

Black's 41 and 43 were good moves; then he made a move to **X** (45). After the game the players were asked what their thoughts were when Black made the 45th move.

White said, "I was pleased that Black made that move, and I was certain that I had won."

Black said, "My forty-fifth move was a planned step after forty-one and forty-three. I was sure I would win."

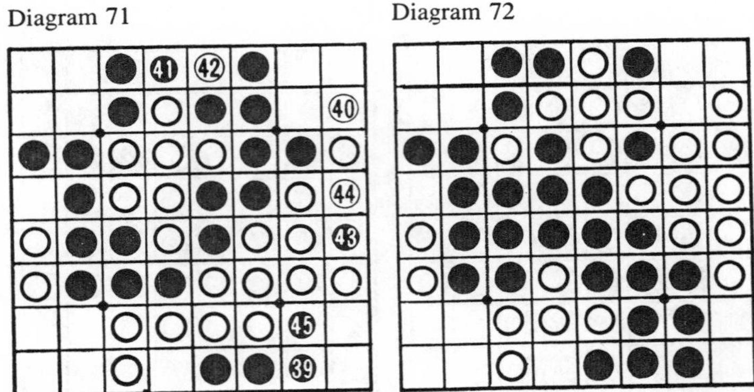

The truth is that in Diagram 72 White has only a slight advantage over Black. White was naïve to assume that because he forced Black to go to the **X** position he was assured of victory. On the other hand, Black's conviction that 45 was a winning move is somewhat naïve as well. He was not aware of a trap. Black firmly believed that White would move to the lower right-hand corner, but he badly underestimated his opponent.

In the actual game White indeed played into Black's hand and moved to the corner position. He should have moved to position 46 in Diagram 73. Diagrams 73 and 74 show how White could have won.

Diagram 73

Diagram 74

Now look at Diagrams 75 and 76. They show how this game proceeded. Black's 45th move to the taboo position proved a good one. On the other hand, White's 46th move to a supposedly formidable corner position could not be used effectively. He simply couldn't flip many black discs, despite the strategic position.

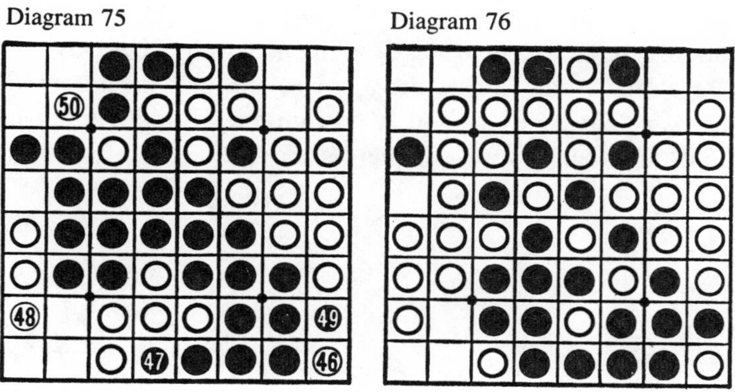

Diagram 75

Diagram 76

Black's 47 and 49 were well-thought-out moves. If Black had made the 47th move to the 49 position, White would have moved to the 47 position, turning the tide in his own favor.

Black's 51st through 59th moves steadily kept White on the defensive without allowing him to regain his advantage (Diagrams 77 and 78).

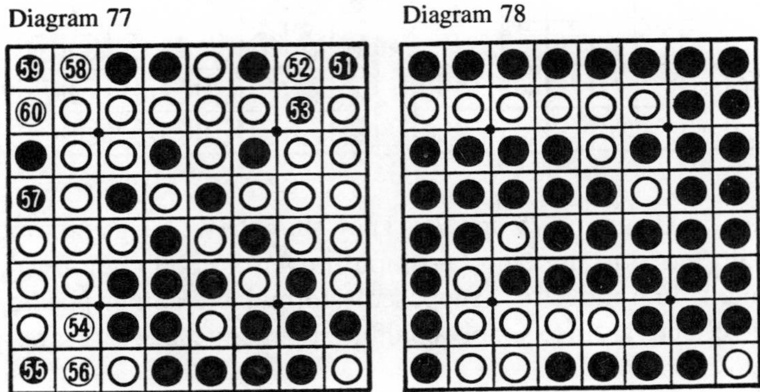

As we have seen, this game started with scrambling for **A** positions. When the game advanced into the final stage, White had a slight edge over Black. In the final stage Black attacked White aggressively and White could not retaliate. This is an example of good **A** position tactics and demonstrates the importance of foreseeing your opponent's moves.

B Can Be Better: Advantages of the B Position

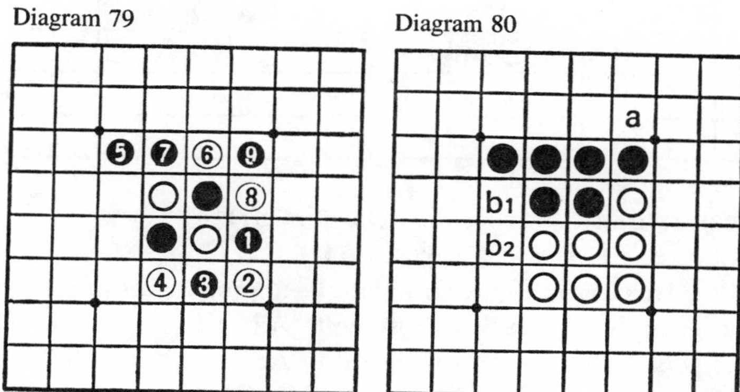

Diagrams 79 and 80 are taken from a game played by title-holder Kaichiro Tsuji and Masahiro Tomoda, an Othello veteran. This is the first game of the two-game match, and Tsuji is White.

Note the black discs in the **b** positions. Black 9 in Diagram 79 is a good move. Black planned it this way: if White went to **b1** (in Diagram 80), Black would go to **b2**, limiting White's 12th move to **a1** or **a7**.

Diagram 81

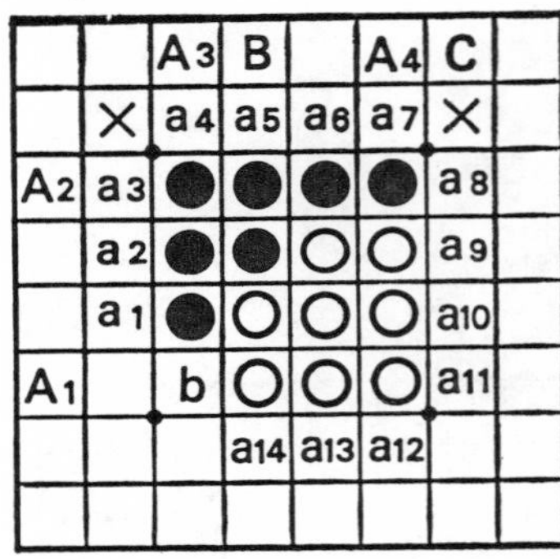

Diagram 82

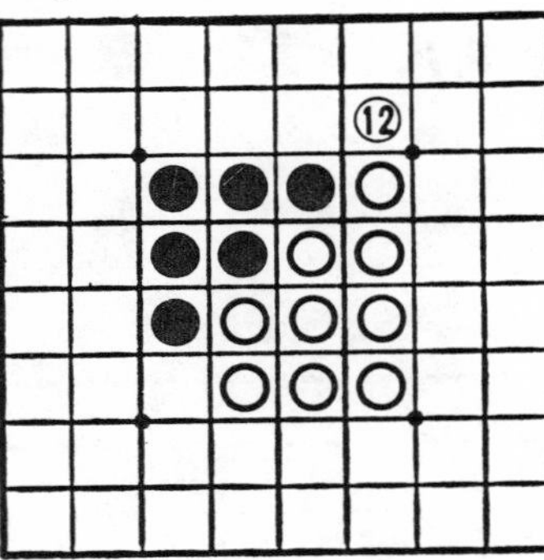

Let's analyze Black's tactics (see Diagram 81).
If White takes **a1**, Black will go to **A1**.
If White moves to **a2**, Black will go to **b**, to prepare for the move to **A2**.
If White goes to **a3**, Black will move to **A2**.
If White goes to **a4**, Black will move to **A3**.
If White takes **a5**, Black will go to **b**, then aim at **B**.
If White moves to **b6**, Black will go to **A4**.
If White goes to **a7**, Black will take **a8** and then **A4**.

These are all good standard moves, which you could figure out with a bit of common sense. But they're not the only moves possible. Take the last one: if White moved to **a7**, the move to **a8** is by no means the only one Black can make. He can go to any one of the positions from **a8** to **a14**. Any of these would provide a good foundation for a later attempt to gain control of **A** and **B** squares and eventually of the corners themselves.

Therefore, as shown in Diagram 80, White could have dared a move to **b1**, allowing Black to go to **b2**, and then could have made his 12th move as in Diagram 82. But White was afraid he'd fall into Black's trap if he moved to

b1. It was reasonable for White to go to position 10 (see #10 below). If Black had gone to **B**, White would have struck back by going to **A**. Black would have gained a valuable **B** position, but at the same time White would be gaining the strategic **A** position.

Instead of going to **B**, therefore, Black made the 11th move as shown below. His intention was to occupy a **B** position without being followed

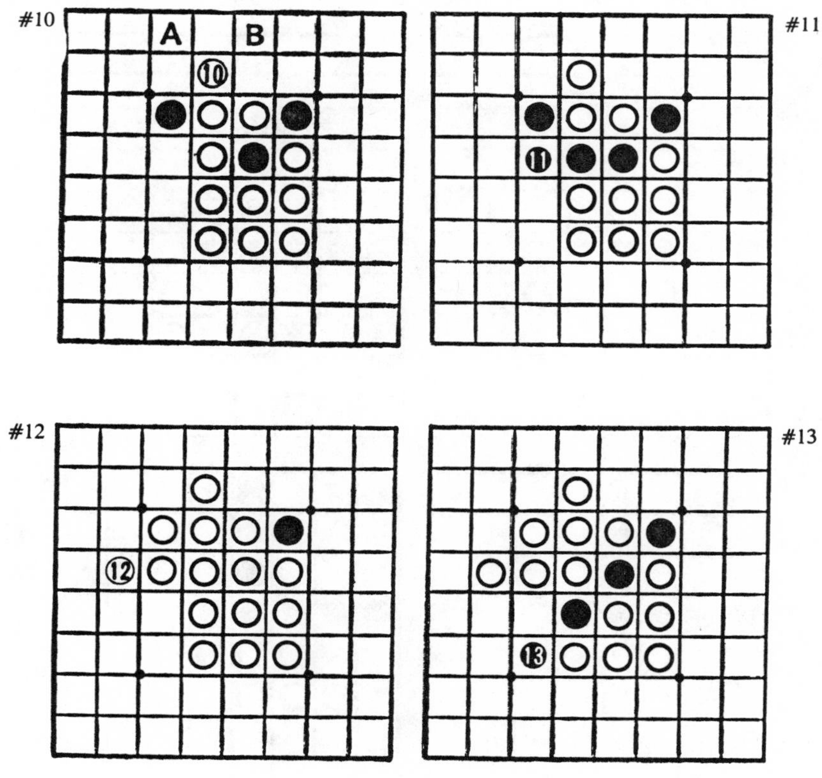

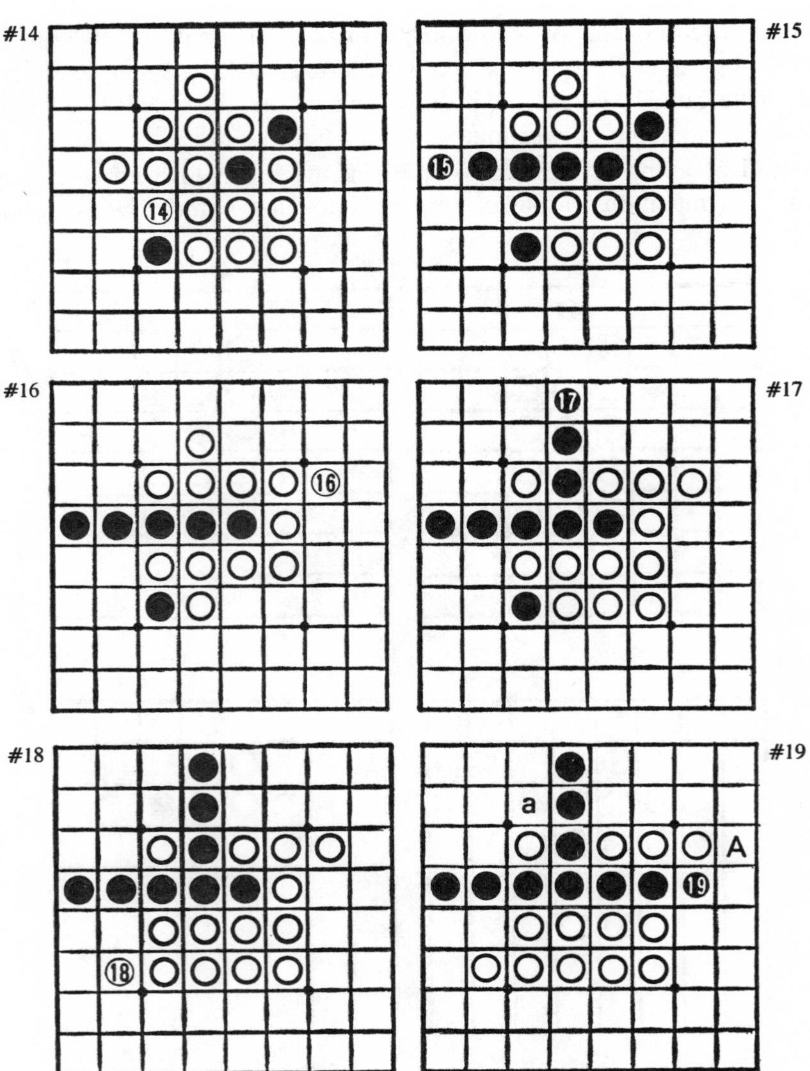
#14
14
#15
15
#16
16
#17
17
#18
18
#19
a
A
19

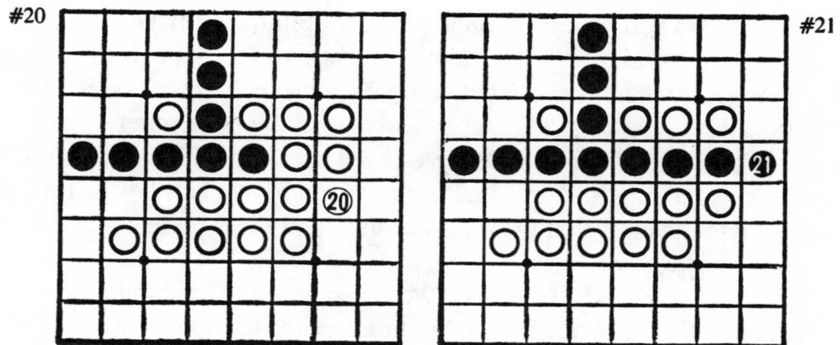

closely by White. Black accomplished this by the 15th move. He also succeeded in establishing unchallenged bases in moves 17 and 21.

Now look back at Diagram 79. One of White's choices was to go to position **b1**. This is not a bad move. Black probably would have gone to **b2**. Then White would make the 12th move to the **a** position. This would have produced the situation shown in Diagram 82. But this is not exactly an unconventional move; Black probably anticipated it.

In the actual match White made the 10th move as shown. His plan was: if Black moved to **B**, White would go to **A**, dealing squarely with Black.

But Black did not go along with White's operational plan. Black wanted an advantageous position like **A** or **B** exclusively, not side by side with White. Therefore, he made the 11th and 13th moves as shown, and by the 15th move he captured the desirable **B** position without being followed by White.

Black succeeded in taking two more **B** positions with the 17th and 21st moves and prevented White from going to comparable positions.

A Difference of Opinion

After the 21st move Black was sure that he had a definite advantage over White and that he could turn the battle in his favor.

However, one expert observer had a different opinion. When he studied the diagrams later, he said, "White could have gone to the **A** position with his twentieth move, but he did not. That could only mean that Mr. Tsuji (White) intended to allow Black to take supposedly advantageous outer-edge positions. Therefore, Black's move twenty-one led him into White's trap, probably without his realizing it. White had an unconventional plan. By the time the game reached the twenty-first move, I am sure White was quite confident that his strategy would work."

Indeed, White made it look as if he were losing in the opening stage, with no useful bases of operation, but in the middle and final stages he somehow managed to turn the situation around. He won in a truly remarkable game.

Mr. Tsuji later said, "Mr. Tomoda played the opening stage of the game quite skillfully, and I was on the defensive. When I took the **b1** position with my second move, he retaliated by taking two **b1** positions with his fifth and ninth moves. My twelfth was too high-handed, and he put me in my place with his thirteenth move. It was a good move.

"As soon as I made the fourteenth move, he went to the **B** position. He took another **B** spot with his fifteenth move, making things difficult for me. But his nineteenth move was a mistake. He should have gone to the **a** position [see

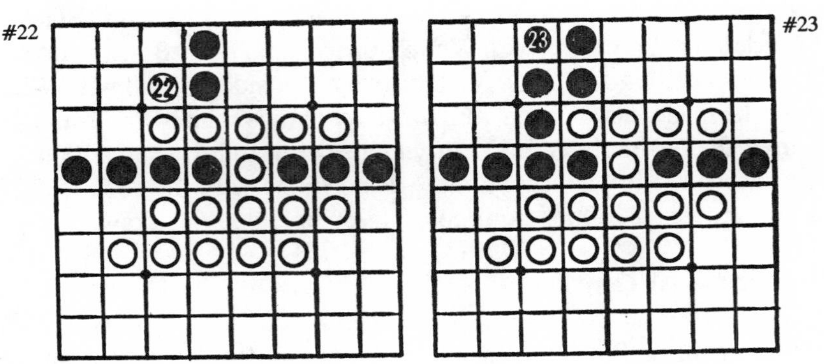

#19 above]. However, my twentieth move was a mistake, too. I should have gone to the **A** position. Because of my error Black took the third **B** position with his twenty-first move.

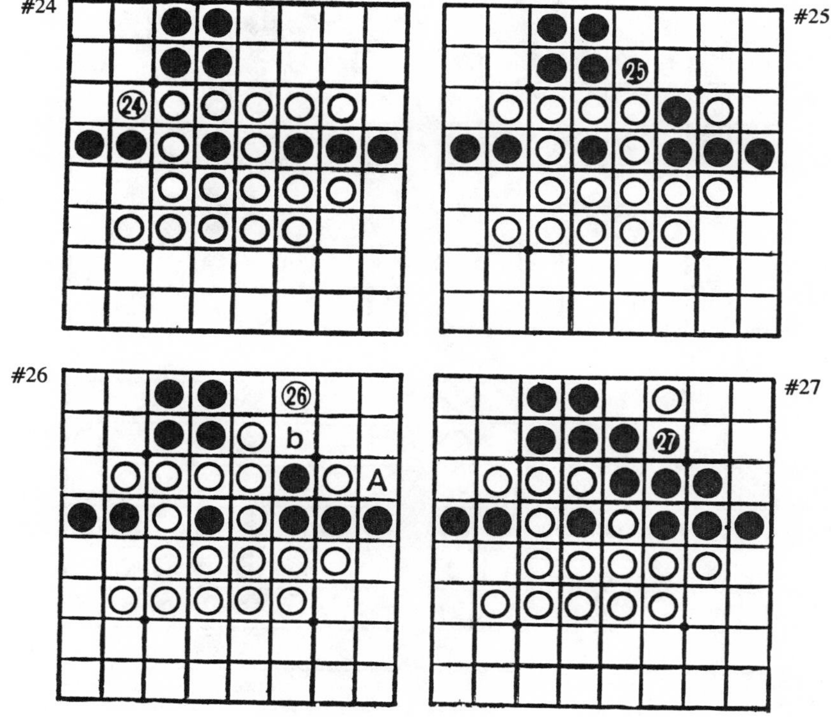

"My twenty-eight was a very bad move. I realized it too late, as I was turning the two white discs over, but of course I could not take it back. At that moment I was resigned to losing the game. But Mr. Tomoda's twenty-ninth move changed the whole picture. It was his fatal mistake. I quickly made the thirtieth move to the **A** position."

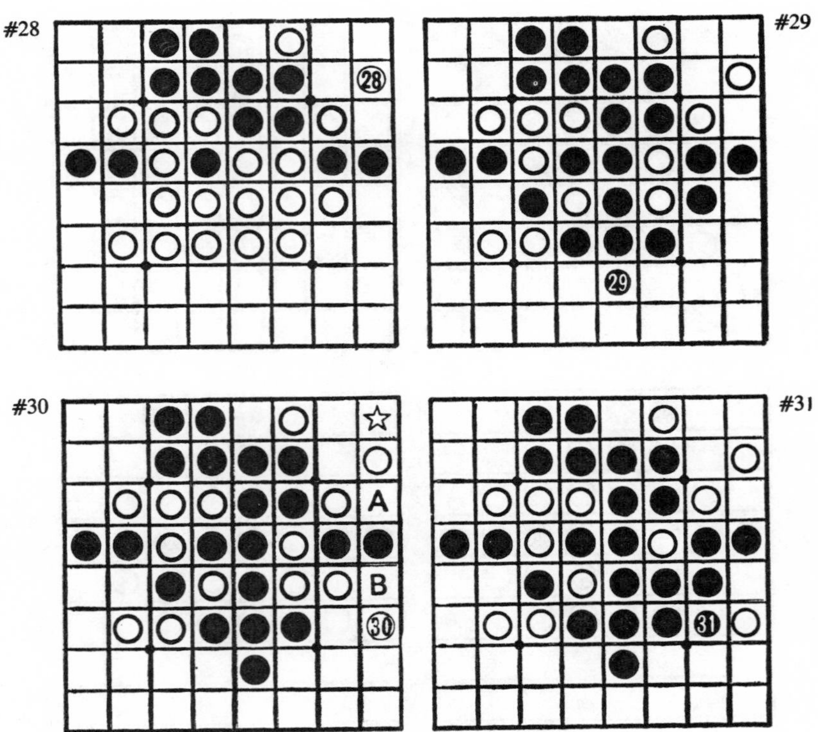

A Border Skirmish

After the 31st move Black and White both played very well. Study the diagrams move by move to see how they fought to gain control of the edges.

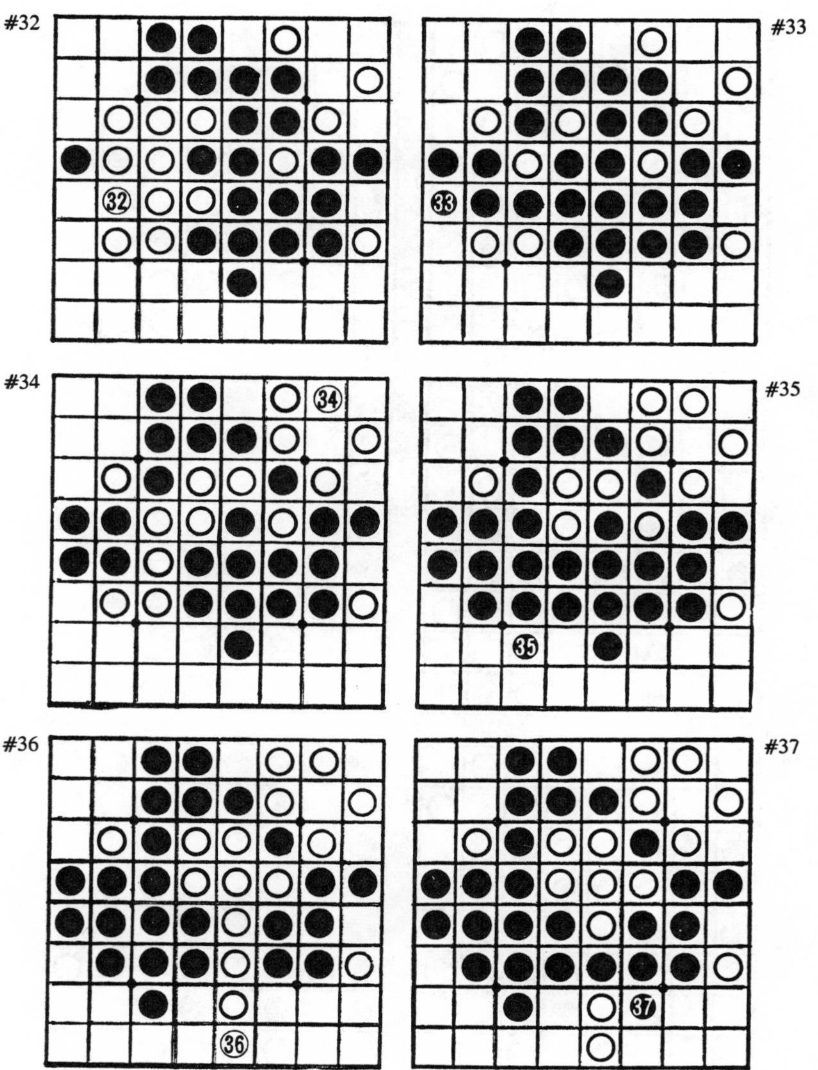
#32
32
#33
33
#34
34
#35
35
#36
36
#37
37

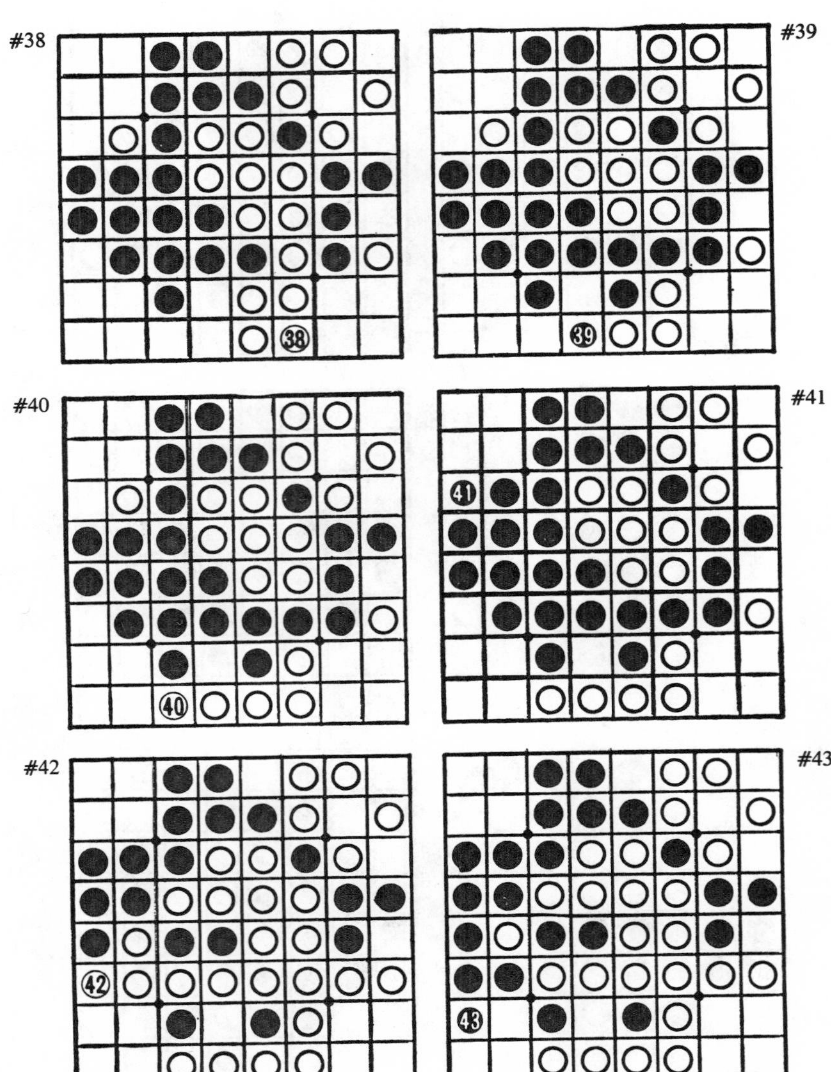
#38
38
#39
39
#40
40
#41
41
#42
42
#43
43

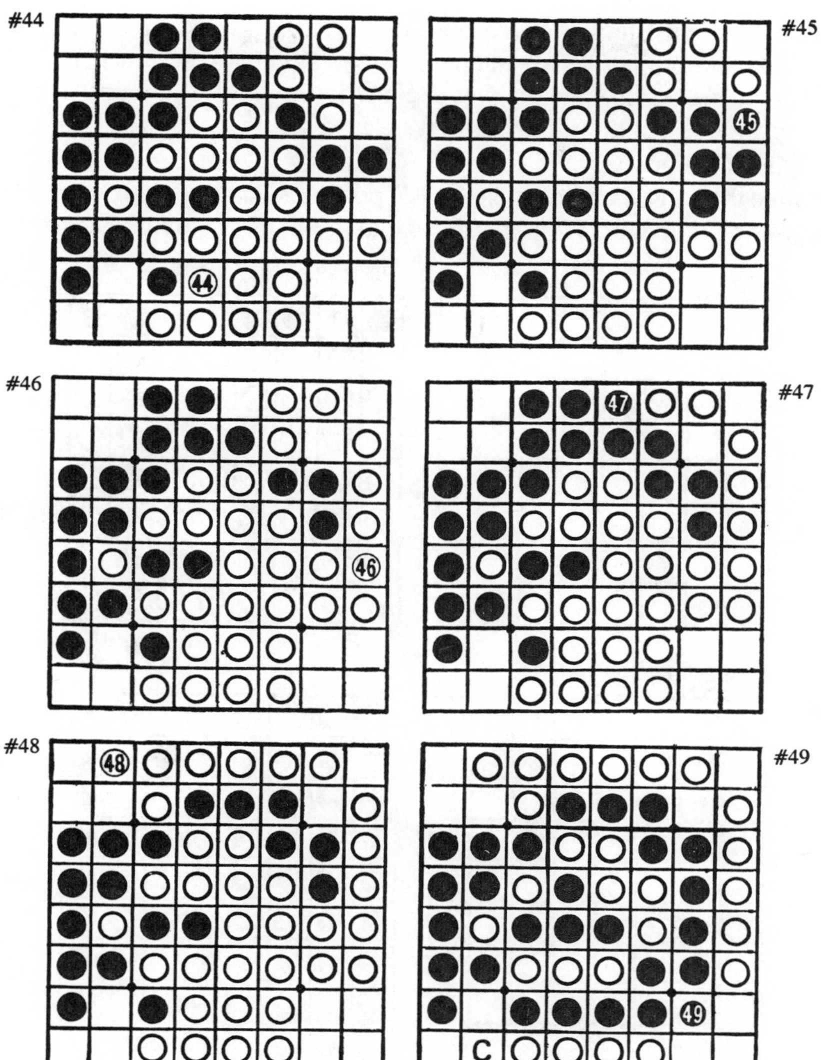
#44
44
#45
45
#46
46
#47
47
#48
48
#49
49
C

White allowed Black to go to position 45 and captured this with his 46. Black's 47 and White's 48 were similar moves. White forced Black's 49 to the **X** position, and White's victory was decided at this point. Diagrams 83 and 84 show how the rest of the game was played. It was a big victory for White, with a margin of 26 points.

Despite the fact that Black took three **B** positions in the opening stage of the game without allowing White to take any outer-edge positions, he could not

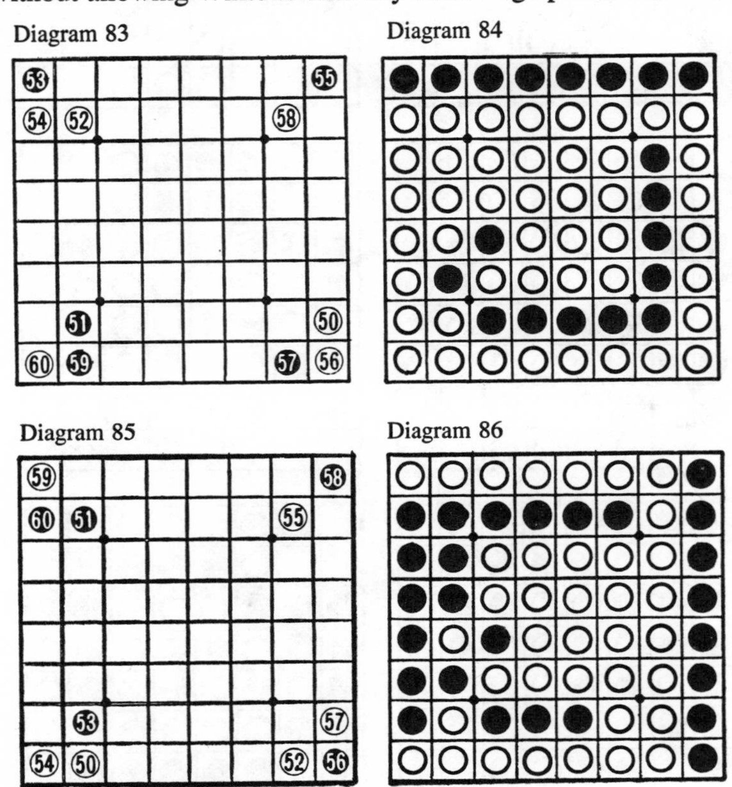

win the game because of his difficulties in the middle and final stages. Nevertheless, White's play in the opening stage was brilliant.

White's 50 and 52 (in Diagram 83) were masterful moves. If White had made his 50th move to the **C** position (#49 in the series of play diagrams), the result would have been Diagrams 85 and 86, and White would have won by only 12 points.

If White had placed his 52 in the lower left-hand corner, as most conventional players would have, the result would have been Diagrams 87 and 88, and also a 12-point win for White instead of the 26 points by which he actually won.

We let two Othello fans play the game starting with the positions shown in #49. Interestingly, this game ended in Black's victory by one point (Diagrams 89 and 90).

White's 50 was a bad move, giving Black a chance to catch up. The 55th move was probably wrong, although many people might think this a good move. White's 56 was a serious mistake. If he had gone to the lower right **C** position, White would have won by 10 points.

Diagram 87 Diagram 88

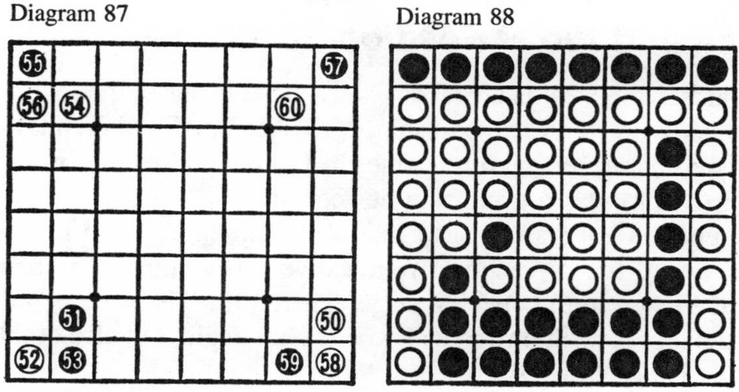

If you study Diagrams 83, 85, 87, and 89, you will see how intense and suspenseful the ending of an Othello game can be. Set up the board back at # 49 in the play diagrams, and see what ending you and your partner can come up with.

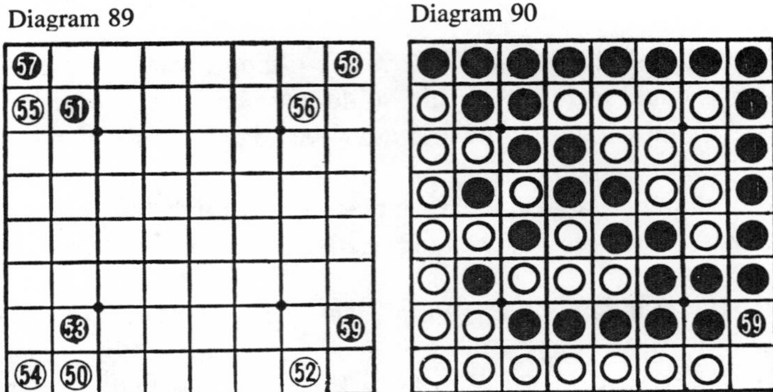
Diagram 89 Diagram 90

Alphabet Soup: A Clash Between the A Position Strategy and the B Position Strategy

The diagrams in this section are taken from a game in one of the semifinals for the All-Japan Women's Championship. Mrs. Kaichiro Tsuji (White) was the strongest woman player, with no games lost in the preliminary rounds. Ms. Shinozaki (Black) was a promising newcomer.

In this game Tsuji started out cautiously, aiming at **A** positions, while Shinozaki aimed for **B** positions from the very beginning. The balance of power was broken in the opening stage. Therefore, this game is not only a good example of **A** position versus **B** position strategies but also of the effect of a broken balance of power.

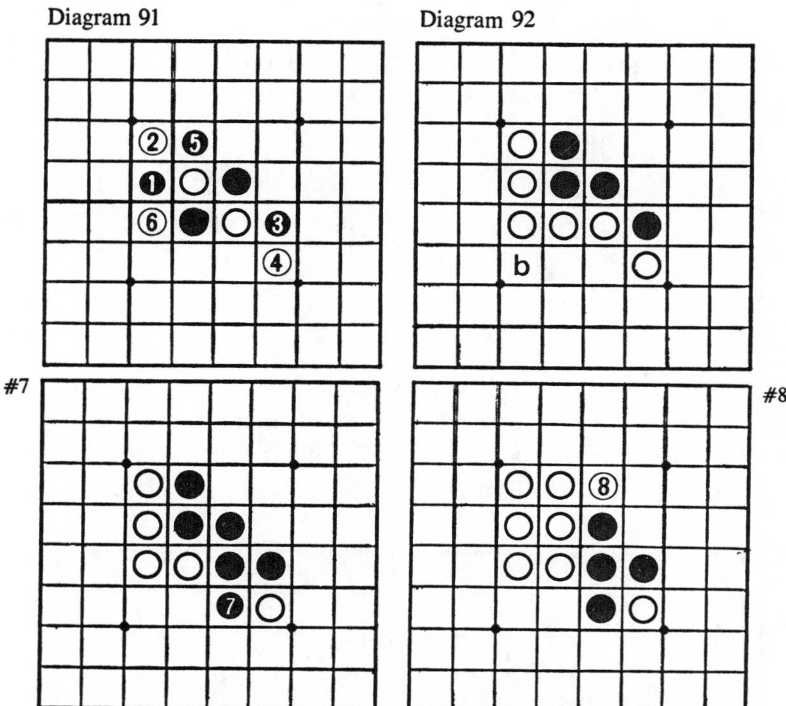

Here is an analysis of the game in Mrs. Tsuji's words:

"When Black made the seventh move, trying to sever the White formation, I thought she was aiming at something, but it was not clear to me what it was. More conventional players would have taken the **b** position in Diagram 92. Then, when she made the ninth move as if she were inviting me to go to the **A** position, her strategy became clear. She deliberately lured me to the **A** position with an intention to disturb the harmony of discs [a balanced number of white and black discs] and eventually lead me to a stalemate.

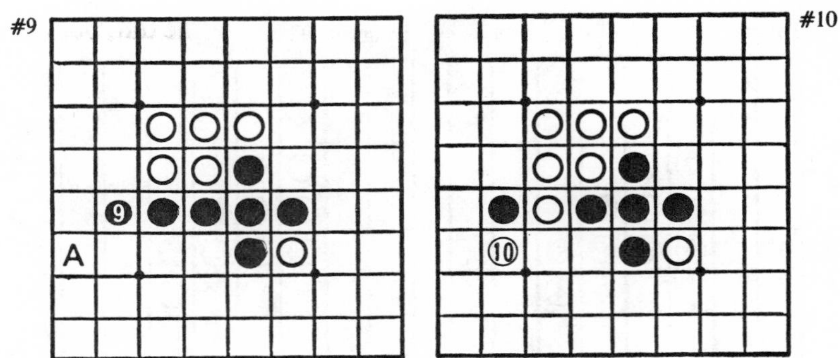

"If I had been playing with anyone else, I would have gone to the **A** position without hesitation, but I had discovered how formidable Ms. Shinozaki was in an earlier game. I just could not make a conventional move. After a lot of thought I made my tenth move as shown above.

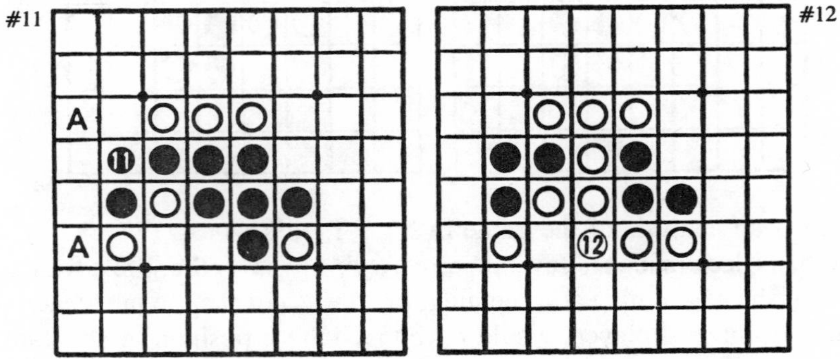

"Black's eleven was a coercive move. It was forcing me to take two **A** positions. What a bold move! Careful not to fall into Black's trap, I made my twelfth move. Black's thirteen was another enigmatic move.

"I could not tell why she made the thirteenth move as she did, but I thought whatever her intentions might be, I would not lose anything by going to the **A** position first. That is why my fourteenth move took the **A** position.

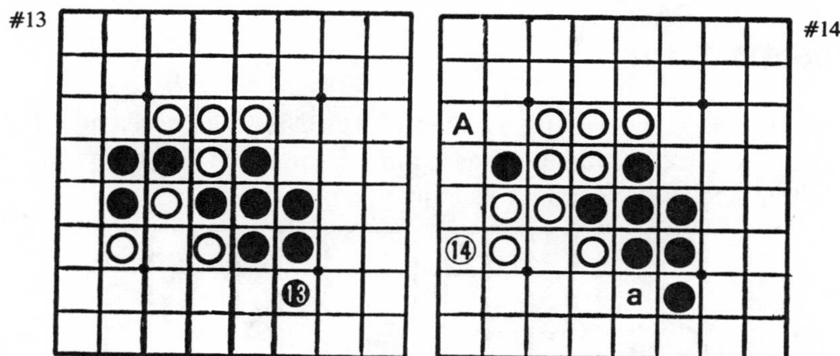

"Black's fifteen was again an unfathomable move. If Black did not want me to go to another **A** position, she would have gone to the **a** position [see #14 above] As you can see [#15], the **A** position was mine to take any time. I noticed that the **A1** position could be mine, too. I thought, 'If I take **A1**, I will have three **A** positions.' Without further deliberation I went to position sixteen as a preparation for the move to the **A1** position. This move

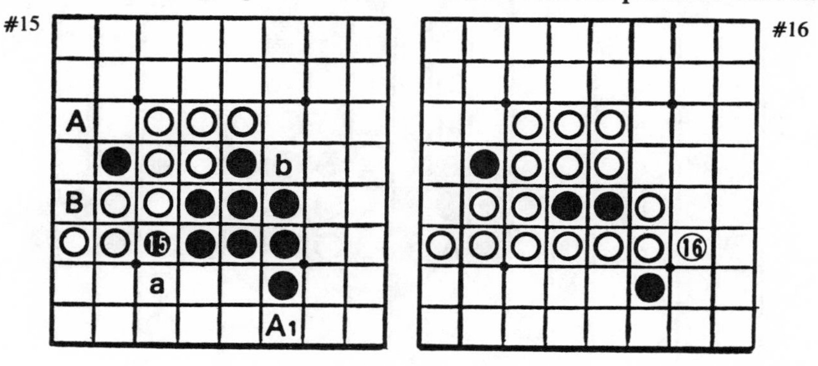

proved to be the direct cause of my difficulties in the opening stage. If I had made the sixteenth move to any of the **A**, **B**, **a**, or **b** positions, I would still have been in good shape.

Whoops! A Trap!

"Black's seventeen was really a clever move. Only after she made it did I realize how serious the situation was for me. Somehow I had been lured into Black's trap and was close to a stalemate.

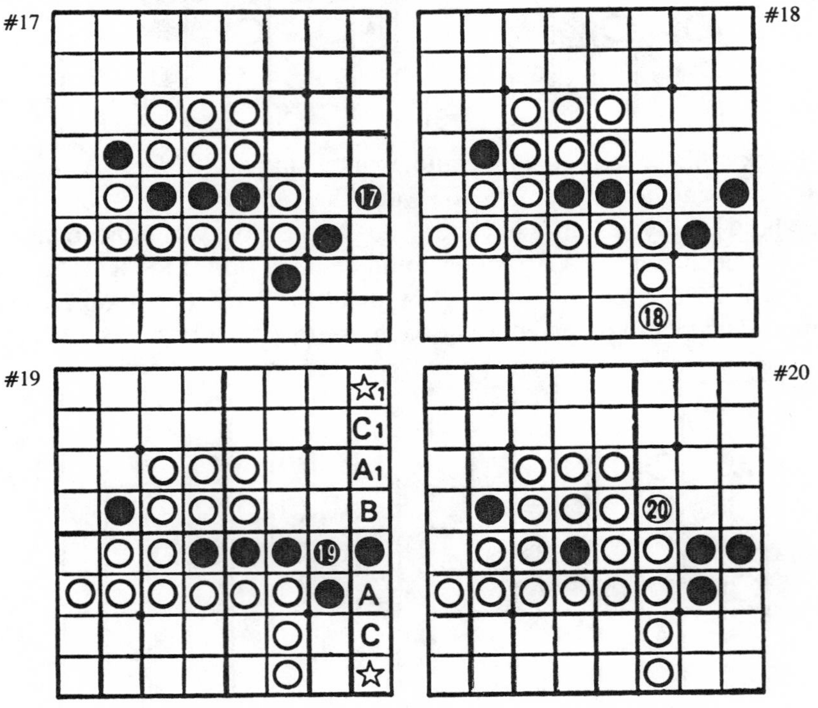

"With my twentieth move I thought of gambling on the **A** position [see #19 above]. But suppose I had gone to the **A** position. If White did not follow my **A**, the position would not be too effective; even if White moved to the **C** position, as I hoped for, there was no assurance that I could go to **C1** and then to **B**. As a matter of fact, such a possibility was slim. Even if it materialized, the moment I took the lower right-hand corner position, Black would go to the **A1** position and then take the upper right-hand corner.

"If we were to scramble for corner positions, the player with more discs on the board would be at a disadvantage, because the more discs you have the greater the rate at which you lose them. So I decided it was too early to take the **A** position at that point. In the opening stage of the game my operational planning was inferior. There were too many of my discs on the board.

"Comparison between the **A** position and the **B** position strategies? Well, in this case the advantage of the **B** position is so prominent that my two **A** positions are overshadowed. Without a balanced number of discs neither the **A** position nor the **B** position is effective.

"The unbalanced number of black and white discs was carried into the middle stage. Both Black and White were wary of the situation. My concern for the balance forced me to make my twenty-second move to the position shown, instead of to the **A** position [see #21].

#21

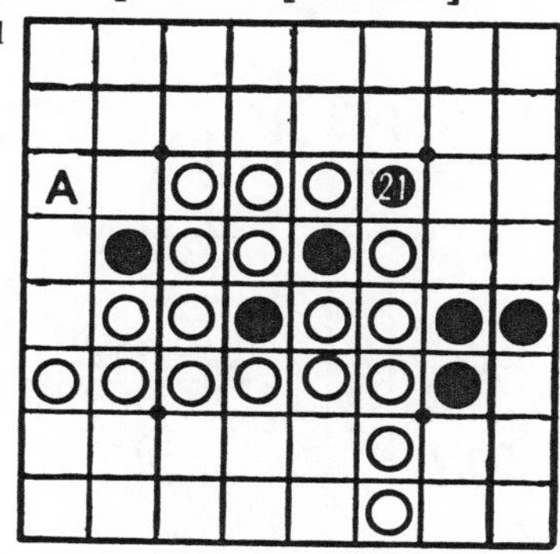

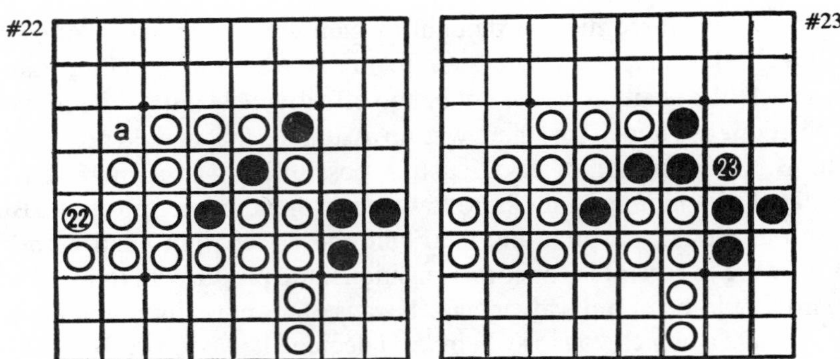

"I was hoping Black's twenty-three would go to the **a** position shown in #22, but it did not.

"The offensive and defensive battle between the twenty-fourth and thirty-fifth moves could have been played in many other ways. Our play was certainly not the most brilliant, but I can say that both Black and White fought very well."

What Would You Do?

Before looking at the diagrams below, can you assess the situation White was in and find a way out?

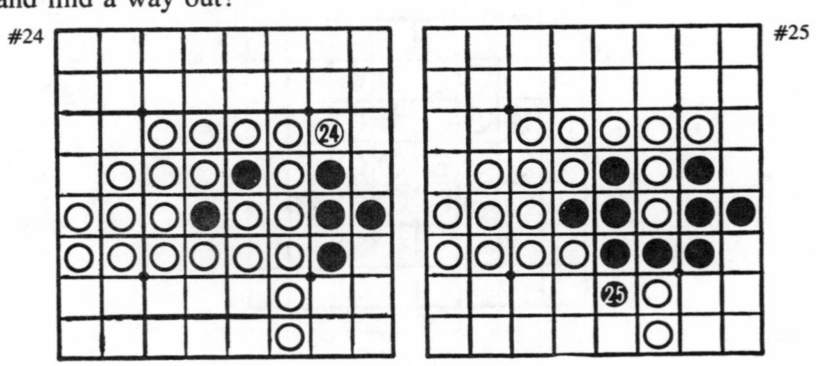

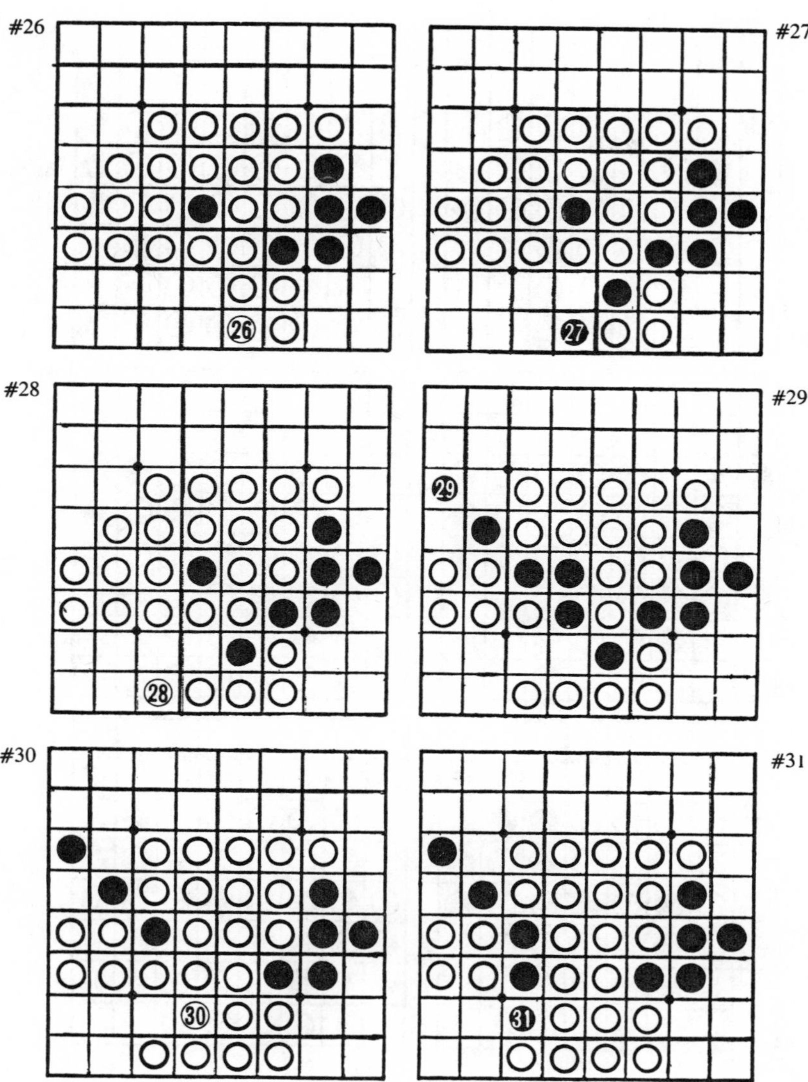
#26
26
#27
27
#28
28
#29
29
#30
30
#31
31

#32

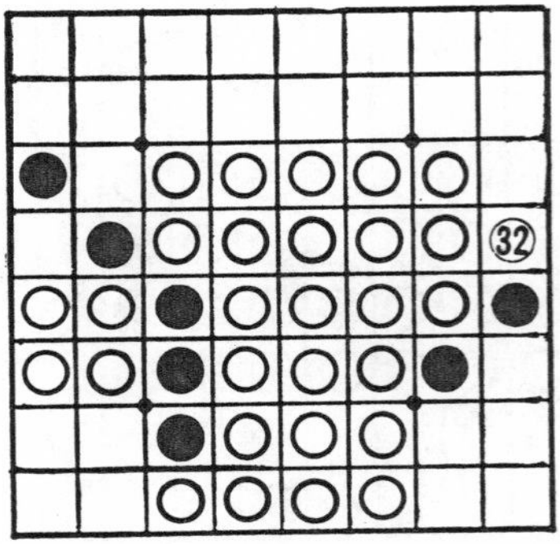

#33

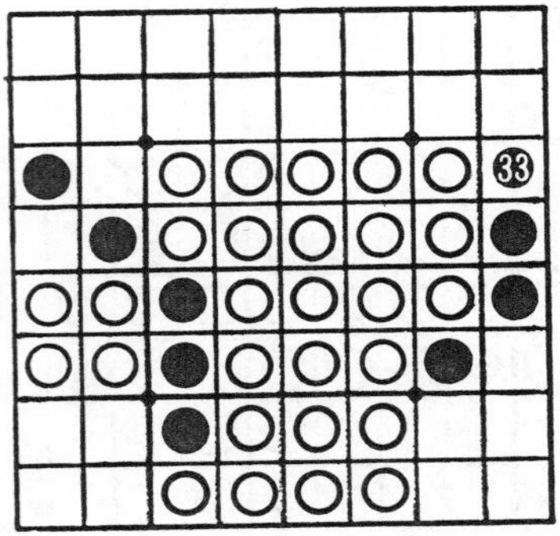

#34

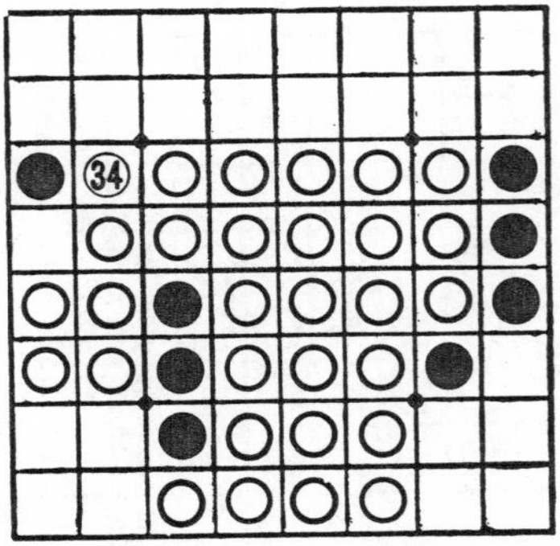

#35

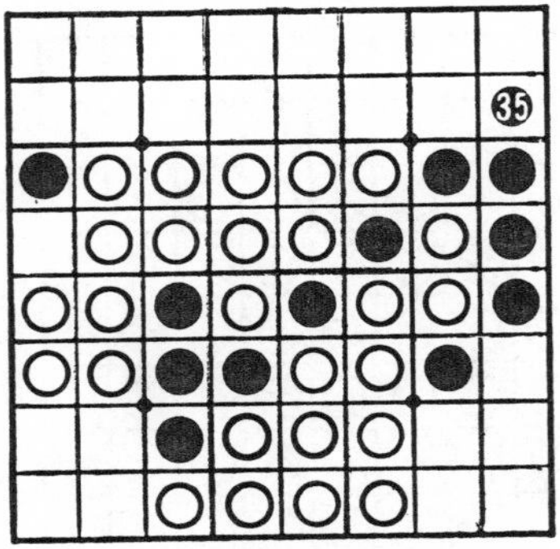

#36

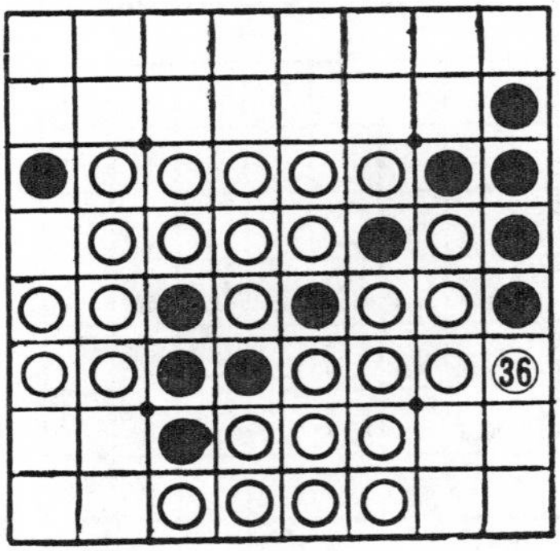

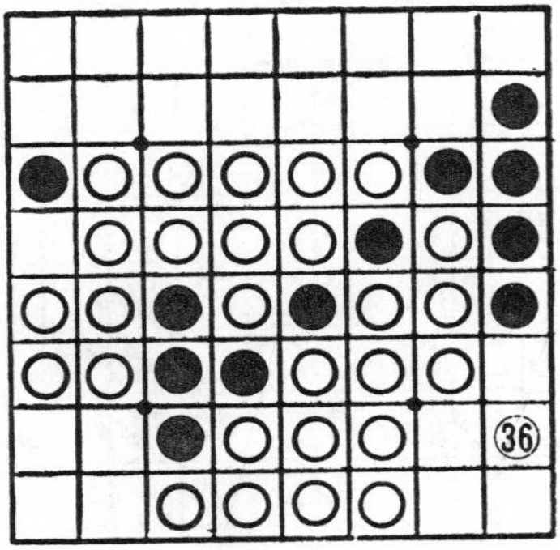

Diagram 93

Mrs. Tsuji continues: ''My thirty-six was a bad mistake. I should have gone to the position thirty-six shown in Diagram 93. Instead I moved to an **A** position [see #36]. This one move canceled out all my good efforts in the middle stage. Black's thirty-seven caused me to make a forced move—move thirty-eight, to the **X** position. The game had not even reached the final stage, but my defeat was obvious.

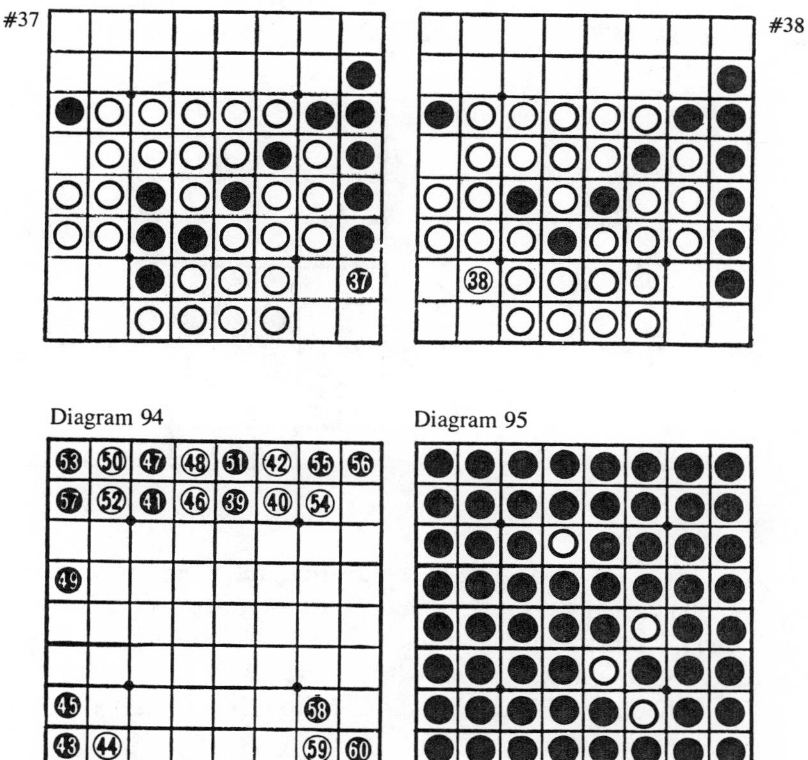

"I tried my best for the rest of the game, but I was no match for Black's skillful play. At the end I had only four discs left. I was truly amazed at Ms. Shinozaki's strength. Her operational planning is calculated accurately, and she is a very forceful player."

C Is for Careful: Two Examples of the Dangers of a C Move

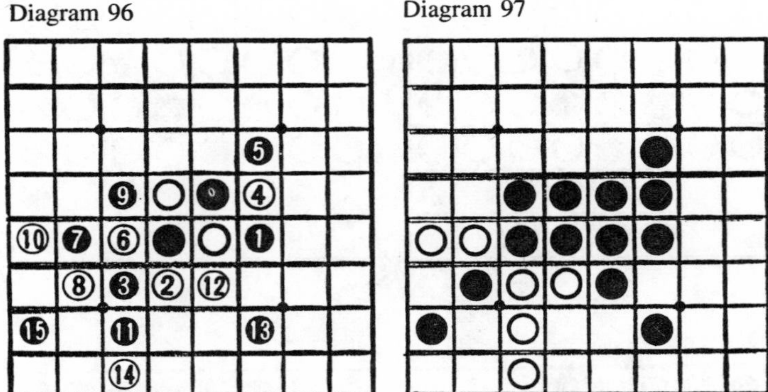

Diagrams 96 and 97 show one of the district preliminary matches for the Second Othello Championship Tournament. Black made his 15th move to the **C** position in Diagram 96. Black made a serious mistake with his 17th move and realized just how serious it was when White's 18 went to the **A** position. After a long deliberation Black made the 19th move, but it was too late. When

White made the 20th move, Black had no way of preventing him from taking the corner position. In Diagrams 98 and 99 Black's defeat is definite.

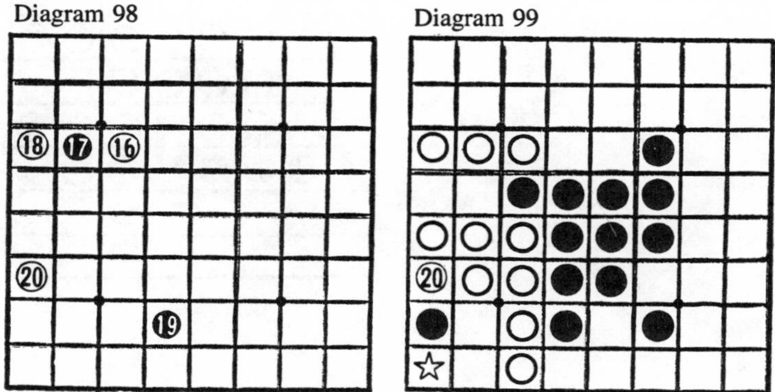

Diagram 100 was taken from an unofficial game. Black has just gone to the **C** position at the upper right. White should now aim for the **B** position and then the **A** position. As a matter of fact, White accomplished this with his 18th and 20th moves. Now the upper right corner is White's, and Black is in bad shape.

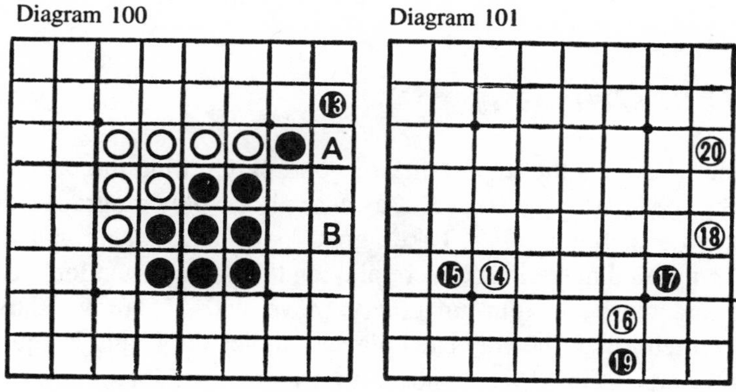

Diagram 102

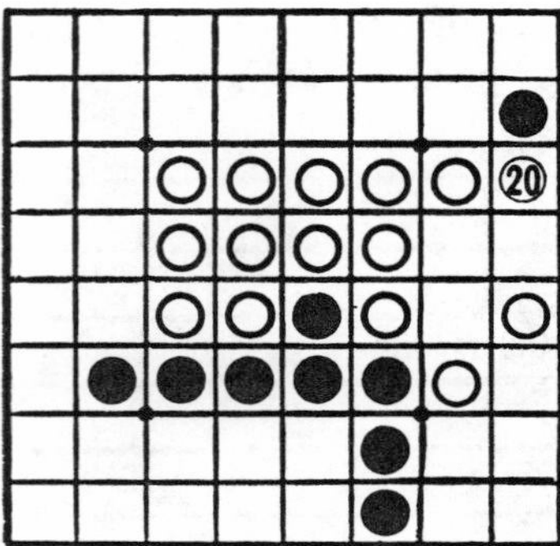

As you can see in these examples, an isolated move to the **C** position in the opening stage of the game is generally dangerous. But if you are a daredevil player, you can try to use the **C** position as a base to prevent your opponent from going to any of the outer-edge positions. Take Diagram 100. If Black wants to gamble on the **C** position, he must go to the **B** position as soon as possible, not allowing White to take the position first.

Play Your Own Way

This game illustrates the importance of good play during the opening stage. Follow the moves step by step. But as with all the play diagrams, don't just look at them one after another. Take a good look at each diagram and think of a move *you* would make if you were playing the game. Then look at the next diagram and compare your imaginary move with the move shown. Pay particular attention to the way each player handles the **C** and **X** squares, and see if you agree with White's moves to **a** and **b** positions.

Ready? Then study the first six moves.

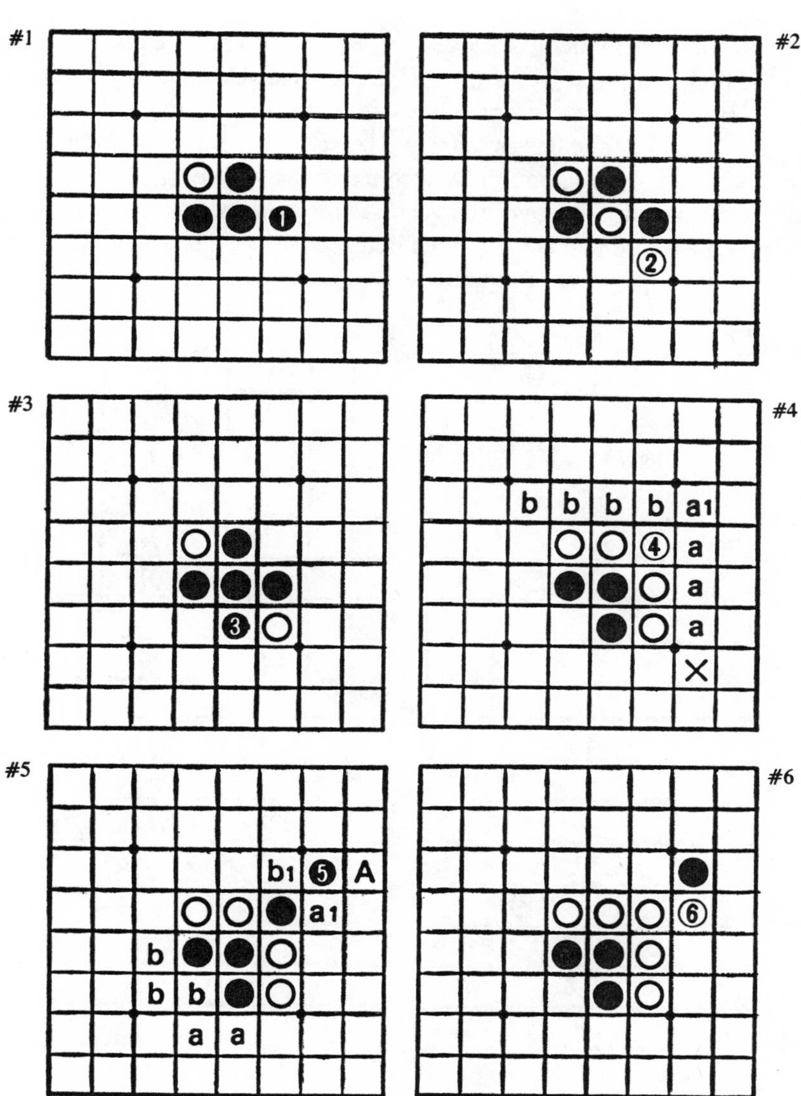
#1
1
#2
2
#3
3
#4
b b b b a1
4 a
a
a
×
#5
b1 5 A
a1
b
b b
a a
#6
6

Black's 5 is high-handed but clever. In #4 there are nine positions Black can go to, including four **b**'s, four **a**'s, and one **X**. Despite four **b** positions available, Black chose the **a1** position with careful planning.

In Diagram 103 White has seven **a** and **b** positions to go to. At this stage of the game you cannot tell good moves from bad ones too easily, but White's 6 was doubtful because it gave away an **A** position to Black. Position 6 in Diagram 103 would have been a much better position. That way White could have taken an **A** position simultaneously with Black.

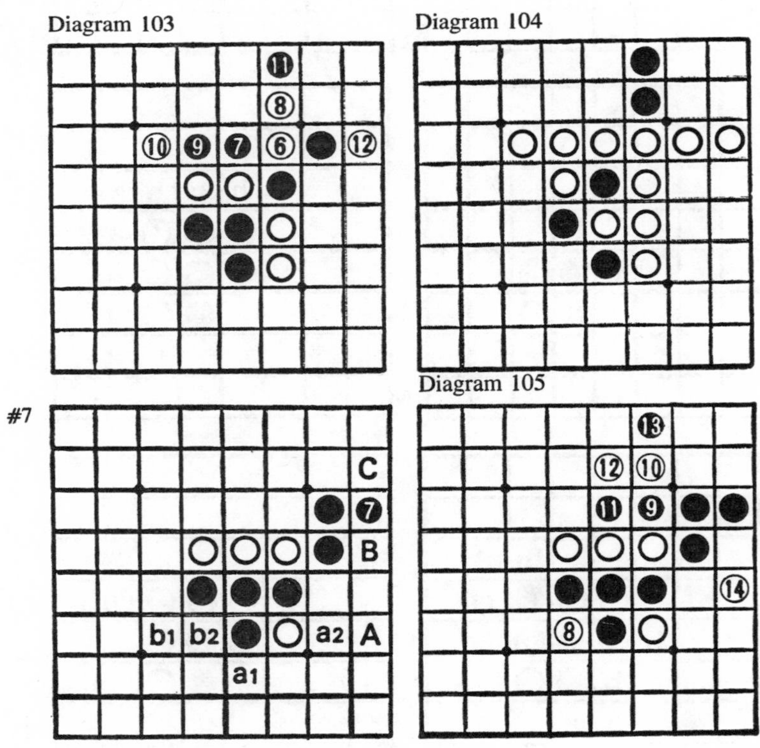

Diagram 106

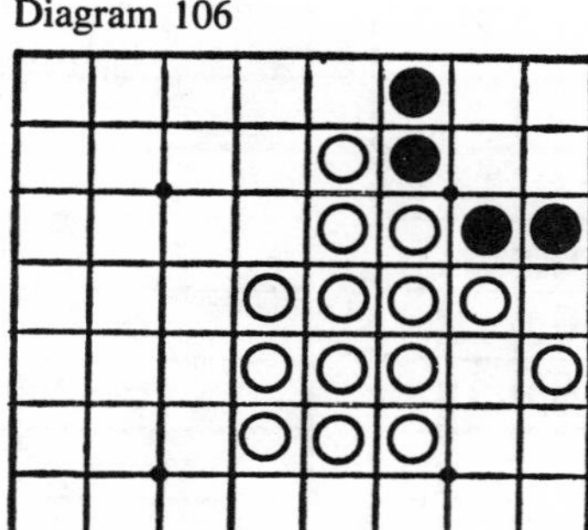

Black's 7 is a good position, enabling him to move flexibly. Black has six positions open to him, including a **C** and a **B** as well as **a**'s and **b**'s. But **C** is out of the question, and in this case **a2** should be avoided. What will happen if White goes to the **b2** position? As Diagram 105 shows, White would eventually take the **A** position (14) and both players would be at equal strength. Just because Black took an **A** position (7) first, it does not mean that the game is decided in his favor. Sometimes **A** positions can be a liability.

But it's a different story if a player takes two **A** positions on a line, with unoccupied **B**'s in between. This is definitely an advantage. That is why we said earlier that **a2** should be avoided in this case. If White goes to the **a2** position, it is obvious that Black will take the **A** position next to it. Therefore, White's 8 was a bad move.

As the play progresses in #9, you can see that White is already suffering. There are ten moves he can make here, but two **C**'s and **X** are out of the question, and the **B** position will just help his opponent.

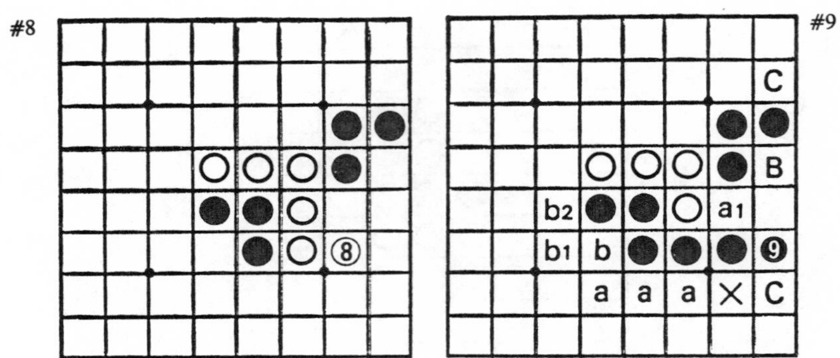

Experience Counts

From this point on the game's changes and switches will increase by geometrical progression, and it is very difficult to foresee everything that can happen. This is where experience and intuition are helpful. If you were an experienced player in White's place, you would instinctively prevent Black from going to the **a1** position. And since Black has established bases on the right-hand side,

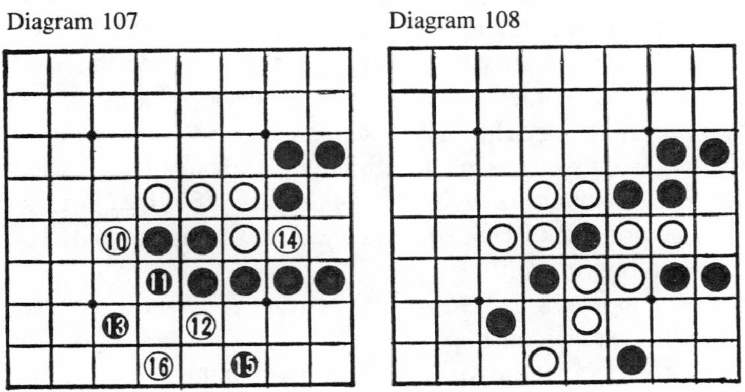

Diagram 107

Diagram 108

you should avoid a skirmish in enemy territory and move the battle to an open, unexplored area. For that reason you would be wise to go to a **b** position rather than to an **a** position.

Can you figure out how the situation would develop if White went to the **b2** position? Play it out on your board, then look at Diagrams 107 and 108.

Moves 14 and 16 will establish White's **A** base. Although Black still has a slight edge over White, the game is far from being decided. Therefore, White's 10th and 12th moves, as shown below, were dubious.

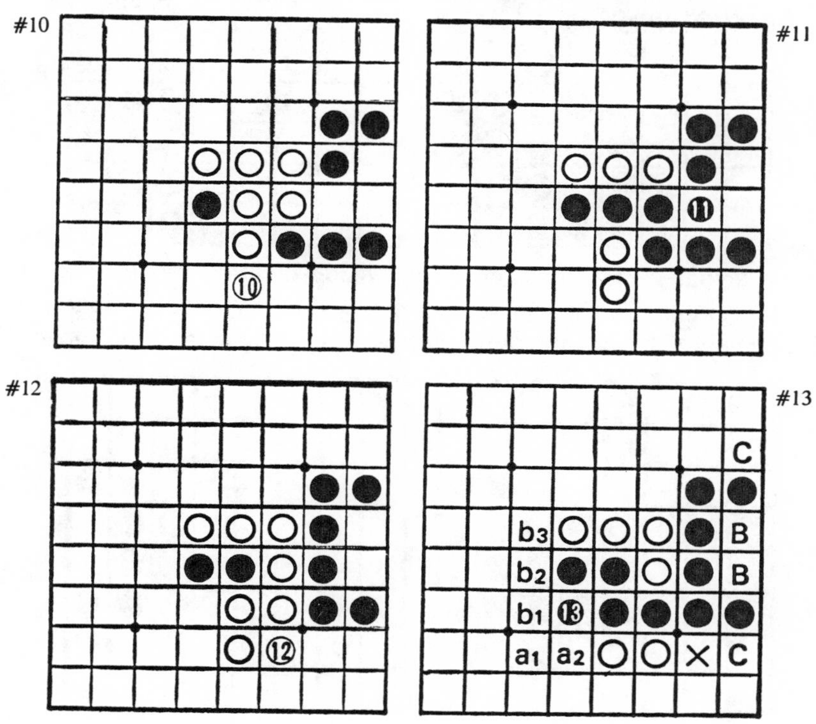

After the 13th move White has ten possible positions available to go to, although five of them are obviously bad. Among the rest, the **b1**, **b2**, **b3**, and **a1** positions have some promise in that they will keep White alive. Suppose he moved to the **a1** position. Diagrams 109 and 110 show that although this would be a difficult battle for White, he would still be capable of fighting.

Diagram 109 Diagram 110

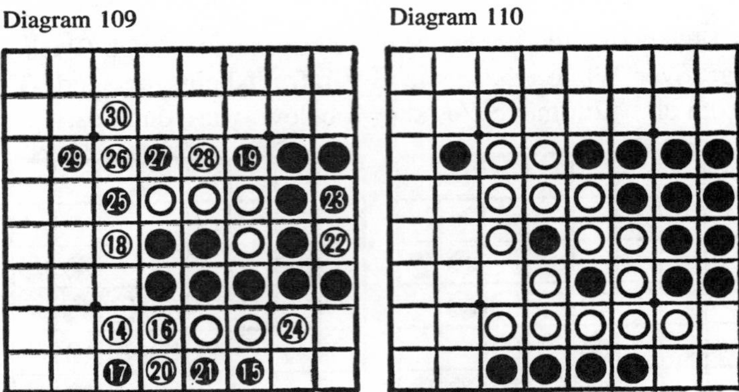

In the actual game, however, White made his 14th move to the worst possible position. As you can see in the play diagram below, White has lost the center area of the board; there is no position left there for him to go to. If he

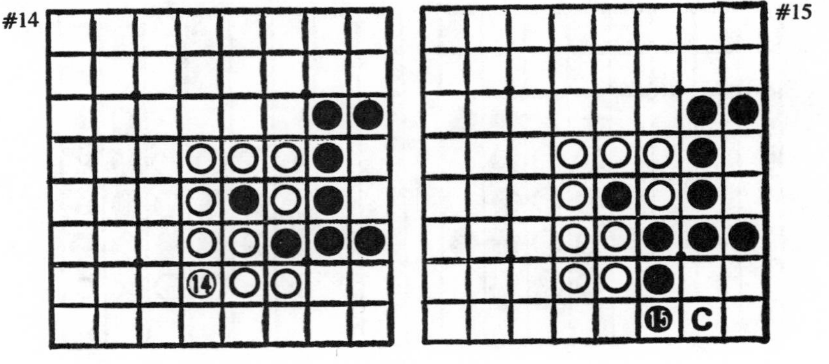

had gone to one of the **b1**, **b2**, **b3**, or **a1** positions shown in #13 above, such a stalemate could have been avoided, even with Black's 15th move. White's 16th move is another blunder.

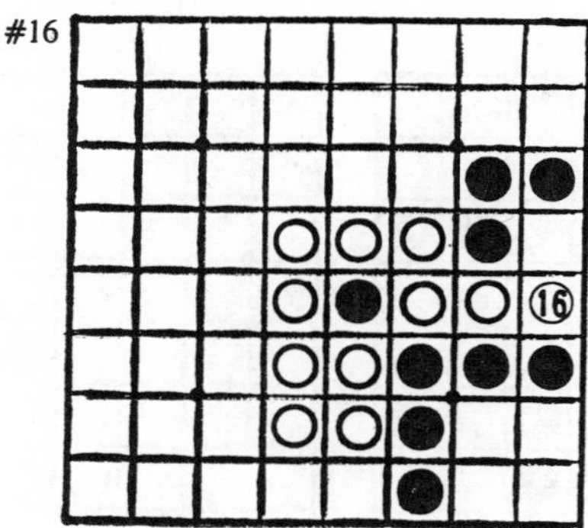

Black later commented: "There was no question that I had won after the fifteenth move. But if White had gone to the **C** position, it would have been difficult for me to destroy him completely, as shown in Diagrams 111 and 112."

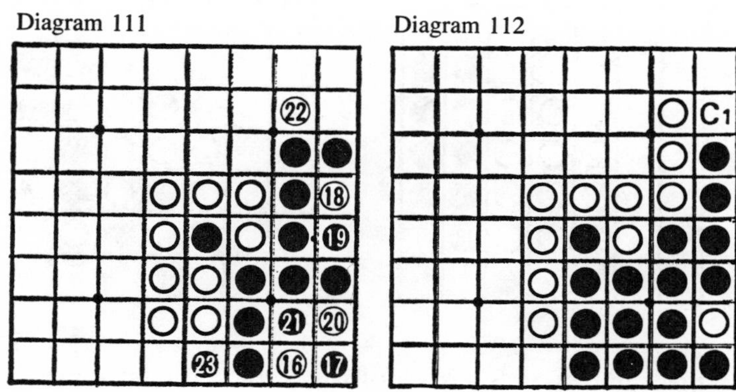

But as we saw, White moved to the B position (#16), and Black immediately outflanked him. Even so, White could have gone to the 18 position and kept fighting.

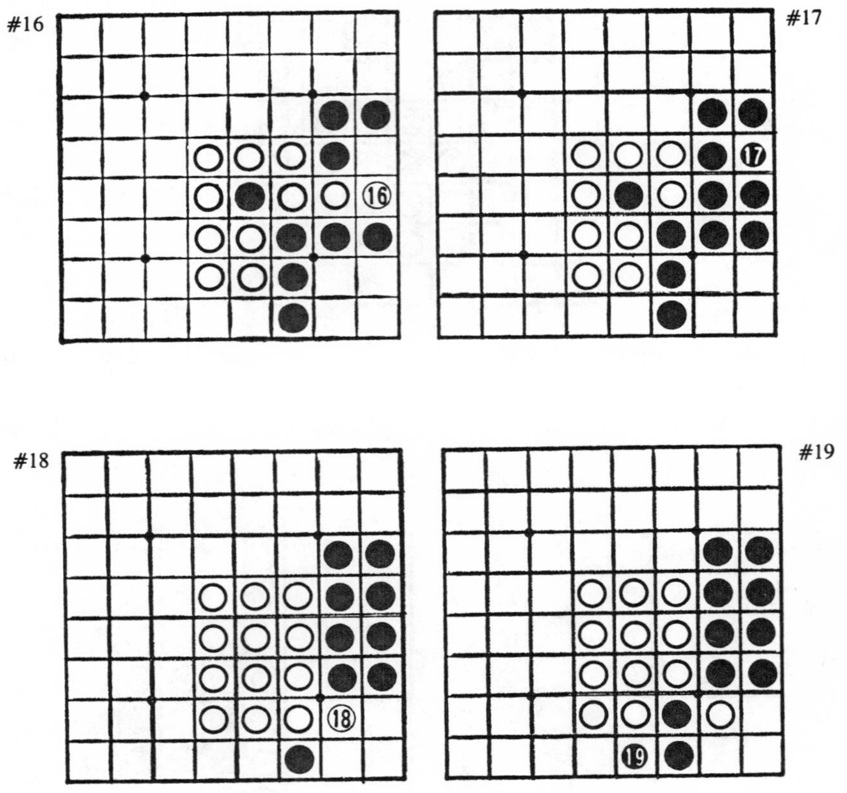

As it turned out, after Black's brilliant 19th and 21st moves, White's complete defeat was clear.

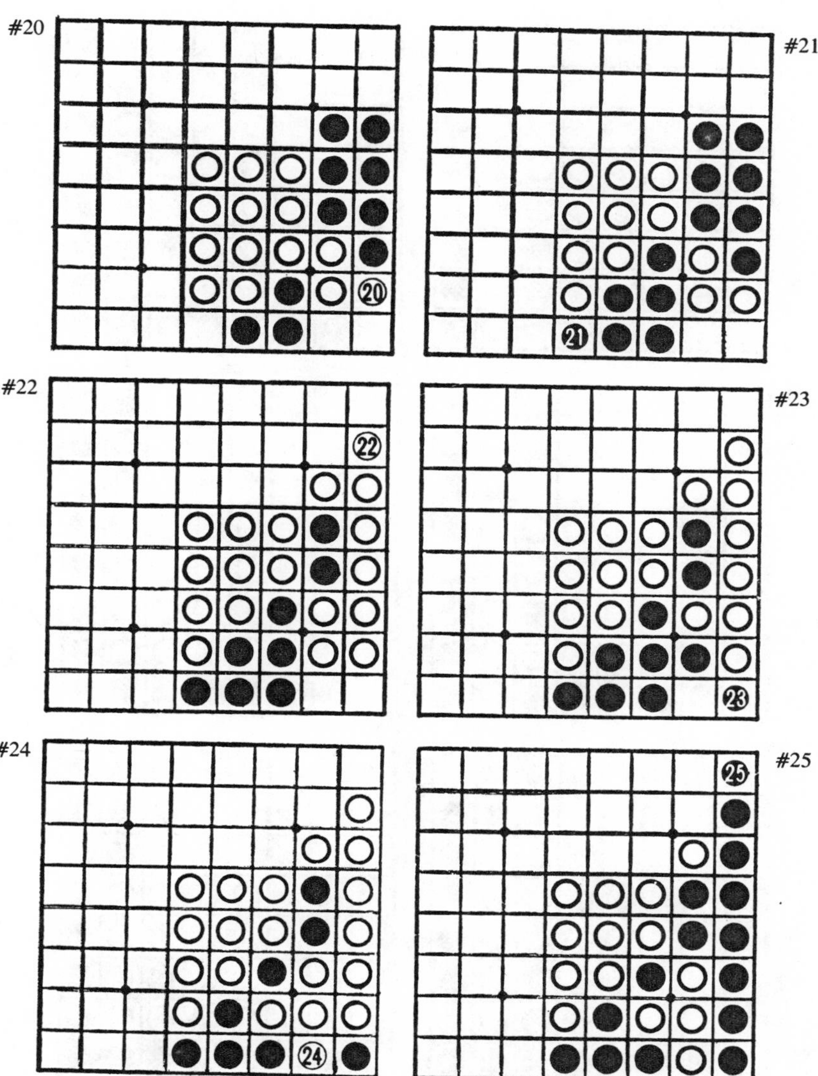
#20
20
#21
21
#22
22
#23
23
#24
24
#25
25

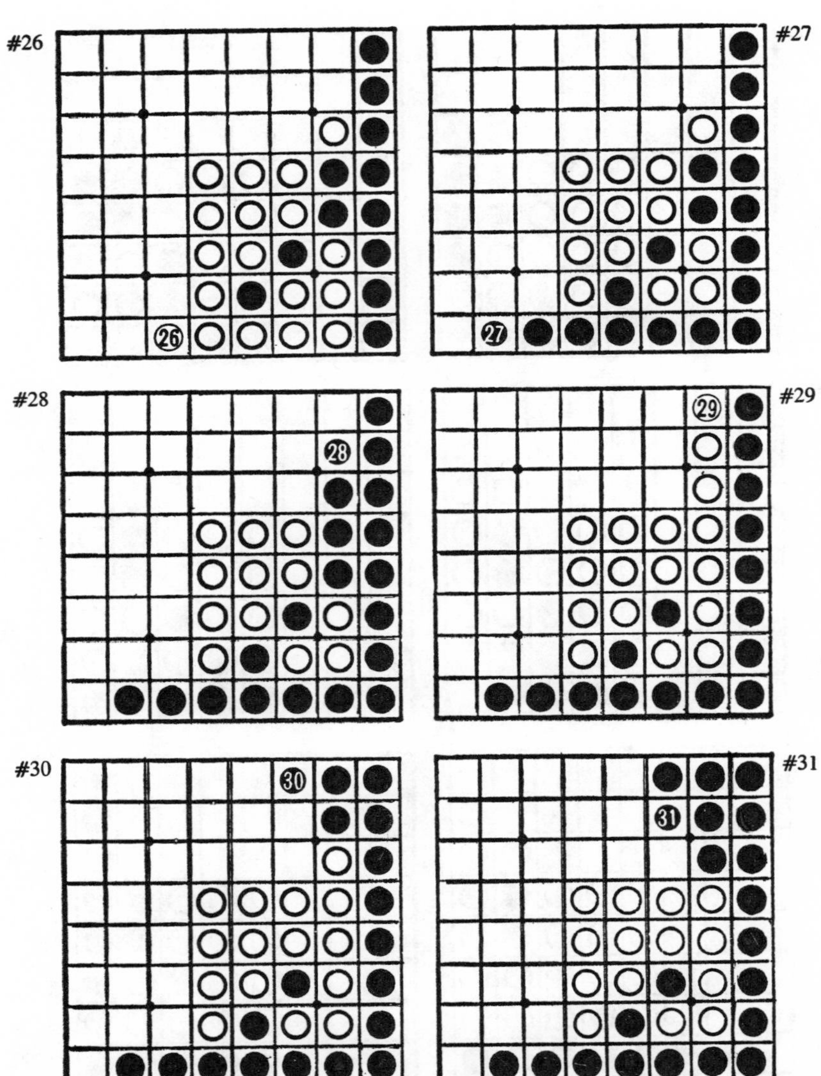
#26
26
#27
27
#28
28
#29
29
#30
30
#31
31

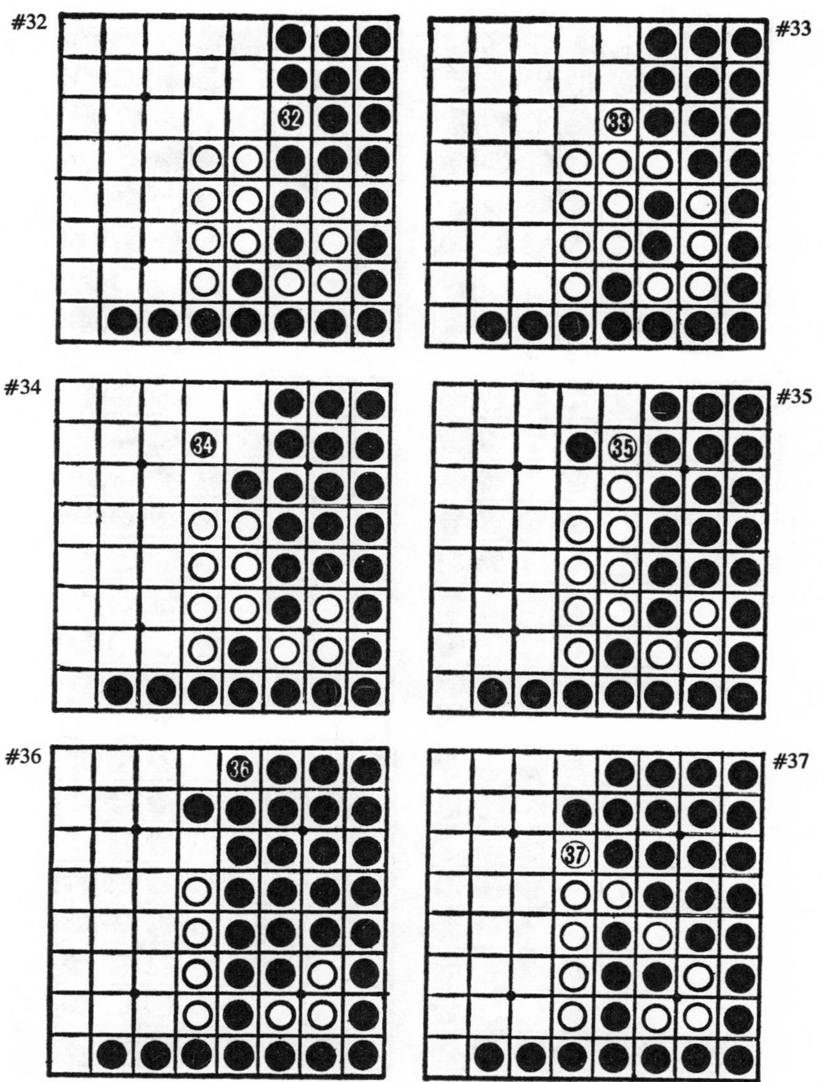
#32
#33
#34
#35
#36
#37

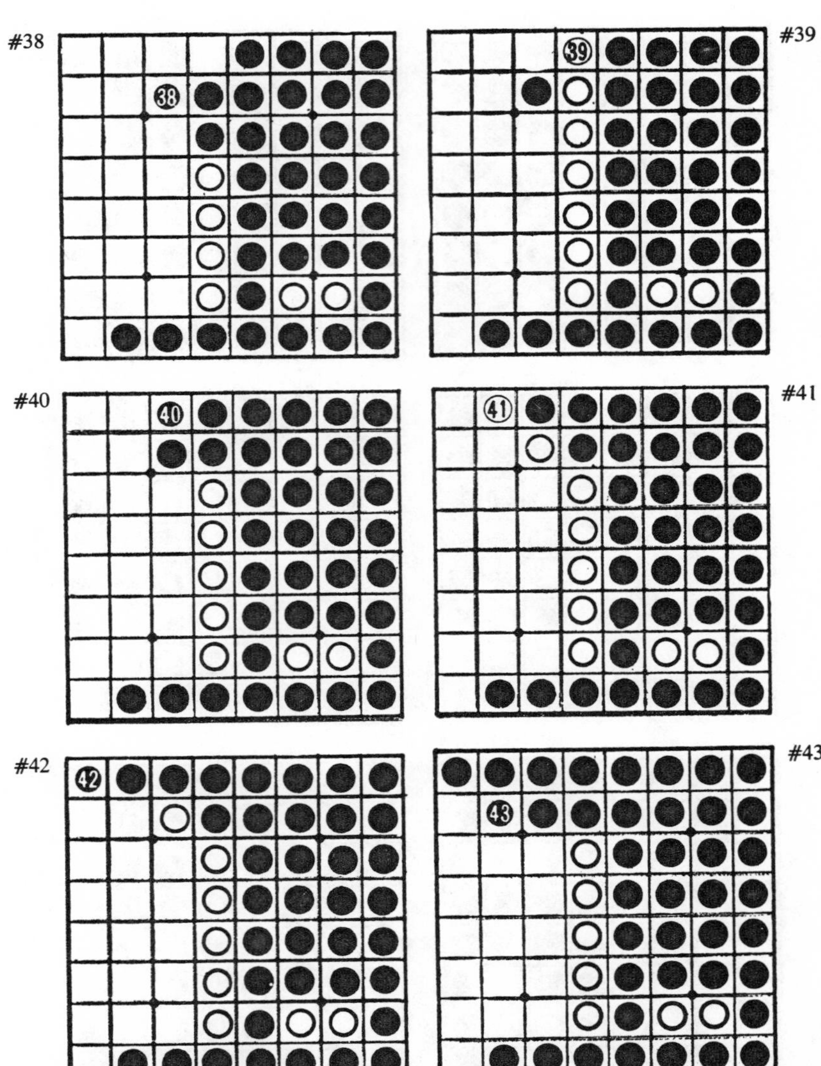

#38
38
#39
39
#40
40
#41
41
#42
42
#43
43

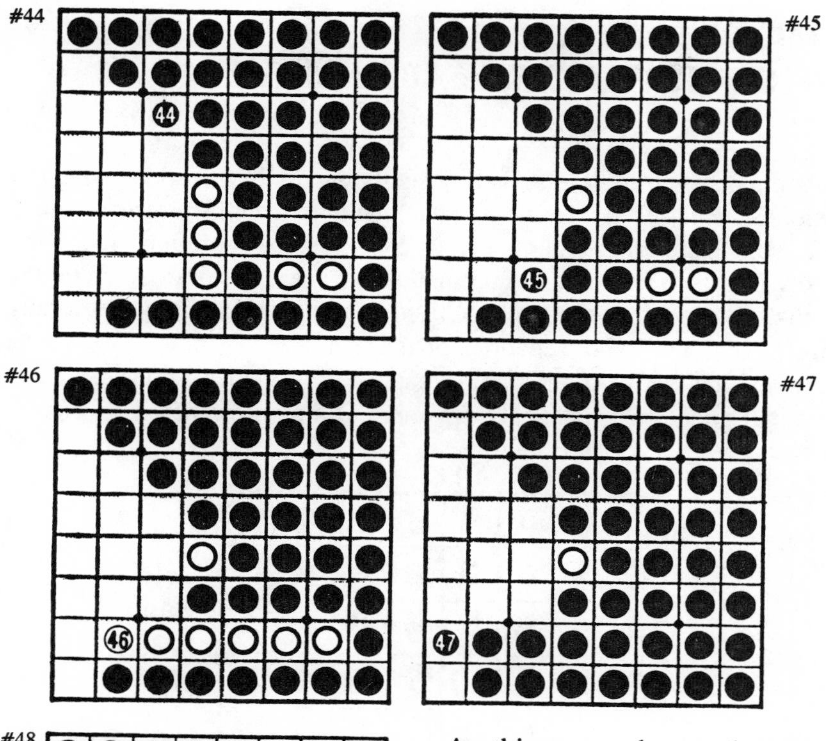

#48

As this game shows, the opening stage of Othello is very important. Even if you avoid **C**'s and **X**'s, as White did in this game, if you take **a**'s and **b**'s without much thought and planning, you can lose the game in the opening stage.

THE MIDDLE STAGE: THE 21ST MOVE TO THE 40TH MOVE

The most intensive struggle in Othello usually occurs in the middle stage of the game. Stay calm. Be ready to attack and to defend your positions. Evaluate each situation as it arises, to find the best solution. Don't be surprised when the board changes dramatically. There are more discs on the board now, so outflanking often results in flipping many discs and totally changing the color of whole sections of the board.

Be free and innovative in the middle stage. Rethink your game plan now. Your original goals may not apply anymore. It's a whole new ball game.

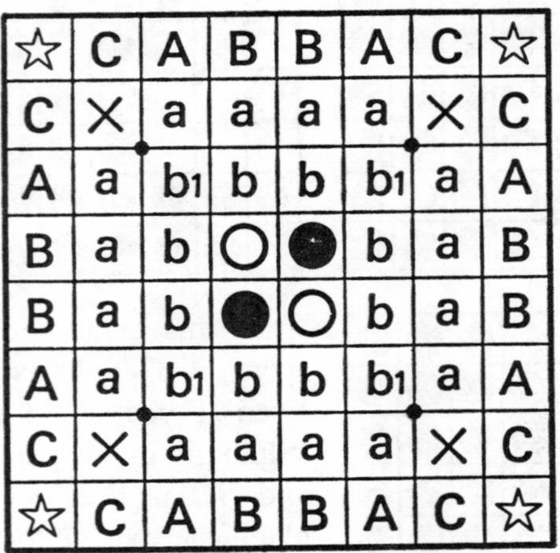

Basic Diagram

Keep in mind the principles of the Basic Diagram, but remember these important differences:

X's and **C**'s: In the opening stage, they were always dangerous moves, and almost always bad moves. In the middle stage they can be very good moves, if they help *you* gain control of corners or protect large areas of the board. But make these moves carefully!

A's and **B**'s: In the opening stage they were good moves. Now they can sometimes get you into a lot of trouble. Remember, the outside edge of the board is not isolated anymore. There are many discs around. If you move to an **A** or a **B** position now, make sure your opponent won't be able to outflank you and gain control of a corner or an edge of the board.

The See-Saw Stratagem (Again)

Now, just as in the opening stage, be careful to keep a balance of black and white discs on the board. Don't try to control too many discs of your color, and don't let your opponent's control get out of hand. The game isn't over yet—this is *not* the time to try to outflank as many discs as possible. Just keep the board fairly evenly balanced, to keep your options open for the final stage.

The middle stage is where most games are decided. If you were fatally damaged in the opening stage, you probably will not be able to recover in the middle, but a minor disadvantage can be overcome. There are more discs on the board now, and the chance of changes in the picture is approximately tripled.

Here are some guidelines and diagrams demonstrating the problems and triumphs of the middle stage.

Winning All the Way

Diagram 113 shows a situation taken from one of the preliminary matches of an All-Japan Championship Tournament. Black has the next move. Which side do you think is winning? There are fifteen possible moves Black can make (his 27th move). Study the diagrams carefully before you decide.

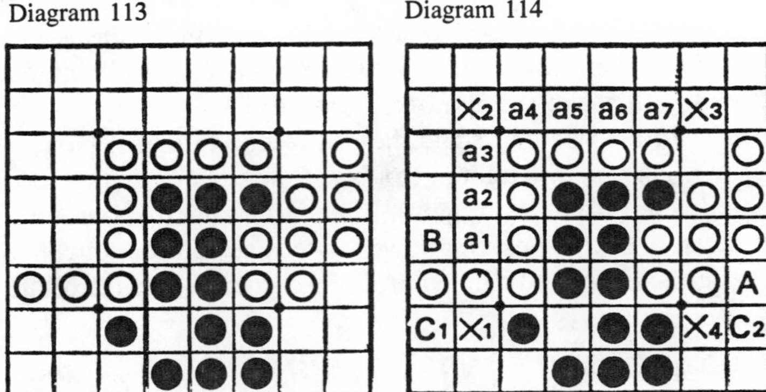

Diagram 113 Diagram 114

What is Black's next move?

We showed the diagram to ten Othello fans and surveyed their opinions. Four thought that Black had the advantage, two thought White had an edge over Black, and the rest said they could not tell who was ahead. Next we let them play the same game, starting with the situation in Diagram 113. Out of five games, three ended in Black's victory, two in White's.

The only answer to the question of who is winning is that in the situation of Diagram 113 Black has a slight edge over White only because he has the next move. In the actual game Black made a move to the **C2** position. This is a position to be avoided in the opening stage because it is a dangerous place for an isolated entry. But in this case it was the best move.

It had to be this particular **C** position, not any **C**. Look at **C1** on the lower left in Diagram 114, for instance. The move to this position would have been a fatal blow to Black. The four **X**'s are out of the question. The **A** position would have invited White to go to the **C1** spot, making things difficult for Black. A conventional move to the **B** position or one of the seven **a**'s would have made it hard for Black to read subsequent changes in situations and to plan future moves. In the middle stage one move can make a drastic and decisive change on the board. Therefore, be cautious each time you play.

White Loses His Cool

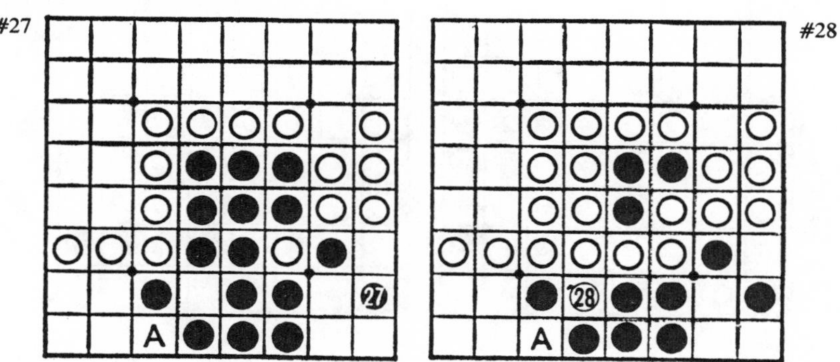

Taken aback by Black's surprise move 27, White made a bad move to position 28. The **A** position would have been better. Diagrams 115 and 116

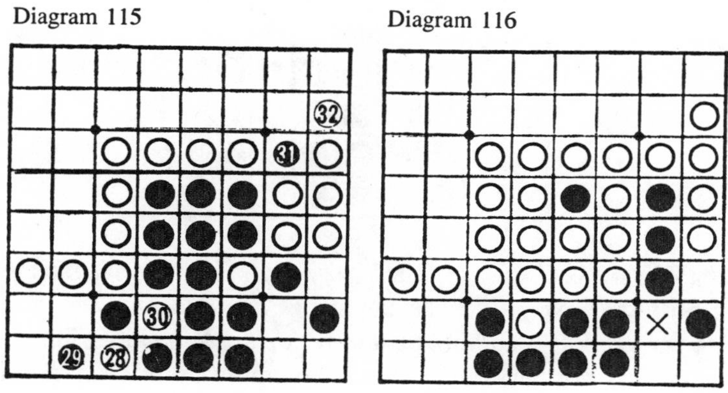

Diagram 115 Diagram 116

show what would have happened if White had gone to the **A** position. In Diagram 116 Black has the next move, but whatever move he makes, White can still go to the **X** position and establish a formidable defense.

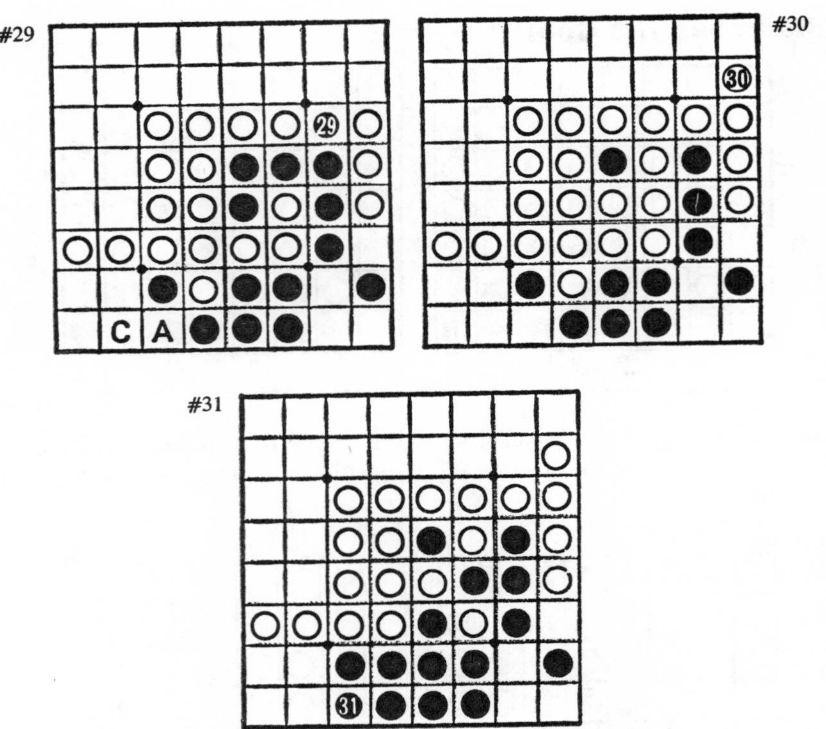

White's 30 is a mistake, since Black's 29 shows his obvious intention to go to the **A** position next (which he could not do with his 29th move). An alternative for White's 30 would be a move to the **A** position. Diagrams 117 and 118 show an imaginary development stemming from White's 30 in the **A**

position—an intense battle with an unpredictable outcome. Another alternative for White's 30 is the **C** position (as shown in #29).

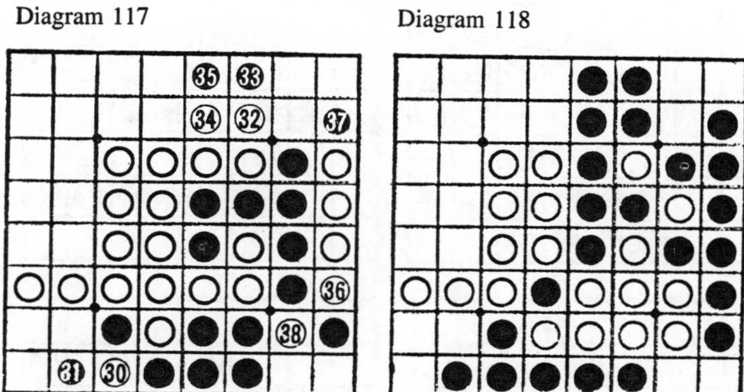

White's 30 in the actual game was what Black was hoping for. Black's next move, 31, clearly shows that White made tactical errors and is losing.

Look at the situation in #31. It is only five moves advanced from Diagram 113, but already it looks desperate for White. Two miscalculations—White's 28th and 30th moves—leave him nowhere to go but to an **X** position. White is definitely defeated.

The following diagrams show Black's aggressive attack on White move by move. See how steadily the white discs disappear from the board. At the end of the game there was only one white disc left, a disastrous ending, hard to predict in Diagram 113.

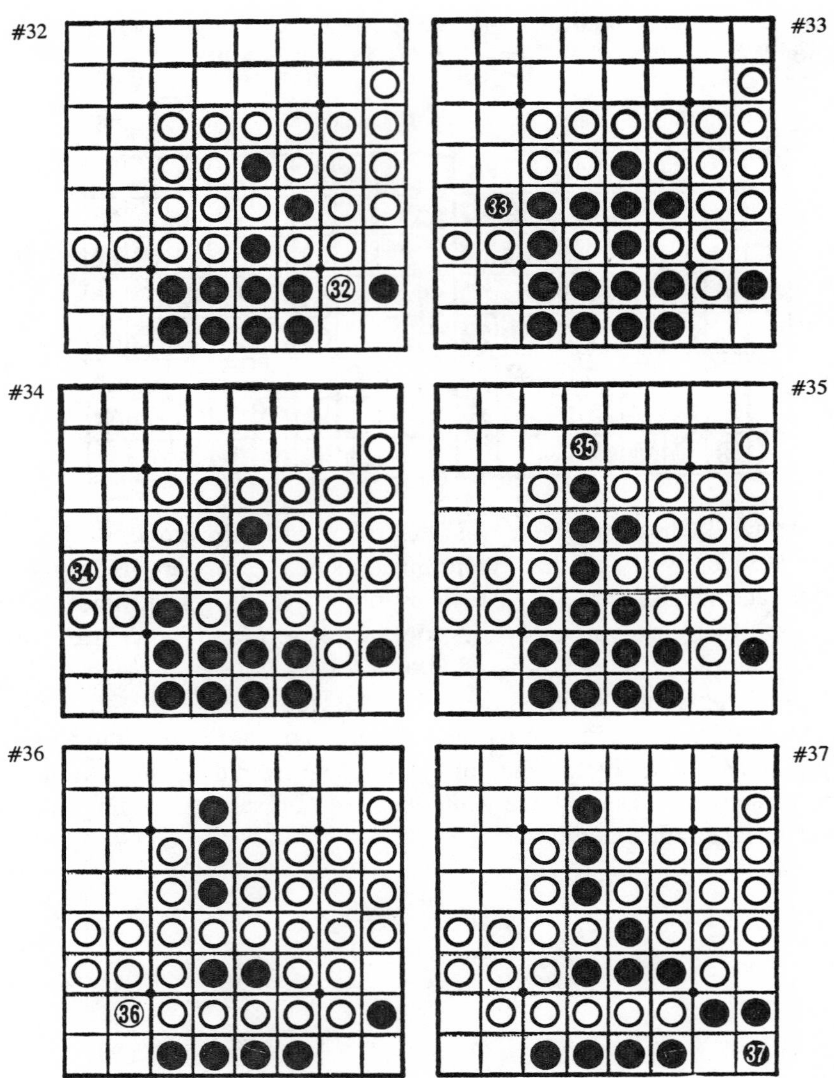
#32
32
#33
33
#34
34
#35
35
#36
36
#37
37

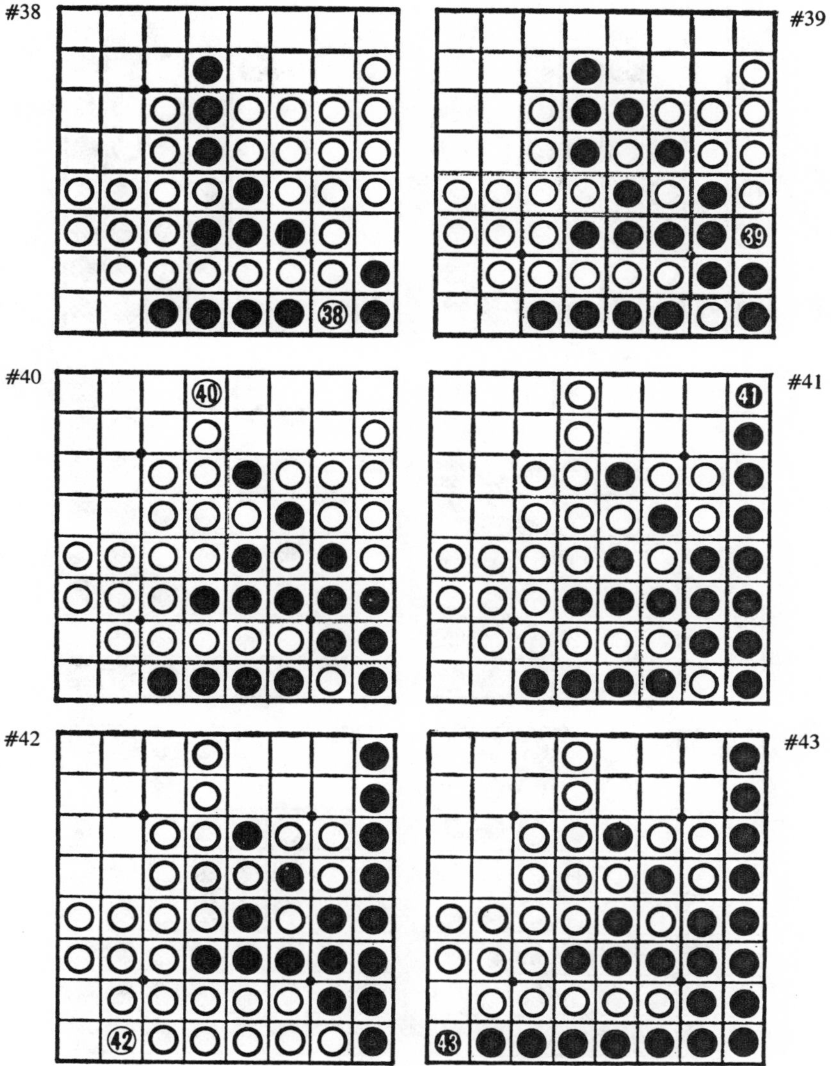
#38
38
#39
39
#40
40
#41
41
#42
42
#43
43

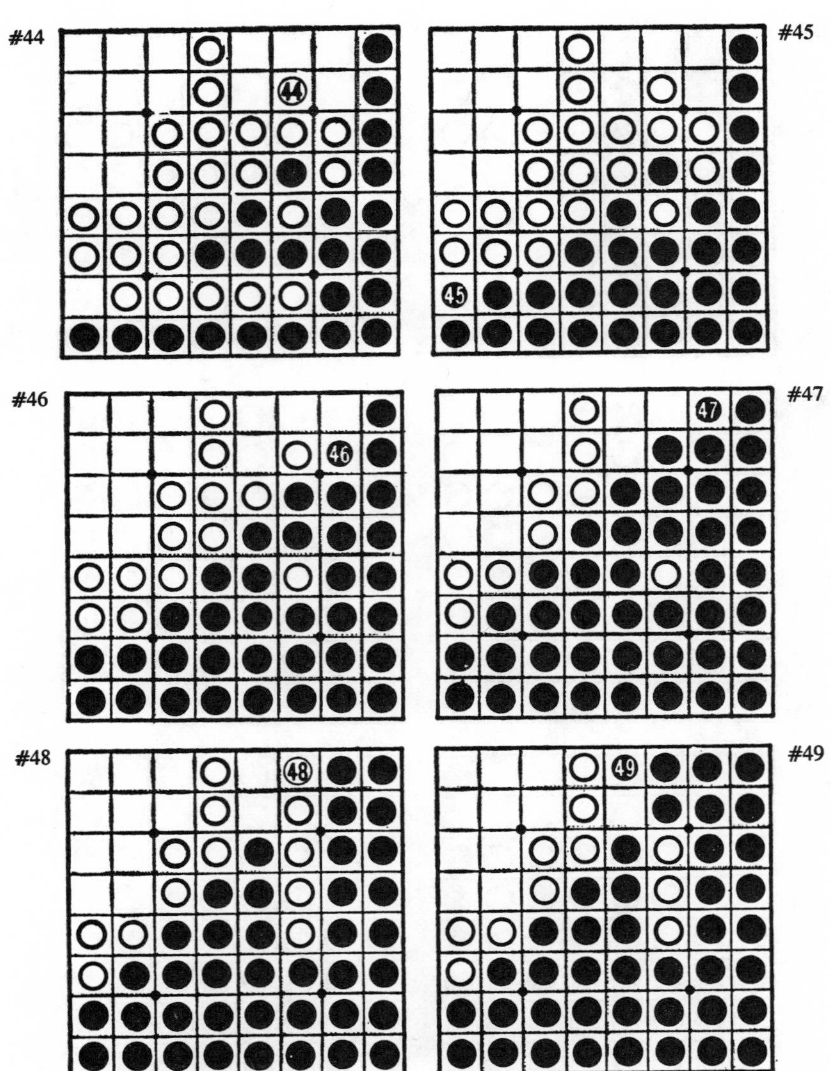

#44
44
#45
45
#46
46
#47
47
#48
48
#49
49

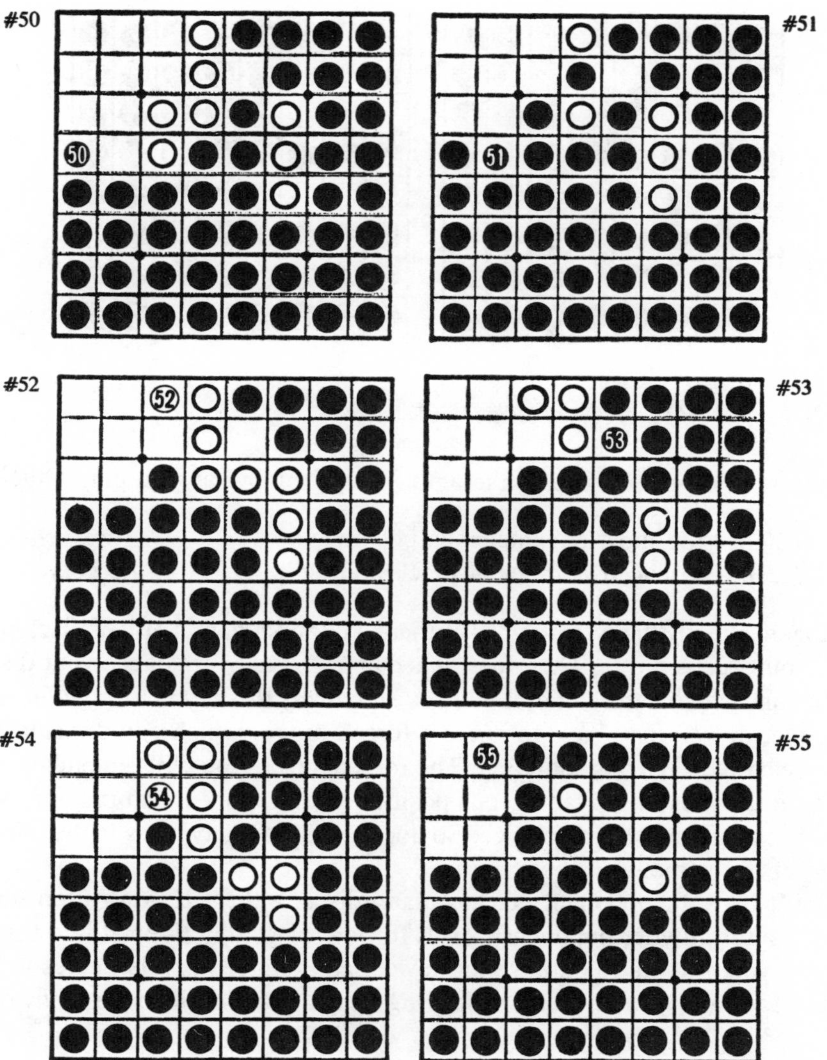
#50
50
#51
51
#52
52
#53
53
#54
54
#55
55

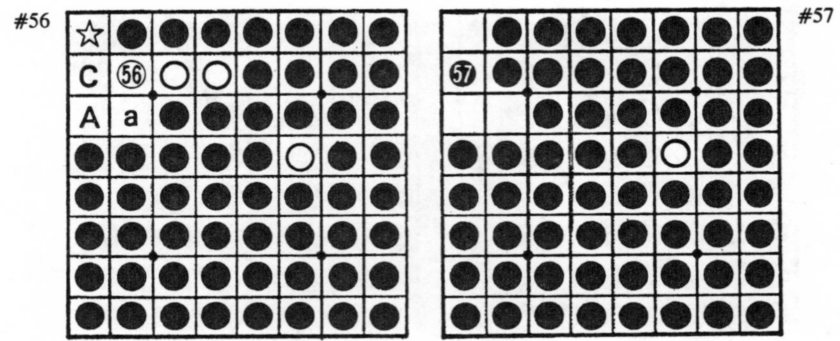

Don't Forget the Balance

There are two major winning factors to keep in mind as you play Othello:

1. Choose the most advantageous positions.
2. Keep a balanced number of black and white discs on the board.

As you already know, you must outflank your opponent's disc or discs each time you make a move. Therefore, it is dangerous to overbalance your discs. In the final stage of the game, if you have too many discs, you may not be able to move, or you may have to make a forced move, which could result in a complete reversal of the situation. The forced move, you will remember, is a move to the most disadvantageous position your opponent can pressure you into, because you have no choice. So don't gain too many discs in the middle stage of the game.

Don't let your opponent get too many discs, either. If you're too timid about capturing your opponent's discs for fear of getting trapped into forced moves, you may find you have too few discs to make flexible moves in the final stage, and you will end up having to make a forced move anyway.

Enough Is . . . Not Too Much

Just what is wrong with having too many discs? Two things. During the opening or middle stages of Othello if you have many more discs than your opponent, you can block your own freedom to move, and you can endanger large areas of the board. But if you have a very sound, well-planned strategy, and if you have placed discs at key points to prevent a last-minute upset, you can safely have a greater number of discs than your opponent.

Inexperienced players often capture many discs during the early stages of the game. Then, in the final stage, the opponent takes a corner position and flips whole rows of discs. Careful, strategic placement of discs can hold these rows and prevent a total reversal of the game at the end—but it requires a lot of planning and thought. Until you know how to protect your discs, it's much safer to keep a balanced number of discs during the opening and middle stages.

Don't Be Greedy

Here is an example of how too many discs on the board lost the game for Black.

Diagram 119

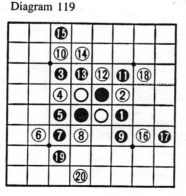

Diagram 120

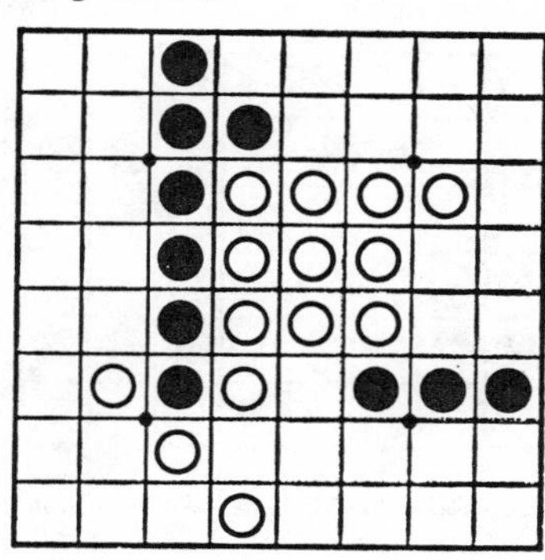

Diagrams 119 and 120 show a phase of one of the semifinals for the All-Japan Women's Championship Tournament. It is the second game of the match. Black is played by Motoko Aimori, and White by Dr. Yoko Kitamura. They have just finished the opening stage of the game, and it is a 50-50 situation.

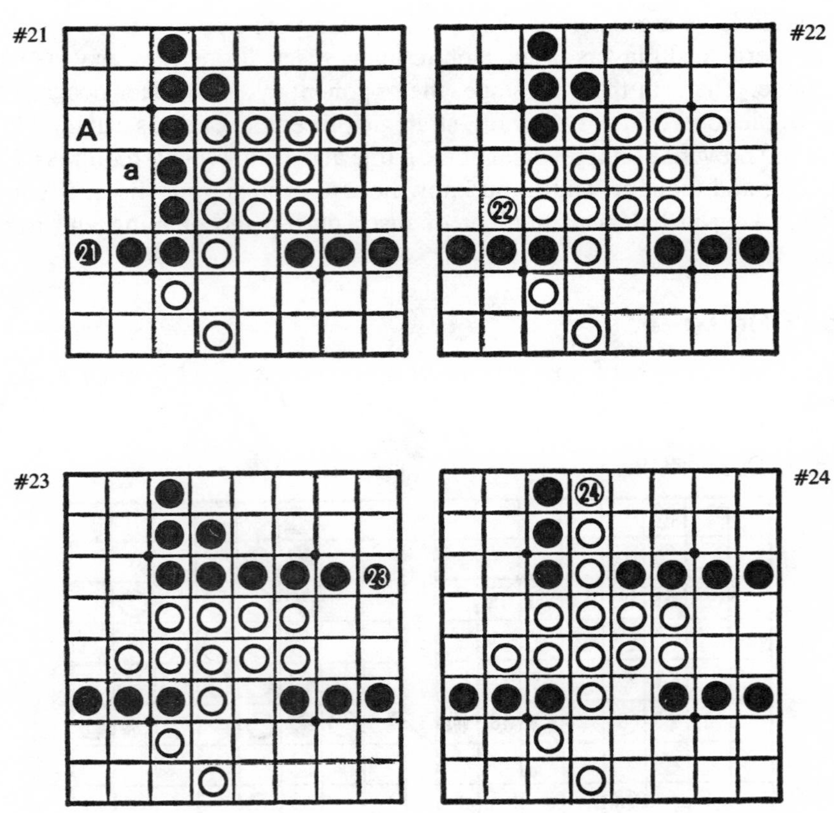

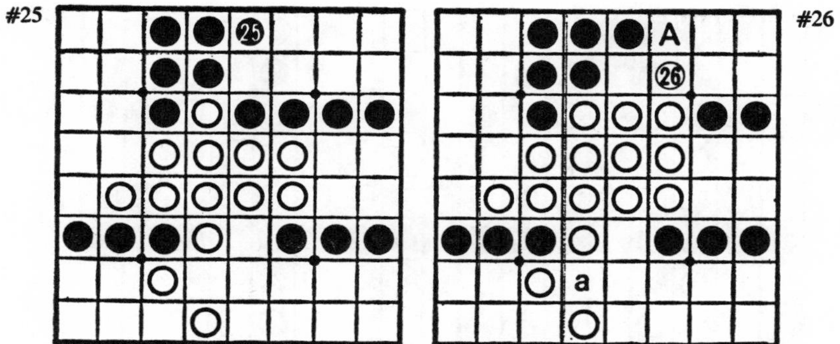

White's skillful play is remarkable. Her 22nd move is exquisite, keeping Black at bay in the left area. If White had made the 22nd move to the **a** position, Black would have taken the **A** position, establishing a base in the left field. White's 24 is an unconventional move. Usually such a position is avoided, but White did not hesitate to go there. Black naturally made the 25th move to the position next to it. White's 26 is provoking Black to go to the **A** position (see #26).

Black Defends Her Move

At this point Black stared at the board for a long time. Later she said, "I was about to go to the **A** position, but when I read the board again I was shocked to discover how bad the situation was for me. If I went to the **A** position, White would go to the **a** position [#26]. Then there would be too many black discs choking up my own rows. So instead of the **A** position I chose the position of twenty-seven [#27 below], which did not improve my prospects much either.

"Black's formation in Diagram 120 was not bad. I suppose my eagerness to take **A** positions with the twenty-first and twenty-third moves worked against

#27

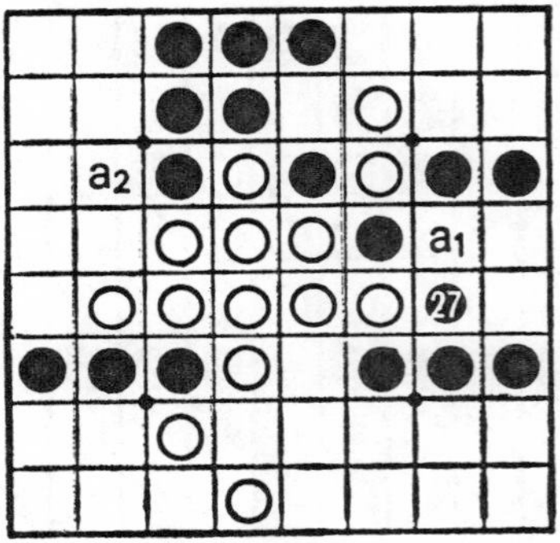

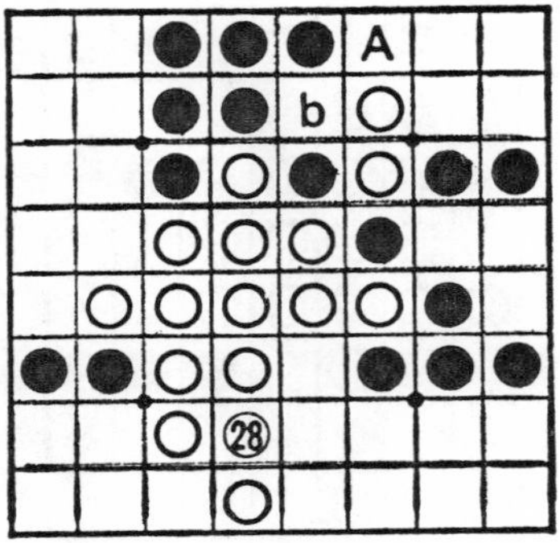

#28

#29

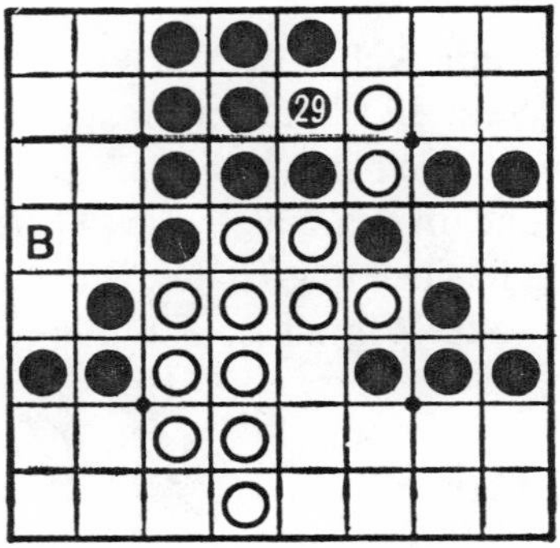

me. But at the time I couldn't predict the possible changes. I didn't have any better ideas.

"When I made the twenty-seventh move, I expected White to go to either the **a1** or **a2** positions. But she moved to the position of twenty-eight [#28 above]. That made me want to go to the **A** position again. But then what would happen? There were many moves White could make, and even if she chose the most conventional **b** position, the result would have been as shown in Diagrams 121 and 122. In Diagram 122 White has many positions to move to, but Black is very close to a stalemate.

Diagram 121

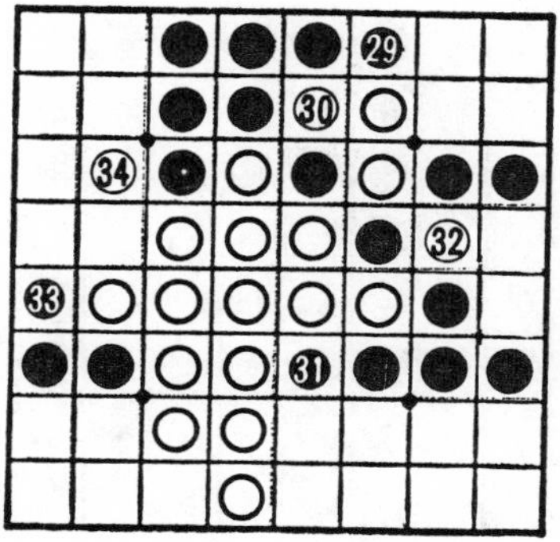

Diagram 122

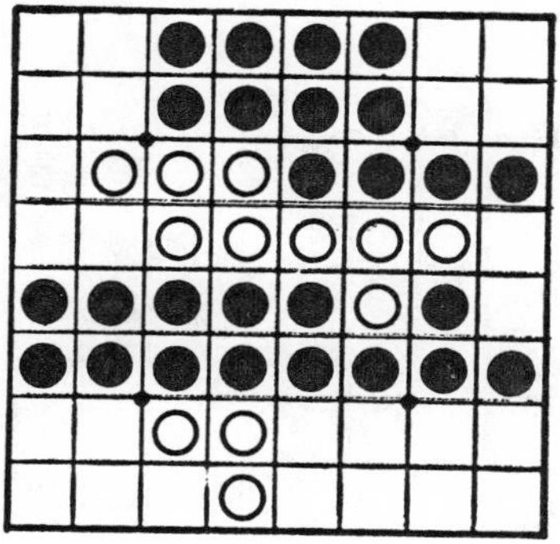

"That is why I chose position twenty-nine. I was sure Black would take the **B** position, but again her thirtieth move was unorthodox and unexpected. For

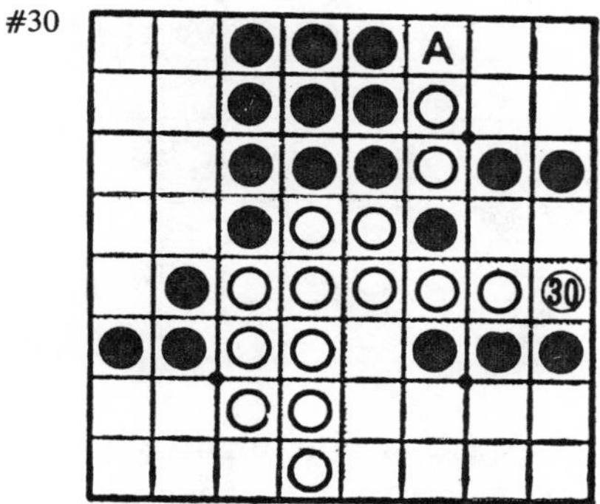

#30

a moment I thought of leaving White's thirty alone and making my thirty-first move as in Diagram 123.

"Black is not necessarily at a disadvantage in Diagram 124, though. If

Diagram 123

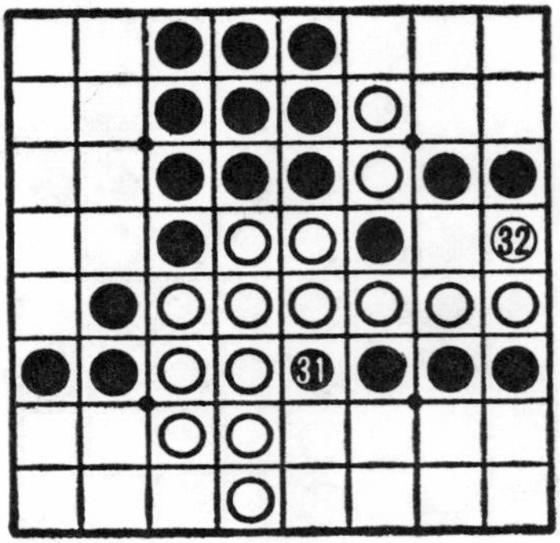

Diagram 124

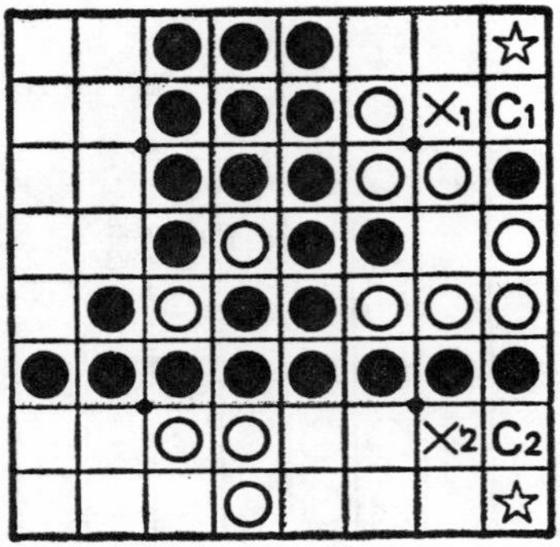

Diagram 125

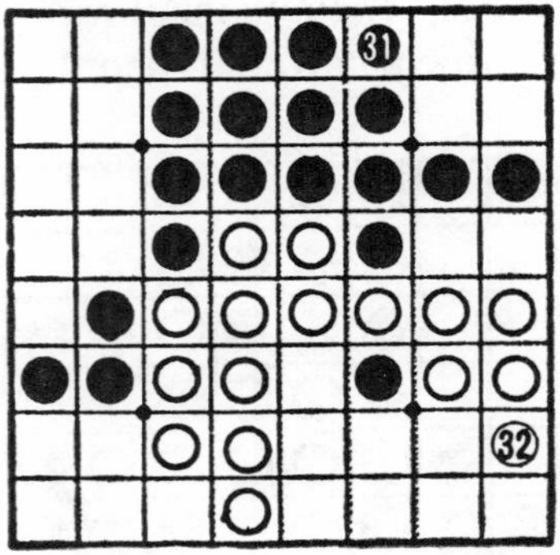

White has to go to the **C1** or **C2** position first, Black can go to the corner, establishing a strong formation. On the other hand, if Black is forced to the **C1** or **C2** position and White takes the corners, it would be disastrous for Black. Anyway, an empty space left between discs can cause a storm in the final stage. I was uneasy about it, faced by such a formidable and unpredictable opponent as Dr. Kitamura.

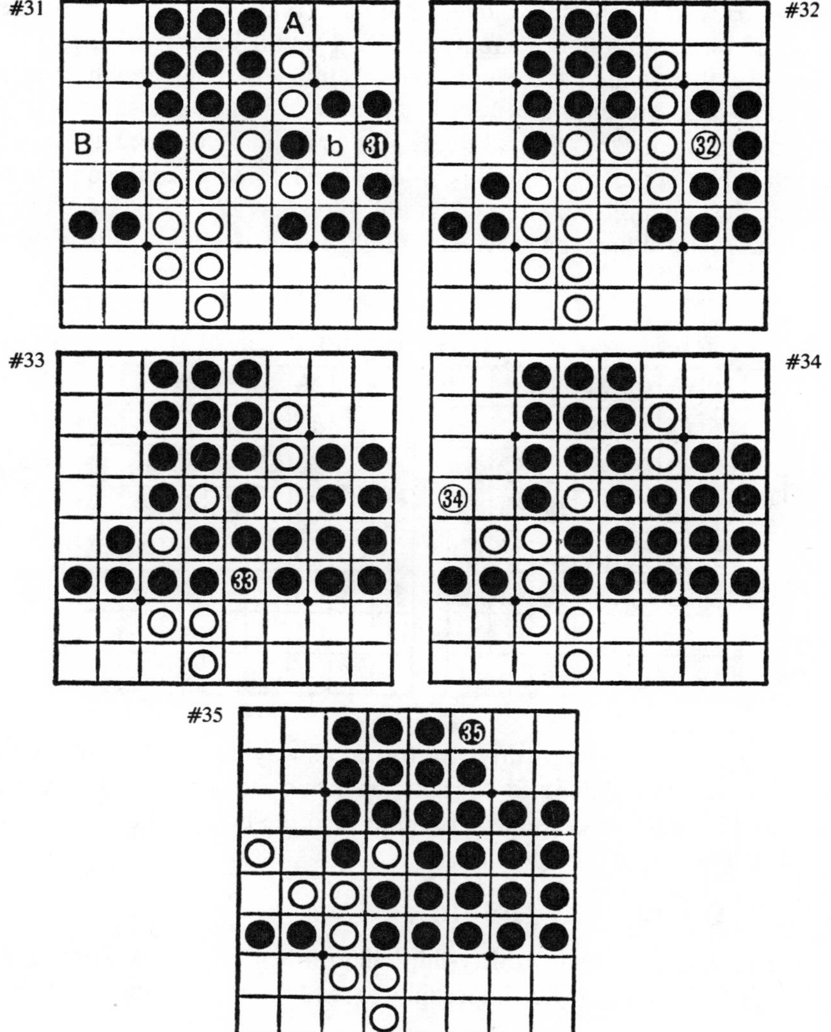
#31
A
B
b
31
#32
32
#33
33
#34
34
#35
35

"Let's go back to the thirtieth move. In order to prevent White from squeezing herself into the ominous empty space, I could have moved to the **A** position. But that would have caused White's thirty-two move to the position in Diagram 125, presenting a puzzling picture. I finally chose to take the empty space myself [see #31 above]. It is an ordinary move, but I thought White probably would go to the **B** position, then I could go to the **b** position, leading to the situation shown in Diagrams 126 and 127. White would be up against the wall. Whatever move she might make, I could go to a corner position.

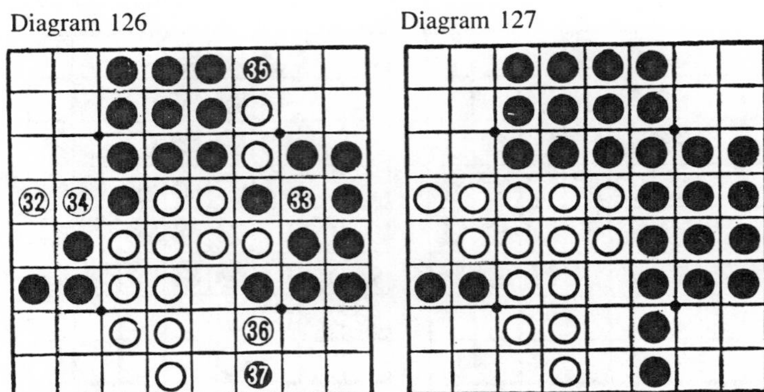

Diagram 126 Diagram 127

"Unexpectedly, White's thirty-two forced its way into the **b** position. I am ashamed to tell you that I did not anticipate this move. Now my dream of Diagrams 126 and 127 crumbled. I had to read the board all over again and make new plans.

When in Doubt, Play It Safe

"I was not sure whether my thirty-third and thirty-fifth moves were the best moves in this situation. It was impossible to read the game accurately because there were so many ways it could turn. My policy is to stick to the principles of the Basic Diagram if I cannot assess the situation clearly. My thirty-fifth move was made accordingly [see #35 above].

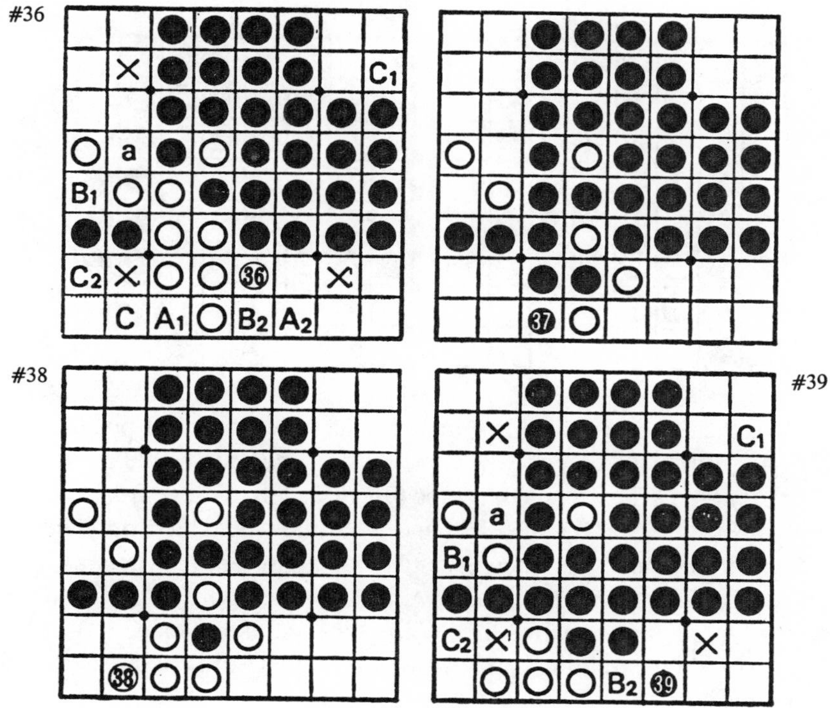

"I was tempted to make my thirty-seventh move to the **C** position [see #36 above], but it would have led to the situation in Diagrams 128 and 129. If White forced the fortieth move to the position shown in the diagram, I would not know how to deal with it. Even if one could read the situation correctly, at this stage of the game one could not predict what it would be ten moves ahead. In Diagram 129 Black has the next move. The diagonal row of five white discs is a very good formation. At this point no one can say that Black has an edge over White.

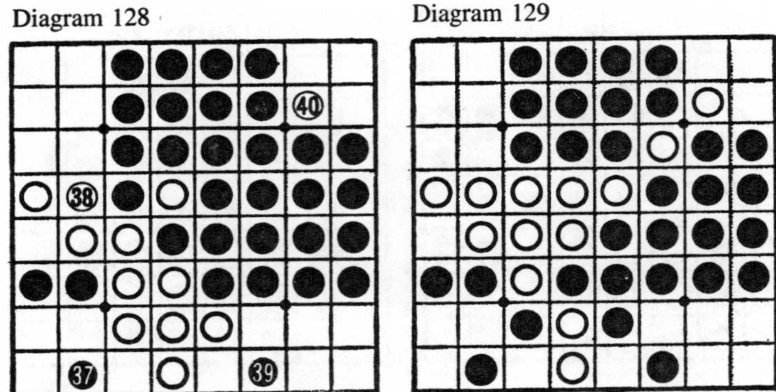
Diagram 128 Diagram 129

"This is the reason I made my thirty-seventh move to the **A1** position: after Black's **A1**, White would go to the **C** position, then Black would go to the **A2** position. By then White would have too few discs left to move freely. Besides unwelcome positions of **C1**, **C2**, **B2**, and **X**, White would have only the **a** and the **B1** positions open [as shown in play diagram #39]. After my thirty-seven, White's thirty-eight was a move I anticipated. Only after I made the thirty-ninth move did I realize that White had one more space left that she could go to without straining herself. I was sorry that I did not pursue my plan to Diagrams 128 and 129, but it was too late.

The Beginning of the End

"Sure enough, White's forty was placed in the spot. Now we still had the final stage to fight, but already my black discs were too many in number, blocking my movement.

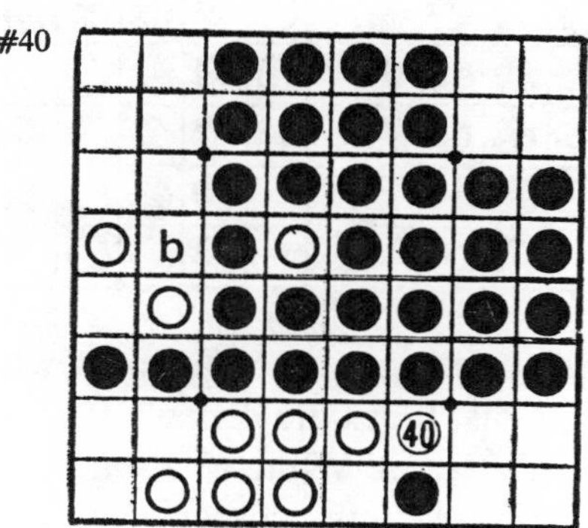

"If I went to the **b** position [#40 above], the situation would have developed as in Diagrams 130 and 131, Black being trapped into making a forced move. I had to make the forty-first move shown in Diagram 132.

Diagram 130

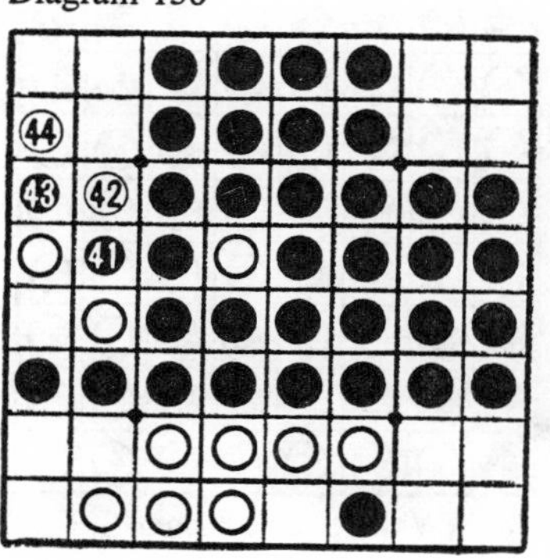

Diagram 131

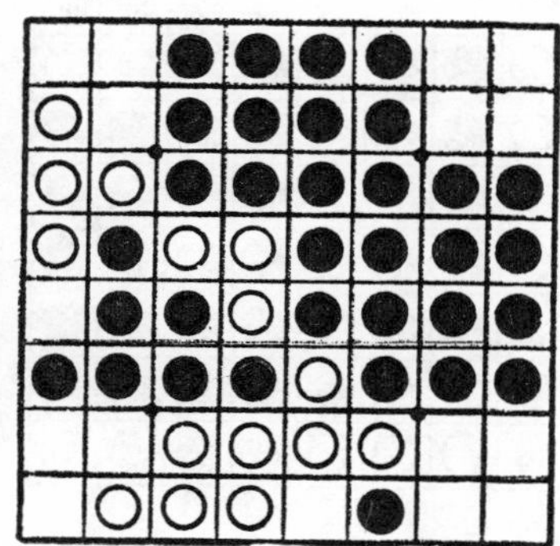

Diagram 132

Diagram 133

"I must admit that Black fell into a predicament when White made the fortieth move. Considering this, Black did very well in the final stage. Black's forty-three and forty-five almost led White to a stalemate. White's forty-six was a clever move, luring Black to the corner position. White squeezed its forty-eight into the slot. Black's forty-nine was a forced move again.

"In Diagram 133 White has complete control of the situation. The board is

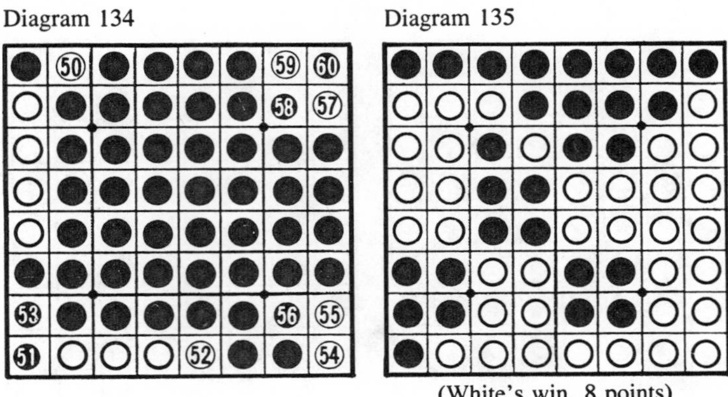

Diagram 134

Diagram 135

(White's win, 8 points)

practically covered with black discs. It has one corner position open. Nevertheless, Black cannot make a single move. On the other hand, seven white discs are placed in excellent strategic positions, ready to swallow rows of black discs."

This game demonstrates the principle that keeping a balanced number of white and black discs is important. If the balance is broken, one side or the other will get into trouble. Usually the player who has many more discs on the board is more likely to be defeated.

Enough Is . . . Not Too Few

In the previous section we saw how too many discs can block one player's movement. The opposite is also true; having too few discs also can limit your freedom and your ability to capture discs in the middle and final stages.

In this section we show how having too few discs on the board in the middle stage can lead to defeat.

From the very beginning (see Diagram 136) White challenged his opponent aggressively. His 8th move took the **A** position. If Black moved to the **B1**

Diagram 136

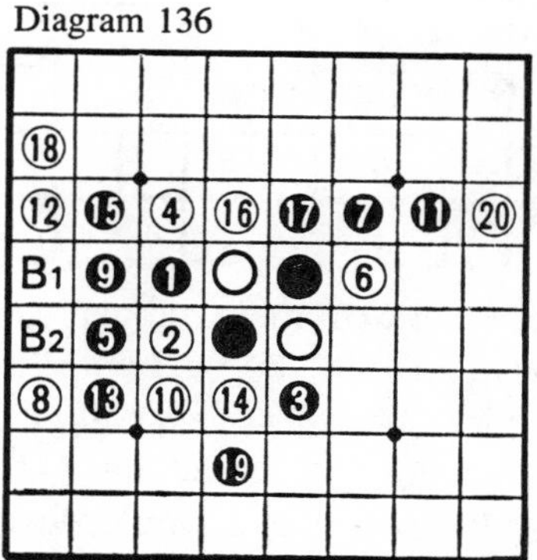

Diagram 137

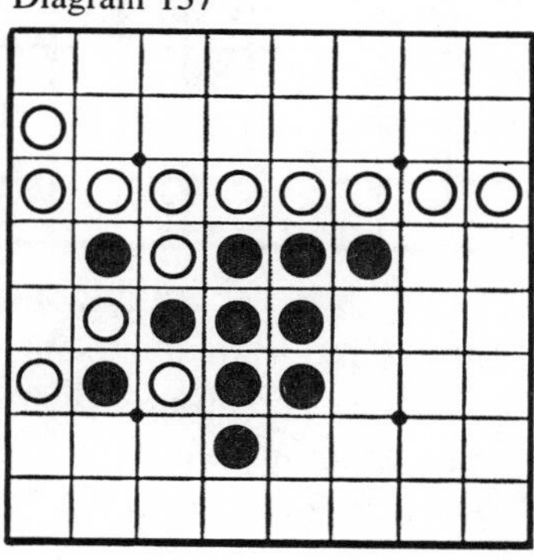

position, White would outflank him from the **B2** position. White was determined to keep Black off the left outer edge. Of course Black was aware of White's intention; therefore he made the 9th and 11th moves elsewhere to see what White would do. White's 12 rushed to the second **A** position, but Black wasn't too worried. He was confident that if he waited patiently for white discs to multiply, he would have a chance to capture them in droves.

Black made a leisurely 17th move, then was amazed to see White's 18th. In the situation shown in Diagram 138 there is nothing to be alarmed at in the position of White's 18 (Diagram 139). White can safely go to the position because if in the future White ever has to make a forced move, Black could not go to the **B1** or **B2** position. If Black takes either of those positions, White can capture it by moving to the remaining **B1** or **B2.**

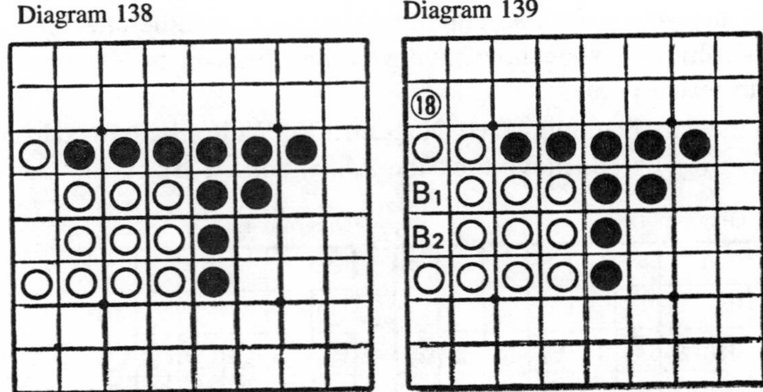

Diagram 138 Diagram 139

But White's 18 is generally considered an extremely dangerous move. If White is forced into a stalemate and has to go to the **B1** or **B2** position, Black will take whichever position is not occupied by White. This will assure Black of the corner position, which will be a severe blow to White. On the other hand, if Black is forced into the **B1** or **B2** position, it would not affect his strength too much.

Even if White has a 50-50 chance to be led into a stalemate, the position of 18 still does not make sense. Unless White were absolutely confident of his control of the game, he would not dare make such a move. No wonder Black fell into deep thought after White's 18th move. White's 20th, following Black's 19th, was another forceful move to the **A** position. The opening stage ended here.

This game is quite different from the one we studied in the previous section. Black discs are floating in the middle without a single base in outer-edge positions, whereas White definitely has a superior formation and is leading Black in the game. It will be interesting to see whether White can maintain the lead through the middle and final stages of the game.

The Wrong Choice

Black had several alternatives for his 21st move. One was to the position of 21 in Diagram 140, which would prevent White's 22 from going to the **A** position. If White went to the **B** position next, Black could go to the **C** position, making White uneasy. If White went to the **a1** position instead, Black could go to the **a2** position.

Diagram 140

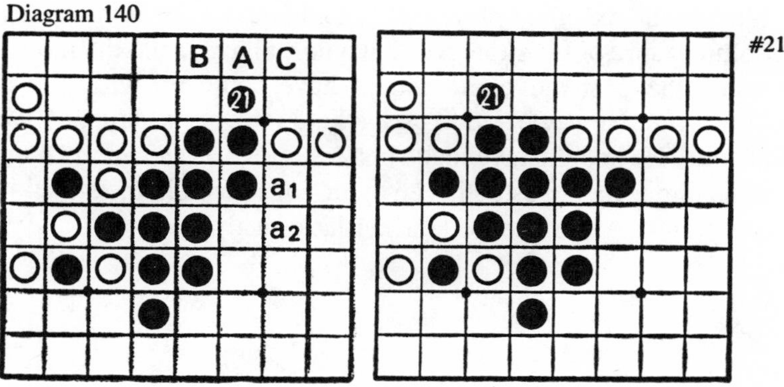

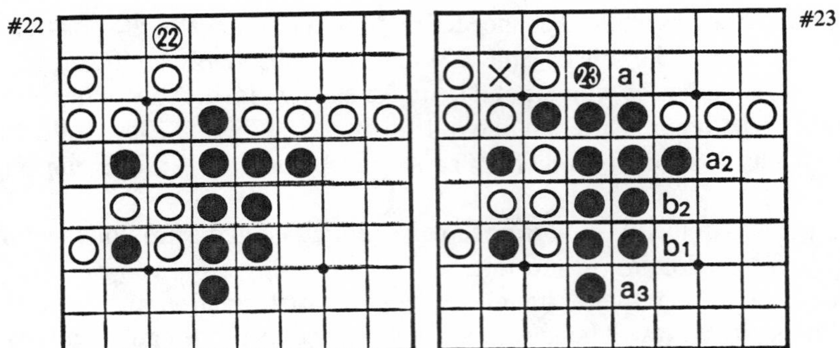

Actually, Black's 21 was a doubtful move because it gave away the desirable **A** position to White. At this point Black read the situation this way: Black's 23 would capture the white disc in the center of a cross-shaped formation (#23 above). The disc would remain black even if White went to the **a1**, **a2**, **b2**, **b1**, and **a3** positions. The black disc could be turned over only when White went to the **X** position, which was exactly what Black wanted.

Black's judgment was faulty, because he assumed that White, not Black, would run into a stalemate. Black had already seen White's 18. And he knew that White was an excellent player. He should have known that unless White was absolutely sure of his strategy, he wouldn't have made the move. Before Black made the 21st move, he should have come up with plans to outmaneuver White. He neglected to take a hard look at the situation and revise his basic plan. He should have made his 21st move as shown in Diagram 140 and tried to find a way to establish an outer-edge base. In the situation shown in Diagram 140, White cannot attack Black easily.

White Keeps Black Running

White's 24 was again a surprise attack on Black, who had to make some forced moves. Black has only the **a** position to go to (see #24). This move will lead to the situation of Diagrams 141 and 142. Black cannot prevent White from taking the corner position. Black's 25 in the **a** position can also result in the situation in Diagrams 143 and 144.

#24

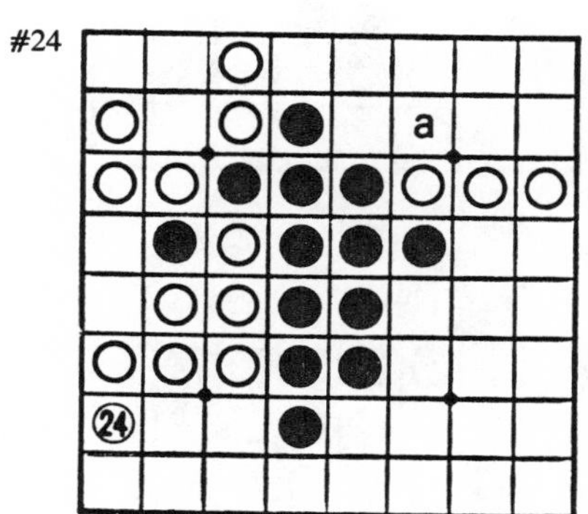

#25

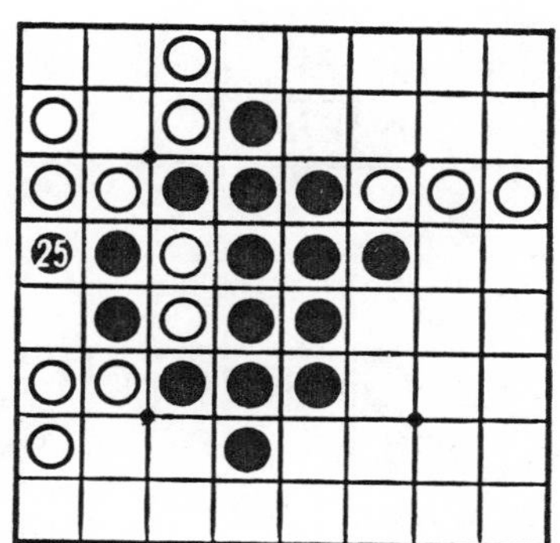

#26

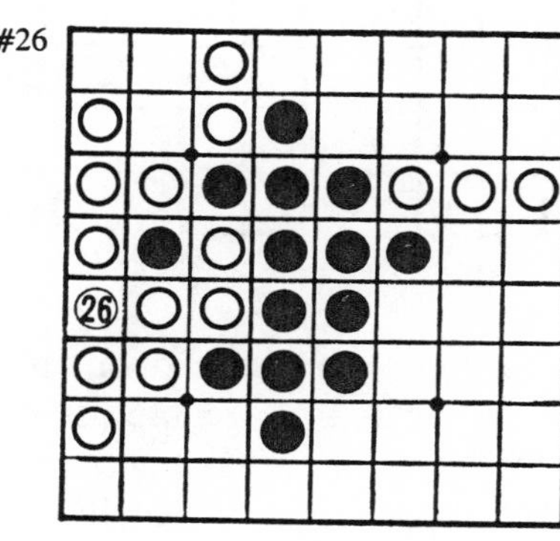

Diagram 141

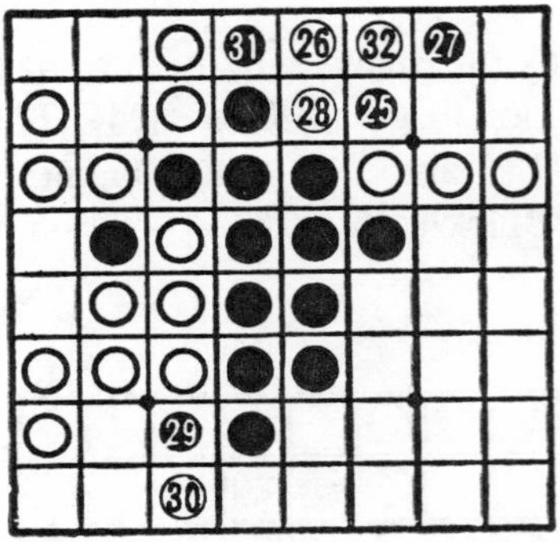

Diagram 142

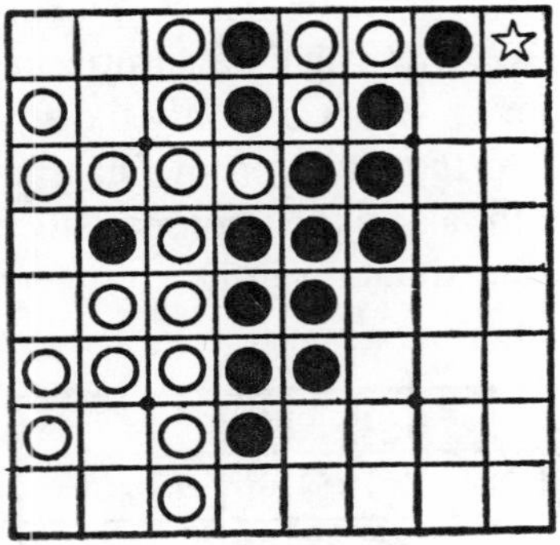

Diagram 143

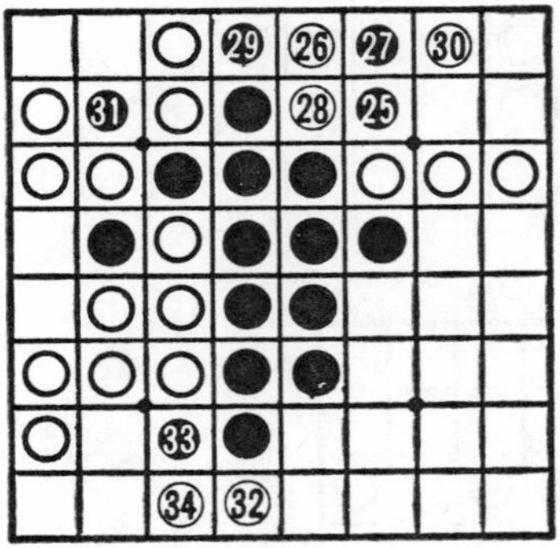

Diagram 144

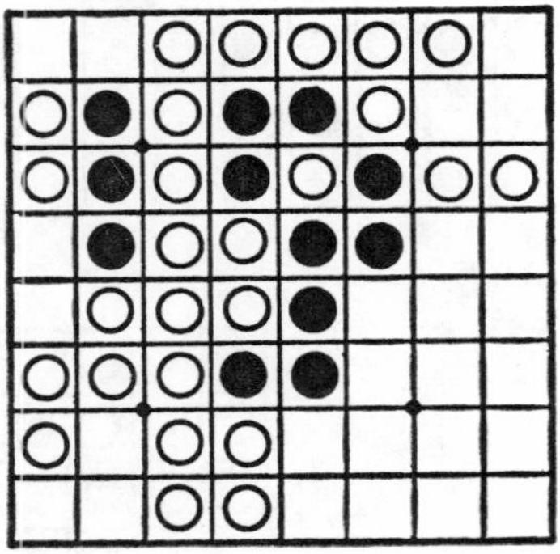

Actually Black made his 25th move as shown, intending this to be a preparation for his 29th. He wanted to squeeze into a space between two white discs. But after White's 30 Black had nowhere but the position of 31 to go to. White's 32 captured Black's 31 immediately, leaving Black without a base.

#27

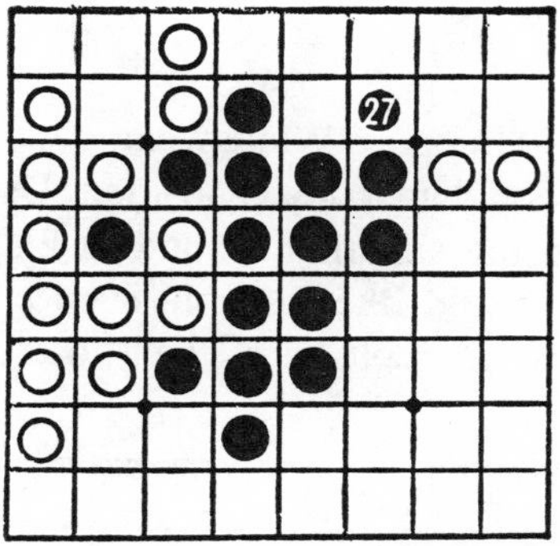

#28

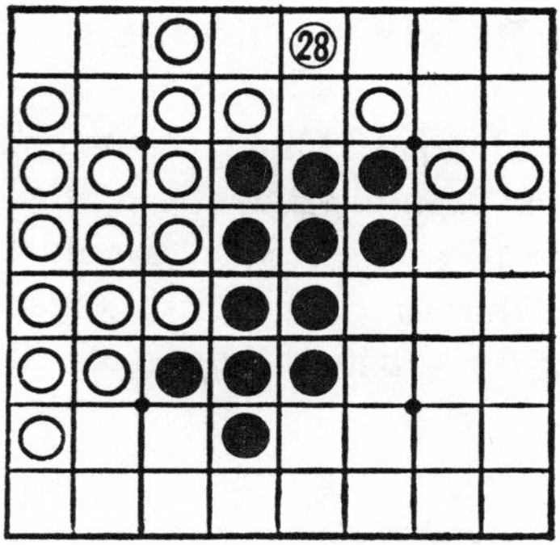

#29

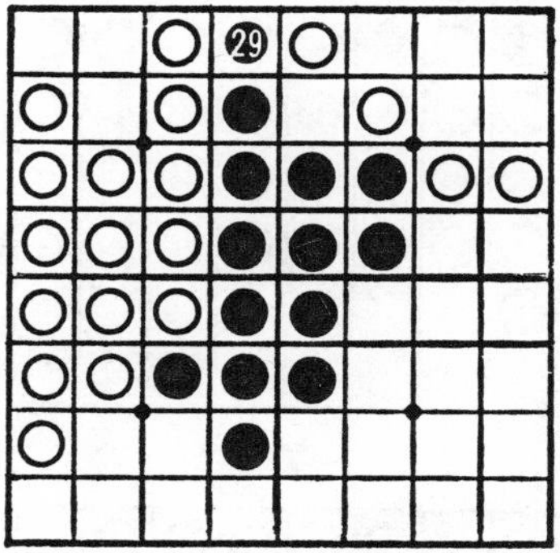

#30

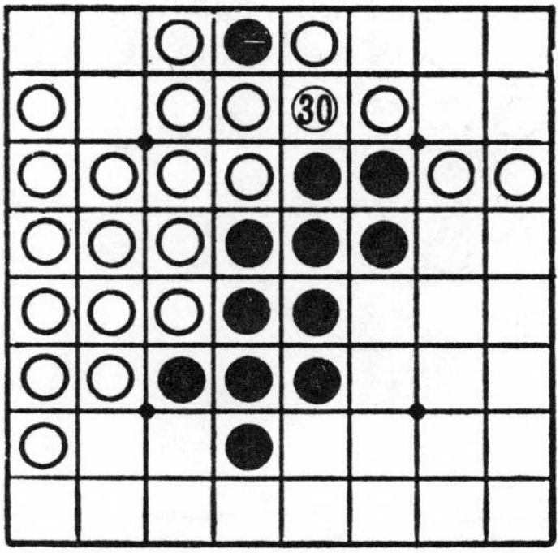

#31

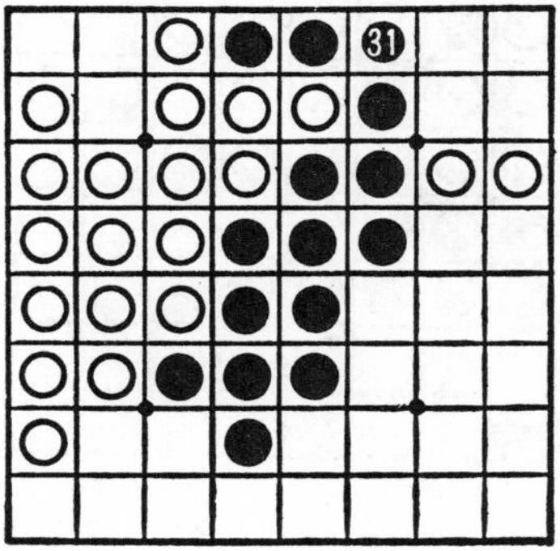

#32

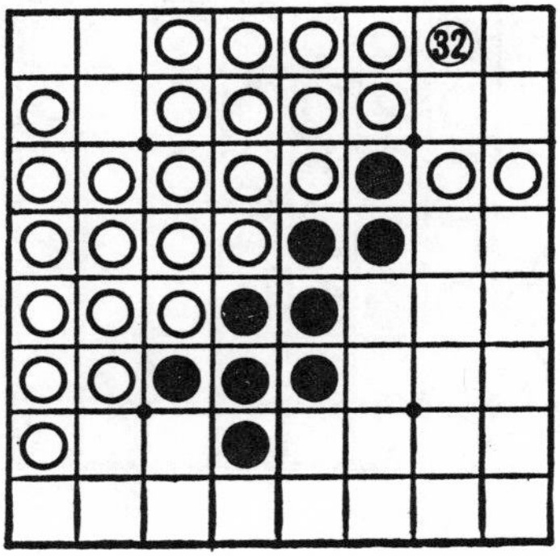

Black's Belated Boldness

Black's bold move 33 made White uneasy. Suppose White went to the corner position and captured Black's 33; Black would go to the **C** position. Using the **C** position as a base, Black would turn the situation around in his favor. White, having too many discs already, would like to avoid such a drastic change in the situation. He would like to keep pushing Black to the end.

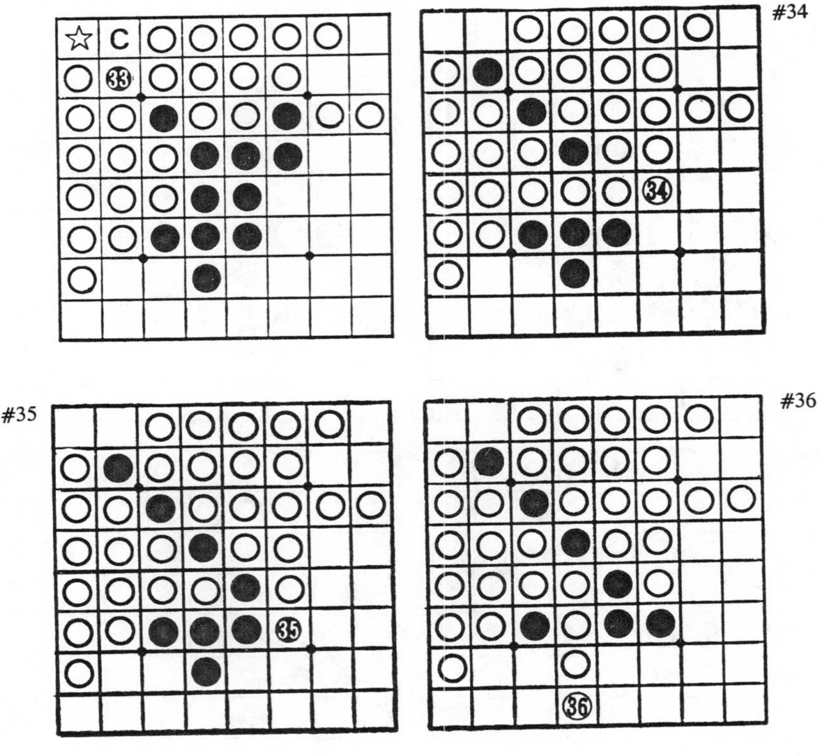

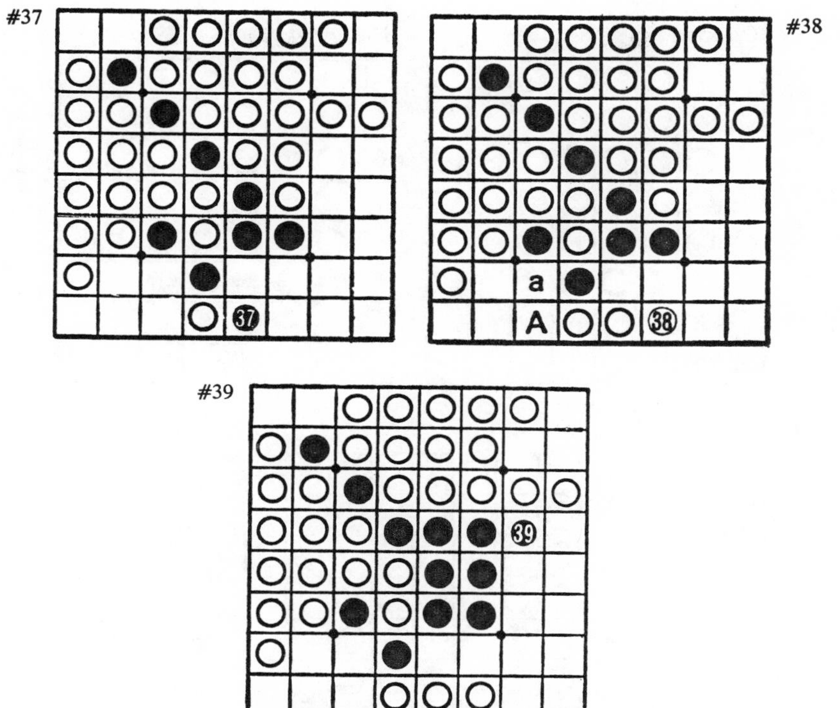

Moves 34, 35, and 36 were all very strong and good, but Black's 37 was a poor move which probably caused his defeat. Black might have moved his 37 as shown in Diagrams 145 and 146. In the actual game Black's 37 was captured by White's 38, and Black could not go to the **A** position. If Black went to the **a** position in Diagram 146, White would capture it right away by going to the **A** position, leaving no good place for Black to move (see Diagram 147).

Diagram 145

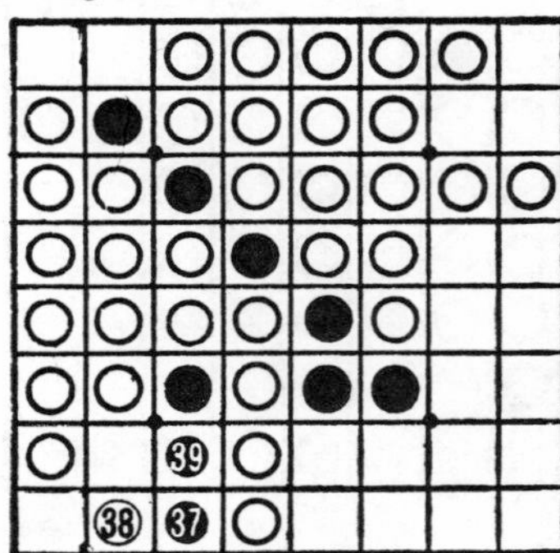

Diagram 146

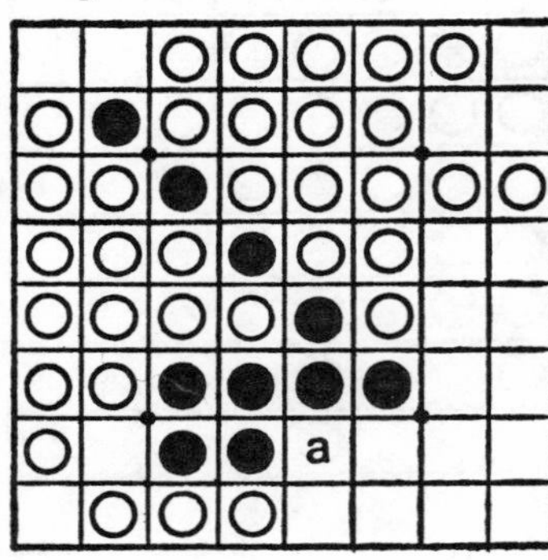

Diagram 147

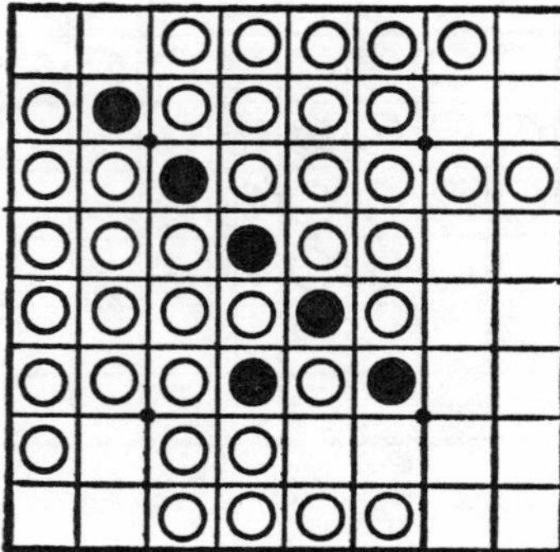

Black had to go to the position of 39 (in play diagram #39) but was immediately captured by White's 40. Black had too few discs to make free moves. White's victory was decided by his 40th move, at the end of the middle stage of the game.

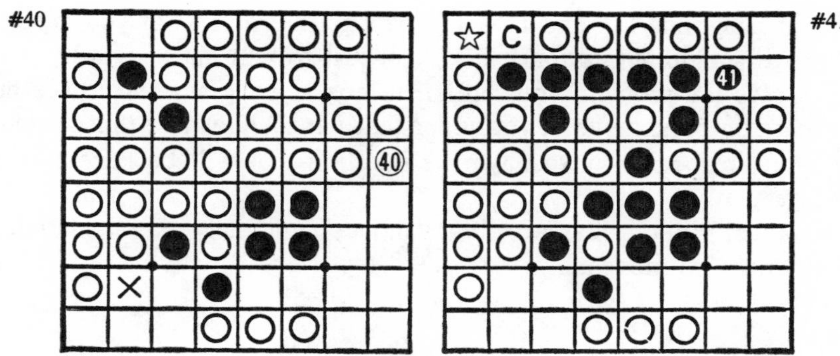

The Post-Mortem

After the game was over, White commented that Black lost the game because he could not establish any outer-edge bases and because his discs were extremely outnumbered by white discs.

Let's continue the analysis of the game just to see how well White played it out. Black's 41 was a very bad move. This move gave the corner and **X** positions to White easily. If Black had moved to the **X** position (#40), he would not have lost so badly.

Diagram 148

Diagram 149

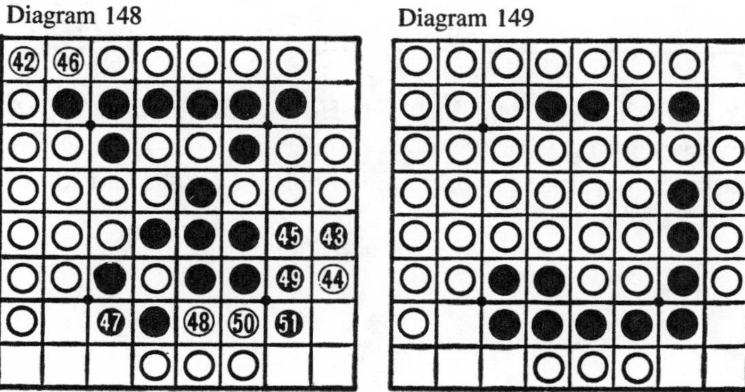

Look at Diagrams 148 and 149. This is a good problem for you to solve. What move should White make next, not just to win but to win by many points? Solve the problem yourself, then look at Diagram 150 to see how White made his 52nd move. If you understand why White made that particular move, you are beginning to have the intuition that will be necessary for final-stage play.

At a glance, White's 52 is an ordinary move, but it really is a foundation for the 56th and 58th moves.

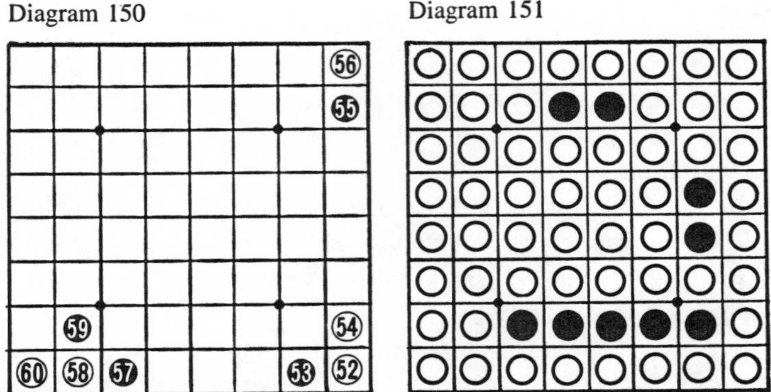

Diagram 150

Diagram 151

The end play of White was brilliant. He overcame Black's defenses and won an overwhelming victory by 46 points.

For a further analysis of the principle of balanced discs and some examples of middle-stage play, see pages 147-156.

Down in the Bull Pen Or What to Do If It Isn't Working

Suppose you play the opening stage of a game very poorly. Will you lose, right then and there? You could.

But suppose you play brilliantly in the opening. Does this guarantee you an edge over your opponent? Sorry. The advantage you gain in the beginning can easily be upset in the middle stage. Stay on your guard!

Suppose you look at your position in the middle stage and realize that you haven't a chance, you're going to lose eventually. What then? Give up?

No—not only because playing a game to its conclusion is the best way to learn but because you can still try to prevent your opponent from getting a high score. If you're playing more than one game, the loss may not be too important if you don't lose by too many points (see Appendix A, Scoring). So shift your strategy to prevent your opponent from winning by too many points. And who knows—he may make a blunder, and the game could be yours!

Putting It All Together–So Far

Here is an example that illustrates tactics used to maintain a superior position through the opening and middle stages (often very difficult to do), ways to pressure your opponent into forced moves, and the timing of occupying the corner positions. This is very important in Othello.

White, the loser in this game, never bothered about **A** or **B** positions. He always kept his attention on a balanced number of white and black discs and made his moves according to changes on the board. He was not trying to win by a big margin but wanted a firm win. In other words, White is a safe player.

Notice Black's 3, which jumped into the **a** row early in the game.

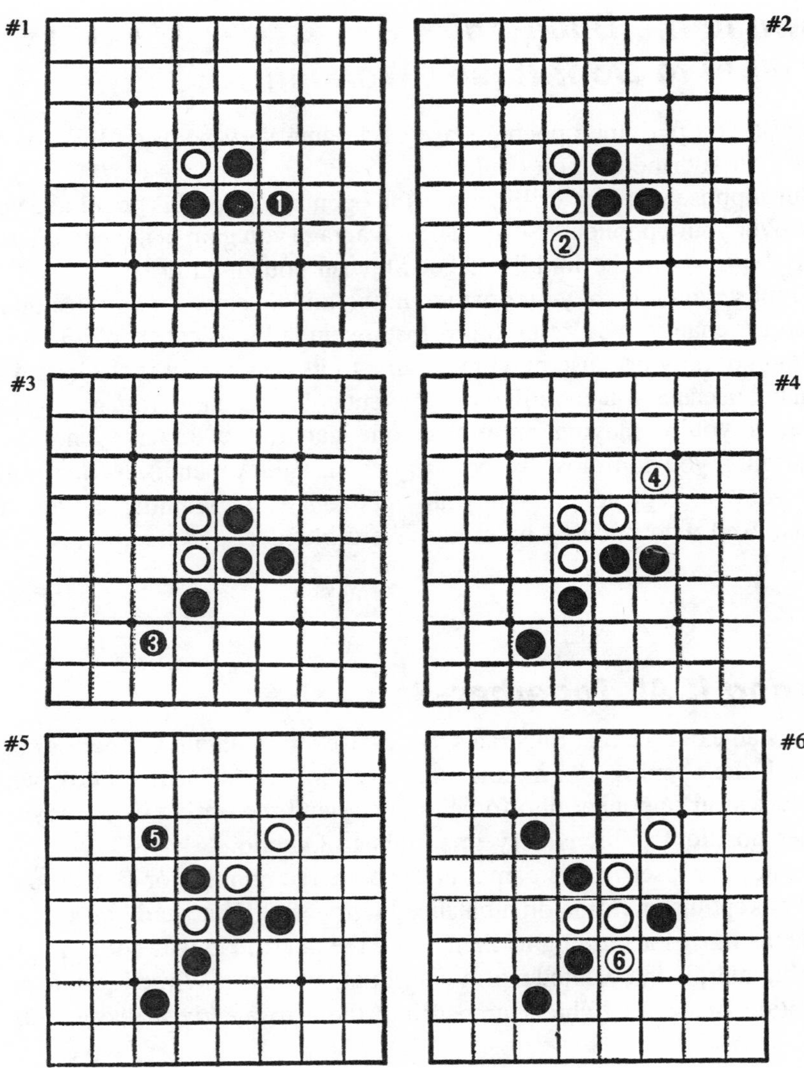
#1
1
#2
2
#3
3
#4
4
#5
5
#6
6

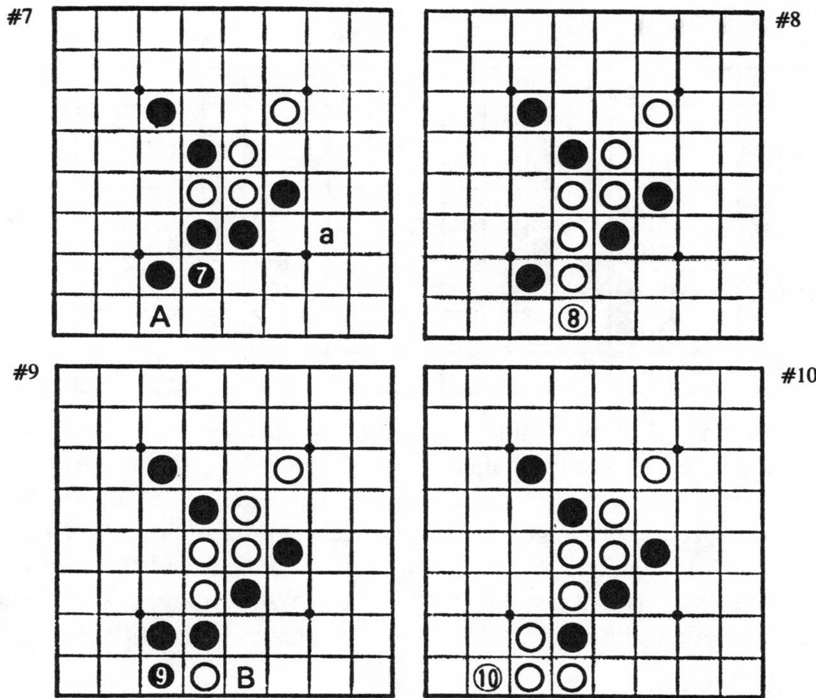

Black's 7 is also an unconventional move. White made his isolated entry into the **B** position with his 8th move, but this was somewhat careless. Why? Because a veteran player would not allow his opponent to go to the **B** position unless it suited the veteran's well-planned strategy. Instead of the **B** position White could have gone to the **a** position (#7 above), aiming for the **A** position next.

Black's 9 was a powerful move unexpected by White. White could not leave this alone. He made the 10th move to capture Black's 9. Black made his 11th move unconcernedly.

Wishy-Washy White

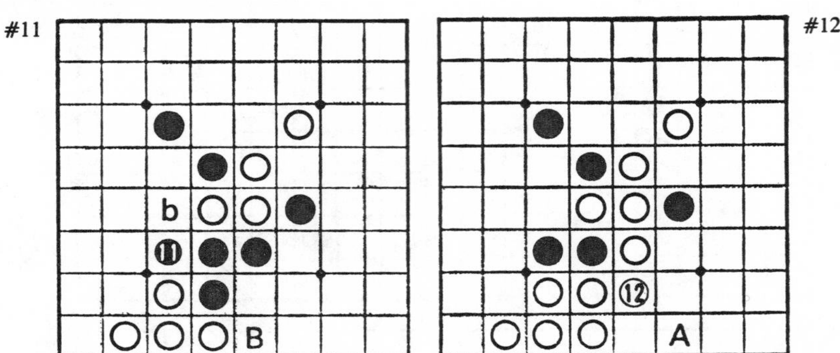

Now the game is in the middle of the opening stage. White's 12 was a dubious move. He should have aimed at the **B** position (#11 above). To get to the **B** position he could have gone to the **a** position. Such maneuvering would have resulted in Diagrams 152 and 153. (In the situation in Diagram 153 White could go to the **C** position first, then to the **a** and **B** positions. It would have been an interesting play, although such moves would make White's formation a bit one-sided.) In the actual game White's 12 gave Black

Diagram 152

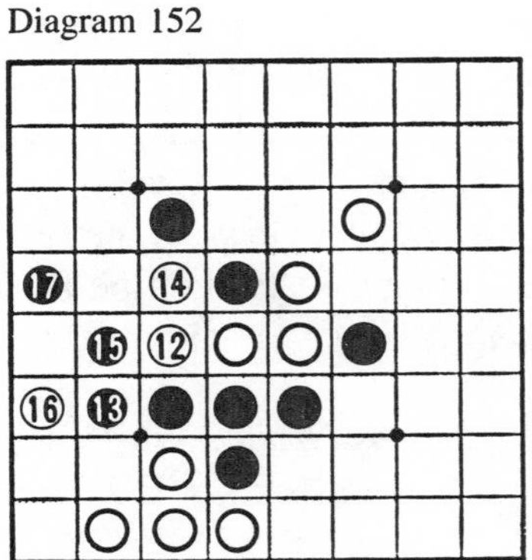

Diagram 153

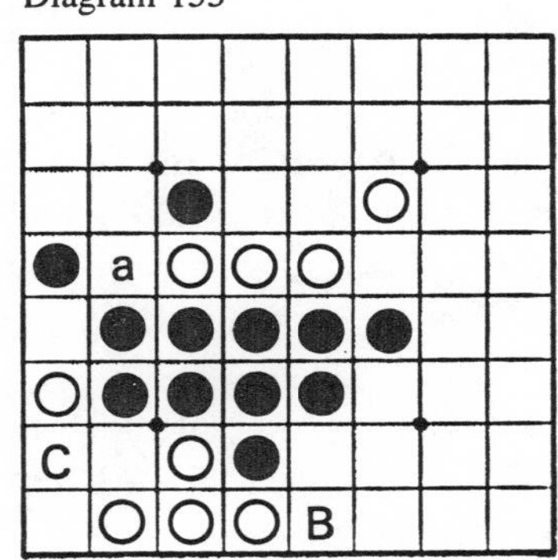

a chance to go to the **A** position. White monopolized the lower outer row with three discs. He should not allow an opening for Black to invade the row

Black didn't go to the **A** position immediately. His 13th move was made to see where White would go.

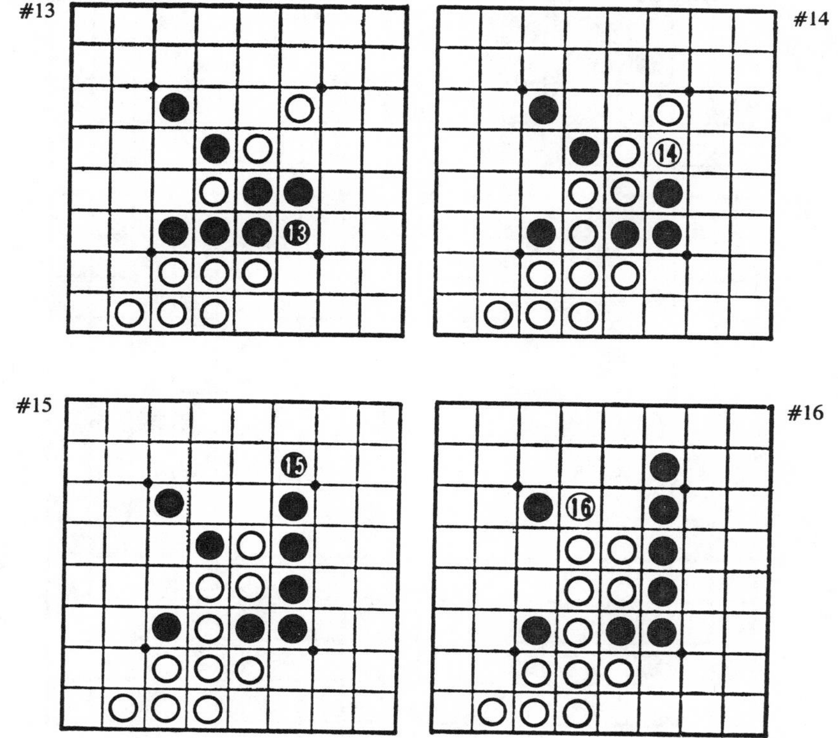

There are many alternatives for the 14th, 15th, and 16th moves. It's hard to say which is best, but Black's 15 was a very forceful move, and White's 16 was defensive.

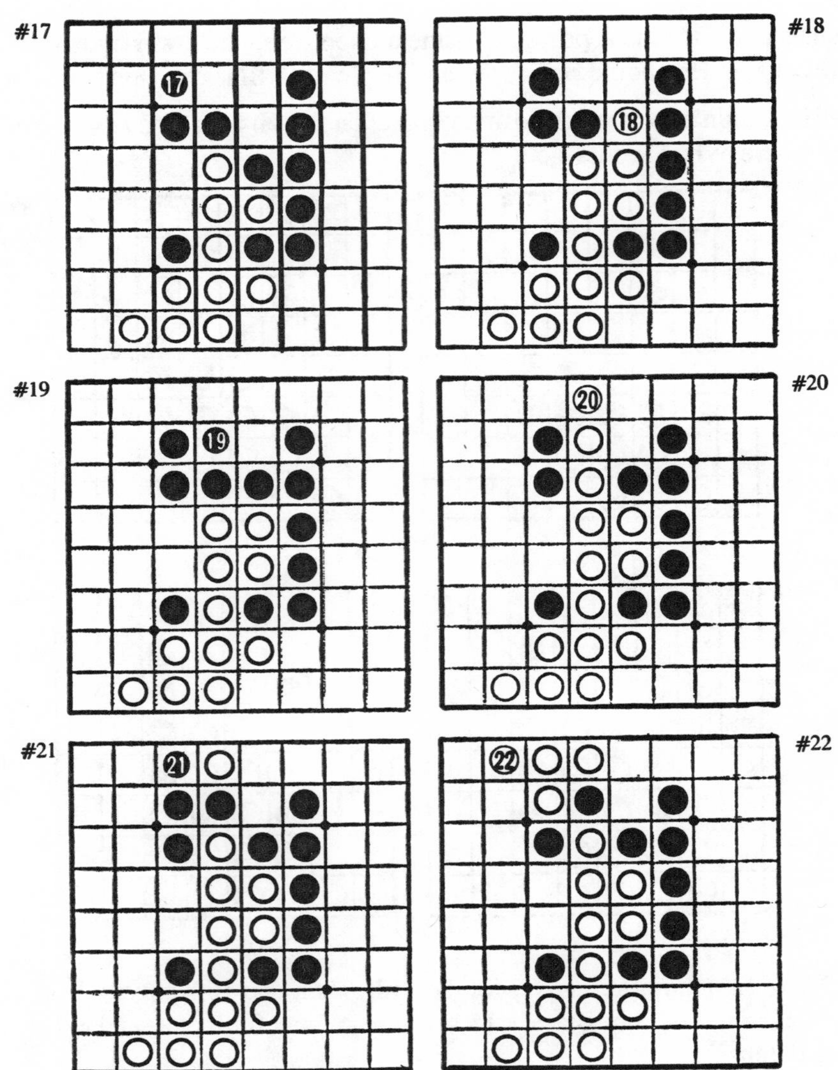
#17
17
#18
18
#19
19
#20
20
#21
21
#22
22

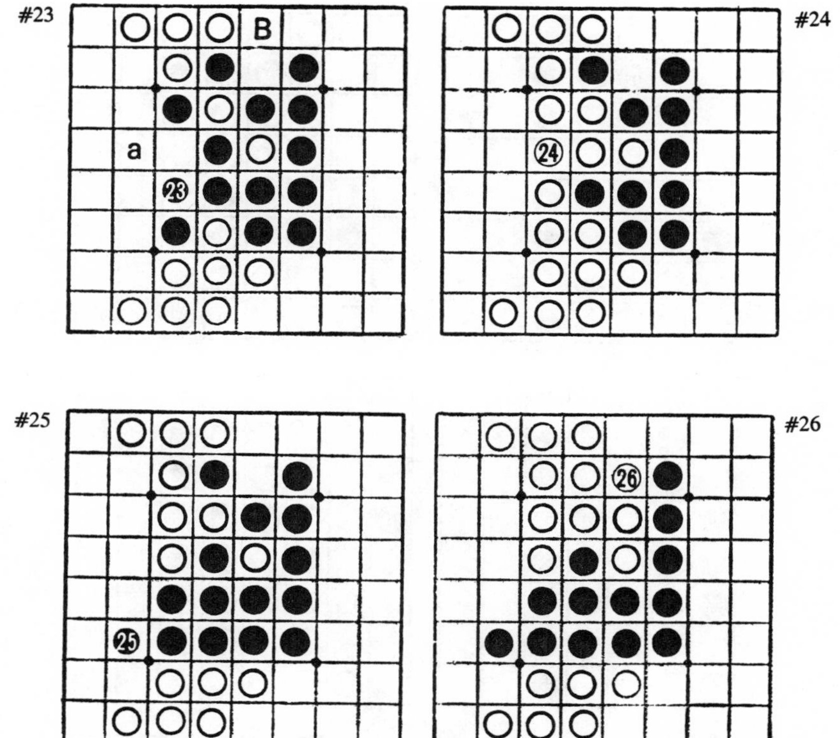

Downward, Ever Downward

White's 24 was his second mistake because it made his formation too one-sided. He should have made his 24th move to the **a** position (see #23) and aimed for the **B** position with his next move. That way he could have kept a better balance in the number of discs and made a better defense against Black's attack.

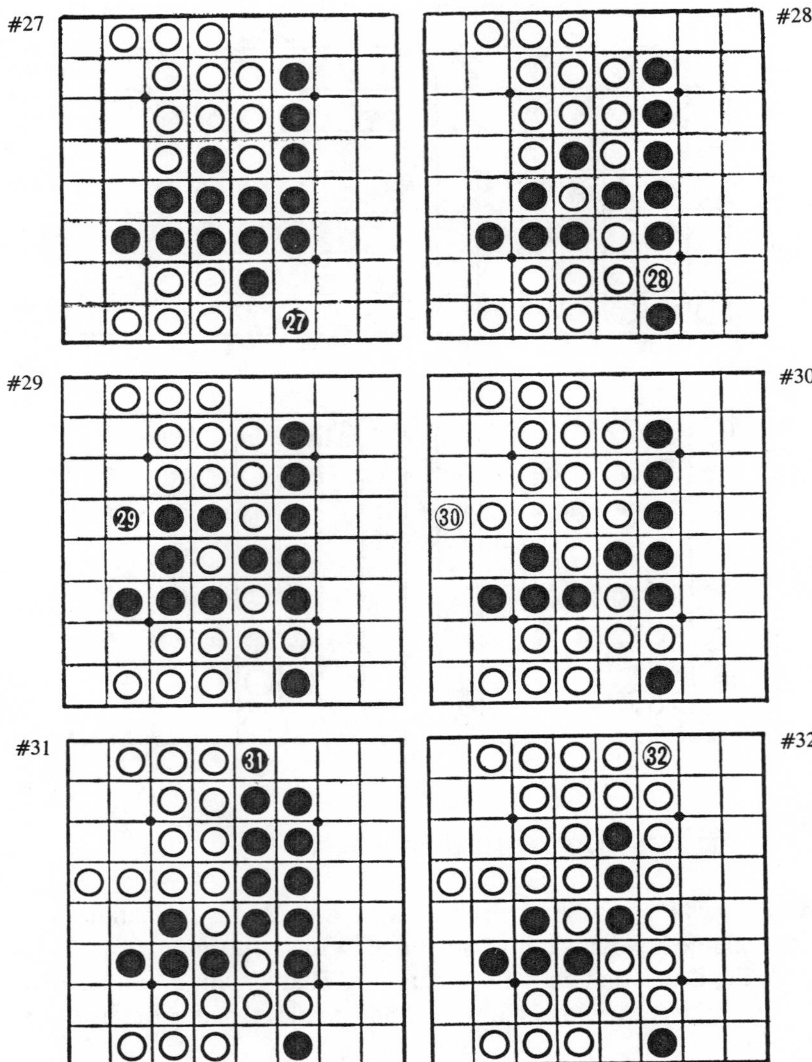
#27
27
#28
28
#29
29
#30
30
#31
31
#32
32

White's following 26th, 28th, and 30th moves were mediocre and unimaginative moves. Black's 31 was a hard blow to White, who had to go to the position of 32. White had run into a stalemate!

White could have made his 26th, 28th, and 30th moves as shown in Diagrams 154, 155, and 156. Such moves would have changed the situation drastically, promising a long and interesting game. As this example shows,

Diagram 154

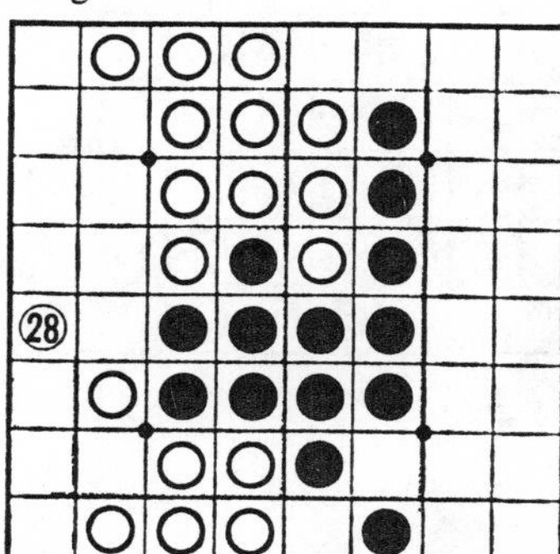

Diagram 155

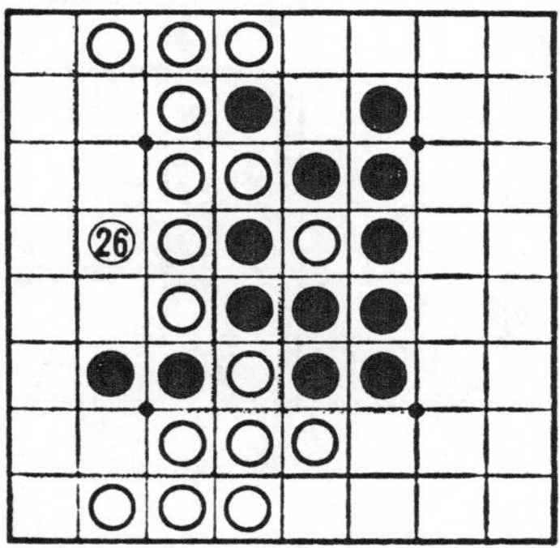

Diagram 156

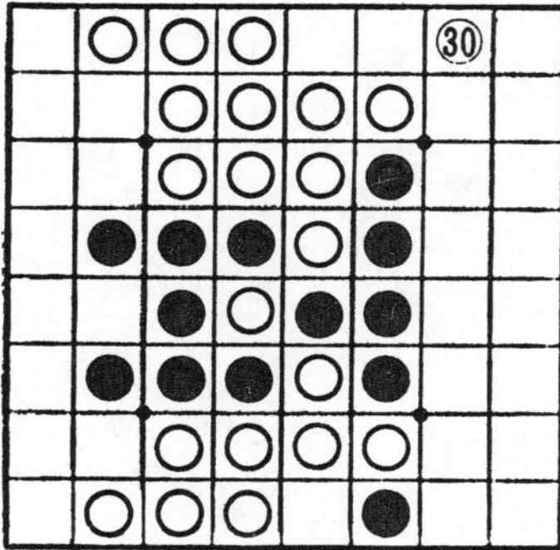

there are many ways a game of Othello can change in the middle stage. A mistake or two will not wipe you out. In a game in which victory or defeat is decided in the beginning of the middle stage, the loser usually has made four or five very bad mistakes.

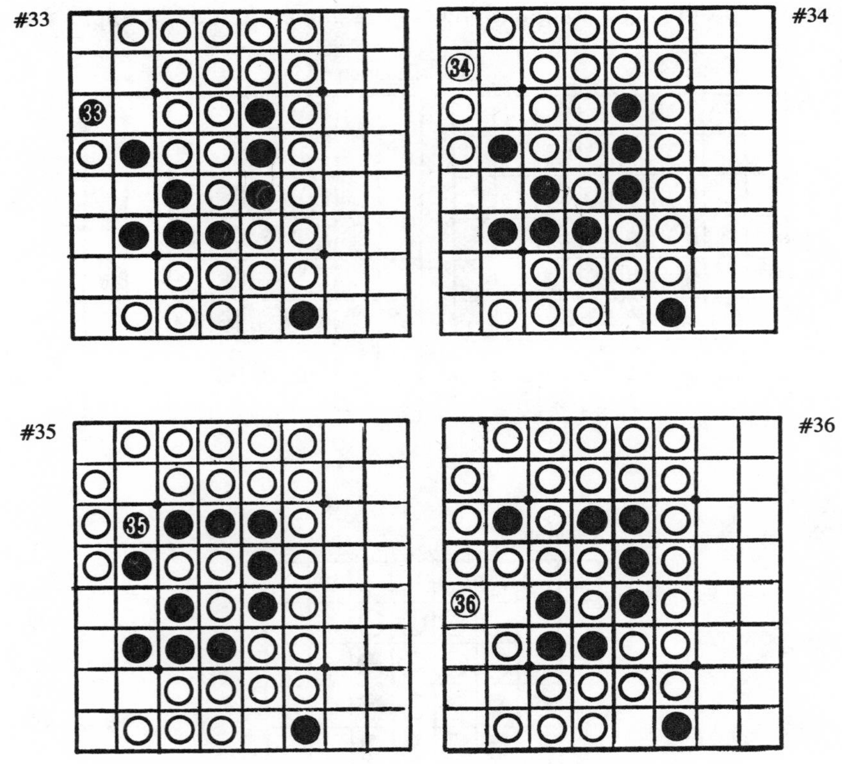

In play diagram #32 Black looks like a sure winner. He kept his advantage well with his 33rd, 35th, 37th, and 39th moves. White's 40 and 42 were forced moves. At this point Black's victory is assured.

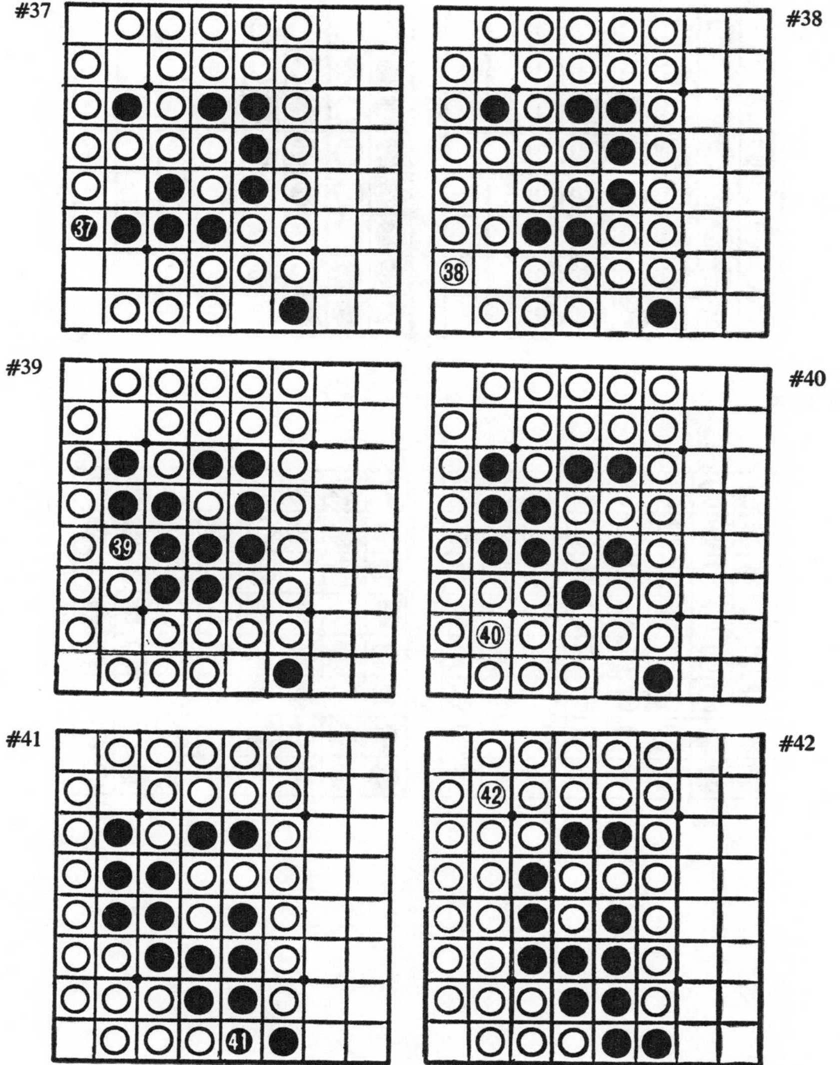
#37
37
#38
38
#39
39
#40
40
#41
41
#42
42

#43

#44

Diagram 157

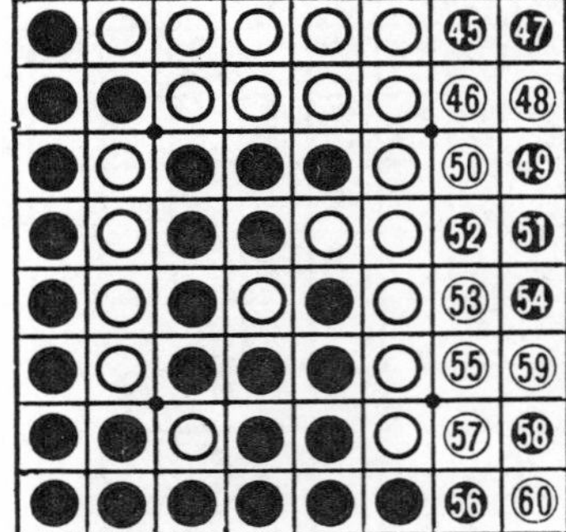

Diagram 158

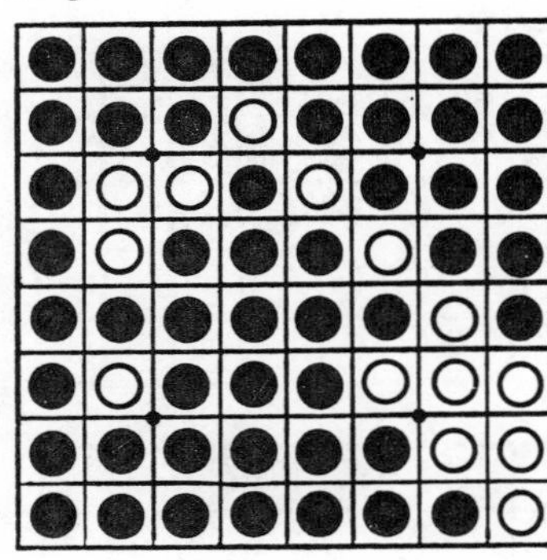

Tactical Alternatives

Othello players disagree about the perfect strategy, but here are some of the favorites. Try them out and find which work best for you—and which to avoid!

The Counterweight Offensive
Or, Balanced Discs Can Be More Important Than the A and B Positions

According to this theory, the most important thing in Othello is to maintain a balanced number of black and white discs. If you try to do this, starting at the beginning of the game, you may have trouble occupying the usually desirable **A** and **B** positions. Your choice here is almost always to maintain not only a balance of black and white discs but a *minimum* of your own discs on the board during the opening stage. This takes priority over efforts to occupy **A** and **B** squares.

The ideal situation, if you can manage it, is to have both a balanced number of discs and to occupy positions **A** and **B**.

The second-best situation is to maintain a balanced number of discs. This is more important here than occupying positions **A** and **B**.

So the Counterweight Offensive theory is:

It is best to have both a balanced number of discs and to occupy positions **A** and **B**.

If you can't have both, it's best to maintain a balanced number of discs.

And if you can't do that, at least try to occupy **A** and **B** positions.

The Counterweight Illustrated

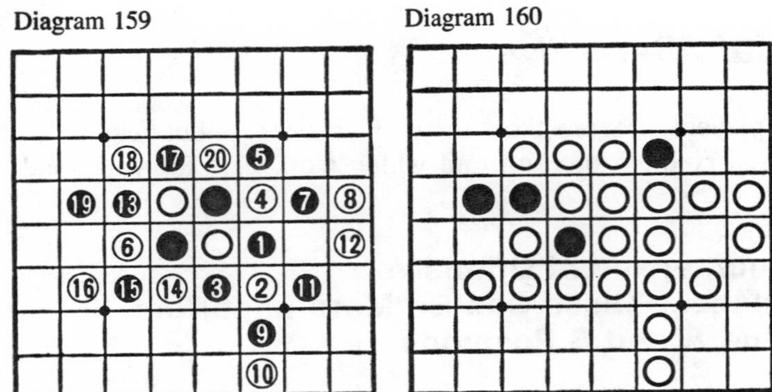
Diagram 159 Diagram 160

Black plays the opening stage of this game (Diagrams 159 and 160) uniquely. His sole purpose is to capture as few white discs as possible. He readily allows White to take **A** and **B** positions. Black's 7, 9, and 11 invite White to establish an ideal formation of the **A** and **B** positions. Tricky, tense play.

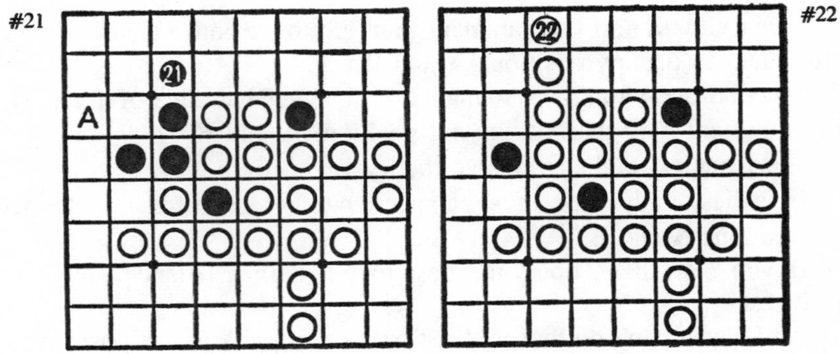

#21 #22

#23

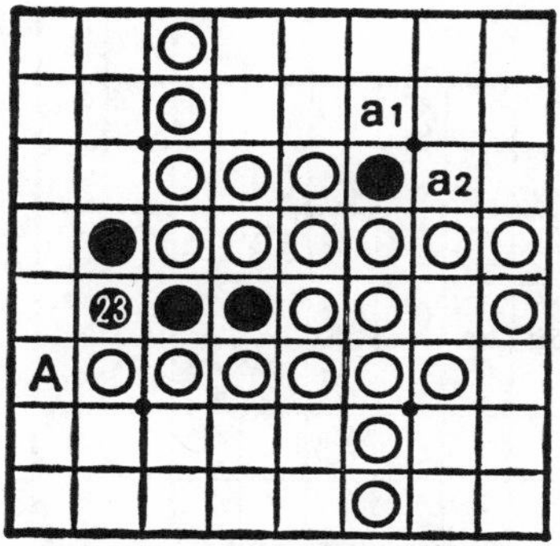

a1

a2

23

A

#24

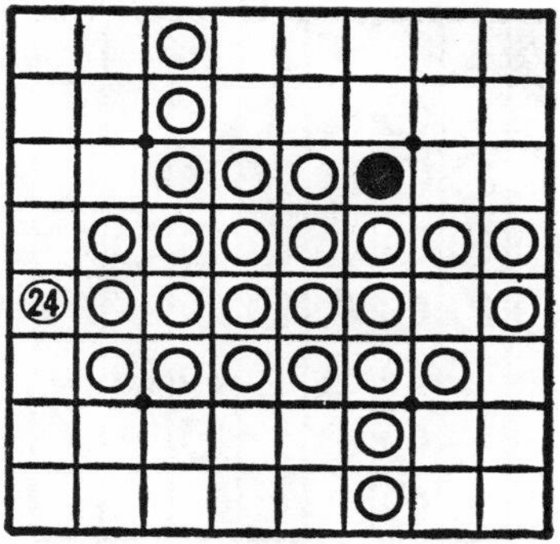

24

#25

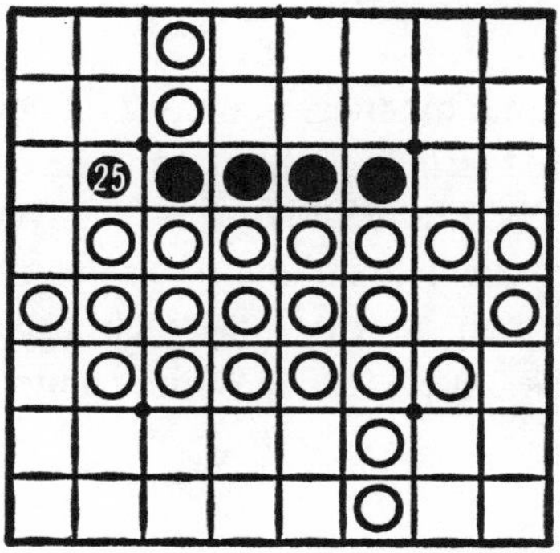

25

#26

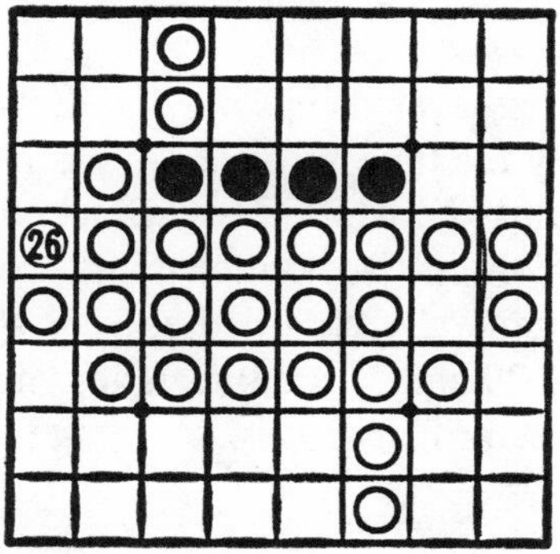

26

#27

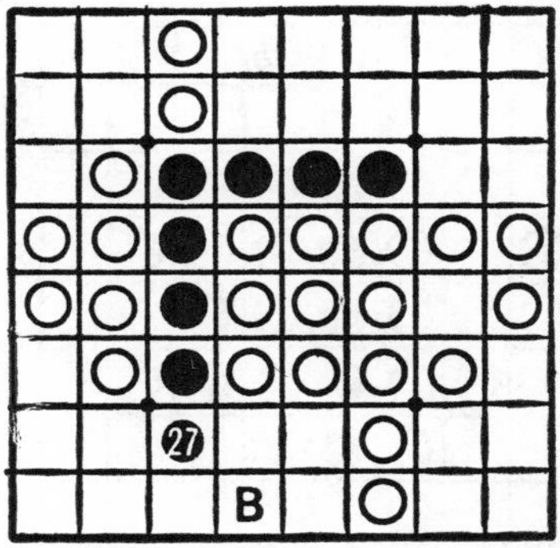

27

B

#28

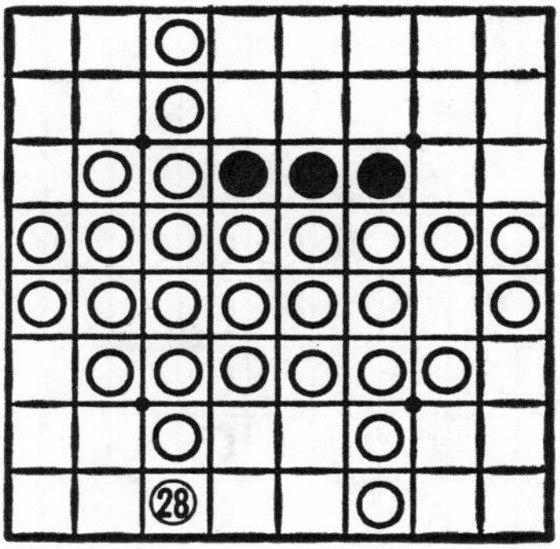

28

#29 #30

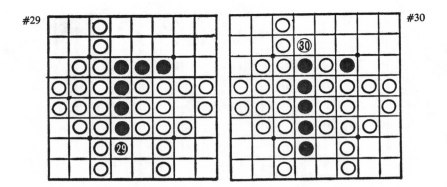

Black, however, keeps playing in the same manner. See his 21st and 23rd moves? By the time White's 24 was moved, Black had only one disc on the board against 27 white discs. Black's 27 is a bold move, inviting White to make the 28th move, establishing two white **A** positions on the same line, which is generally regarded as very bad maneuvering on Black's part.

Black's 29 and 31 are interesting moves. At this point White cannot find a way to steamroller Black.

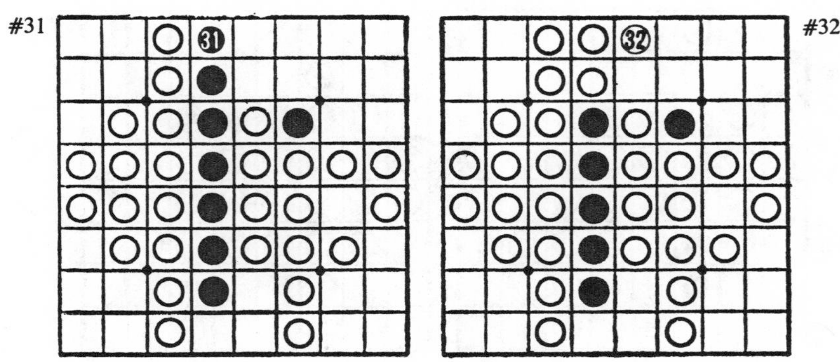

#33

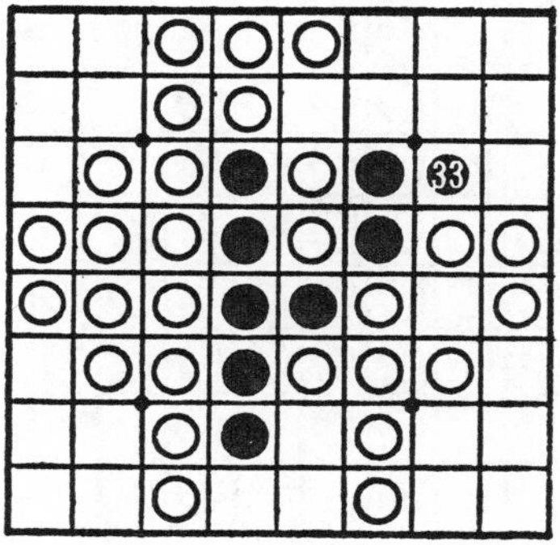

#34

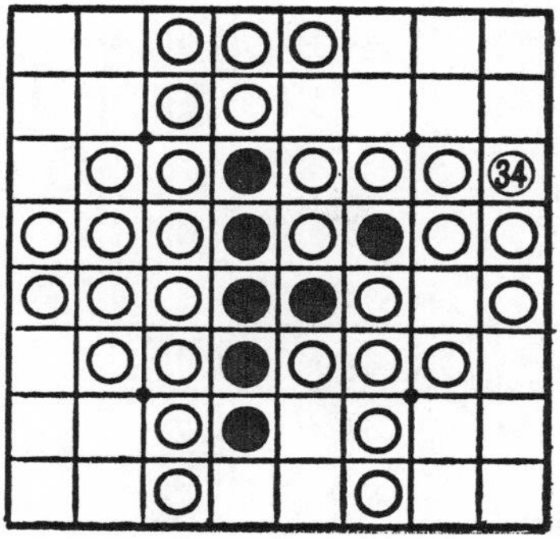

#35

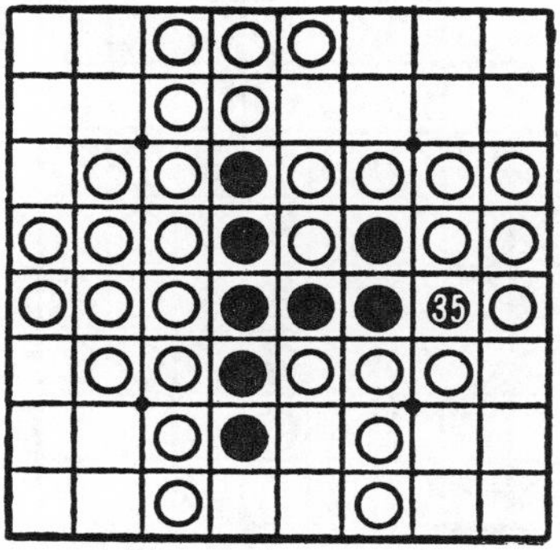

#36

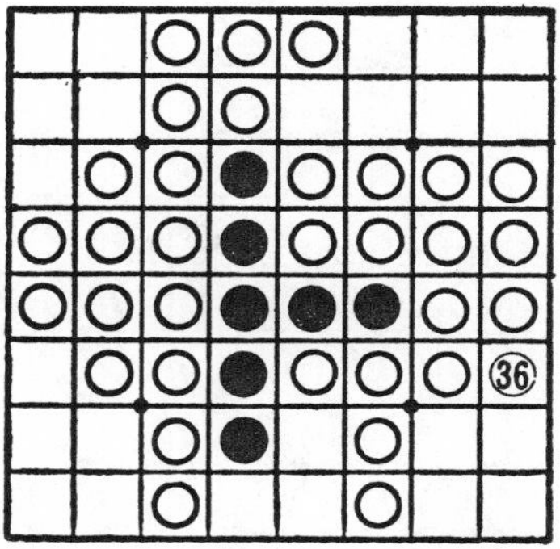

#37

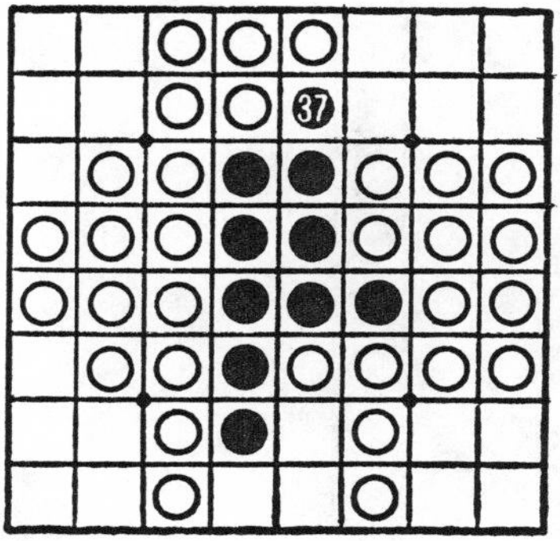

#38

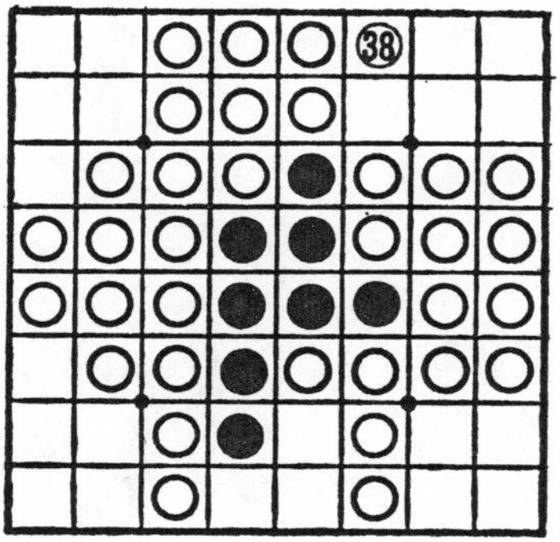

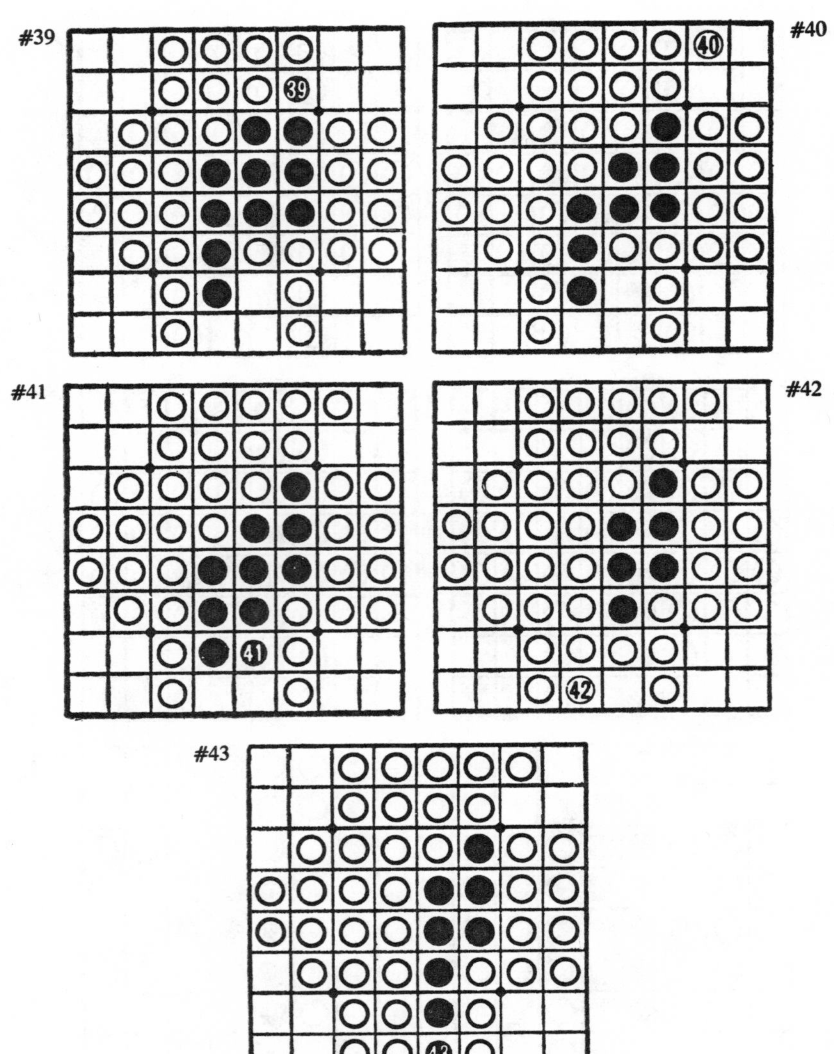
#39
39
#40
40
#41
41
#42
42
#43
43

Virtues of a One-Track Mind

Black's single-minded strategy to break the balance of black and white discs has succeeded. Black's 43 caused White to make a forced move. Black's victory is secure now. White lost because he was too occupied with taking **A** and **B** positions and neglected to retain a balance of black and white discs.

This game explicitly proves the theory: The balance of discs is more important than **A** and **B** positions.

Note: It isn't always a good idea to try to have fewer discs on the board than your opponent has. Remember, though, that no matter how many desirable **A** and **B** positions you take, if you overbalance your discs, you may face a fatal situation in the final stage of the game.

You Are There

The following play diagrams show the progress of the remainder of the game move by move. They are good examples for you to study.

#44

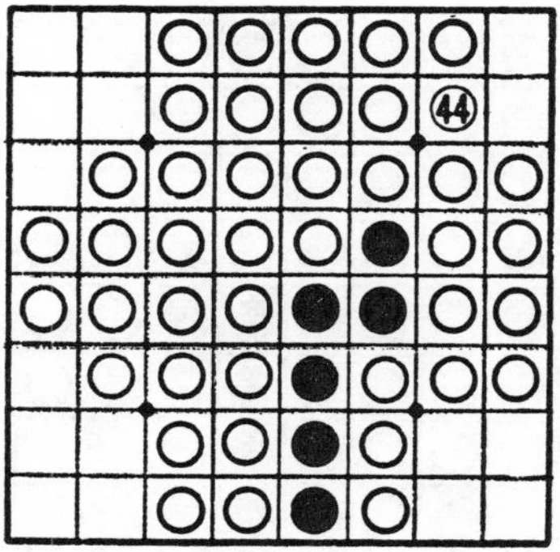

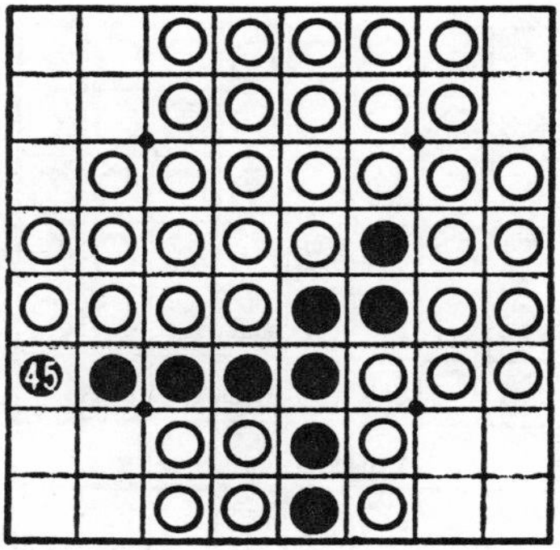

#45

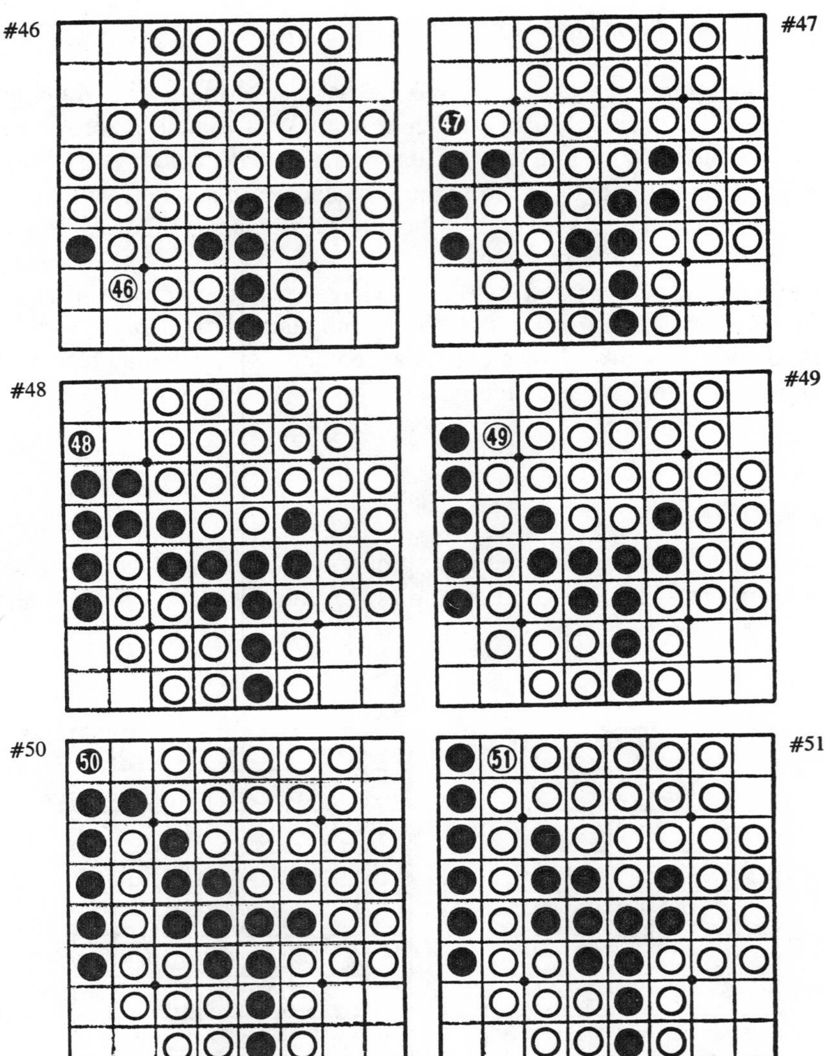
#46
46
#47
47
#48
48
#49
49
#50
50
#51
51

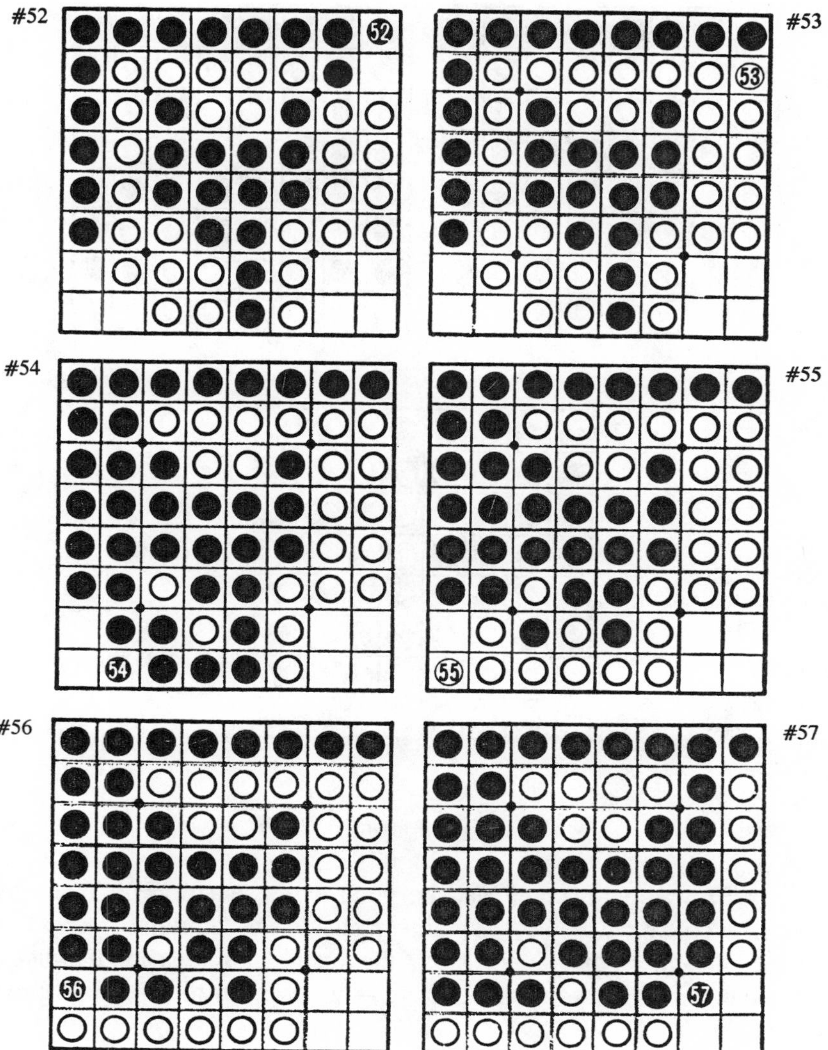
#52
52
#53
53
#54
54
#55
55
#56
56
#57
57

#58

#59

#60

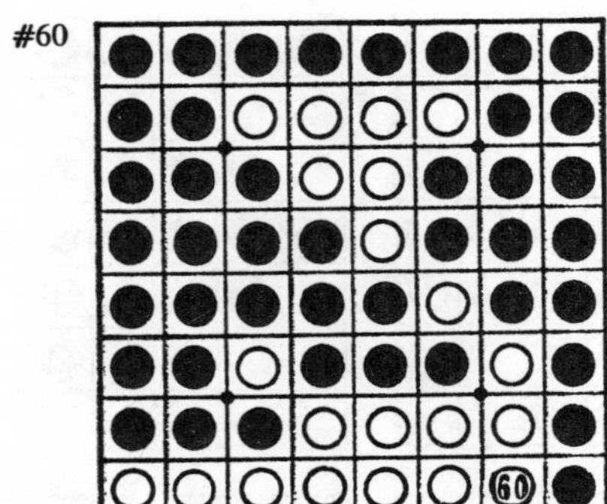

(Black's win,
22 points)

Black's 57 was a mistake. Had he gone to the position of White's 58 instead, he would have won by 28 points, instead of by 22 points. Don't be off guard until the end of the game. One of the intriguing things about Othello is that you can't ever let your guard down—not even in the last few moves.

Forcing the Issue: An Example of Forced Move Tactics

In the game outlined here White does an excellent job of getting **A** positions. Once she takes them she can keep up her powerful offensive to the end. On the other hand, she is also good in the reverse tactics; that is, she allows her opponent to take **A** positions, while she plots to force him into a stalemate, disturbing a balance of black and white discs, which upsets the situation in the final stage of the game.

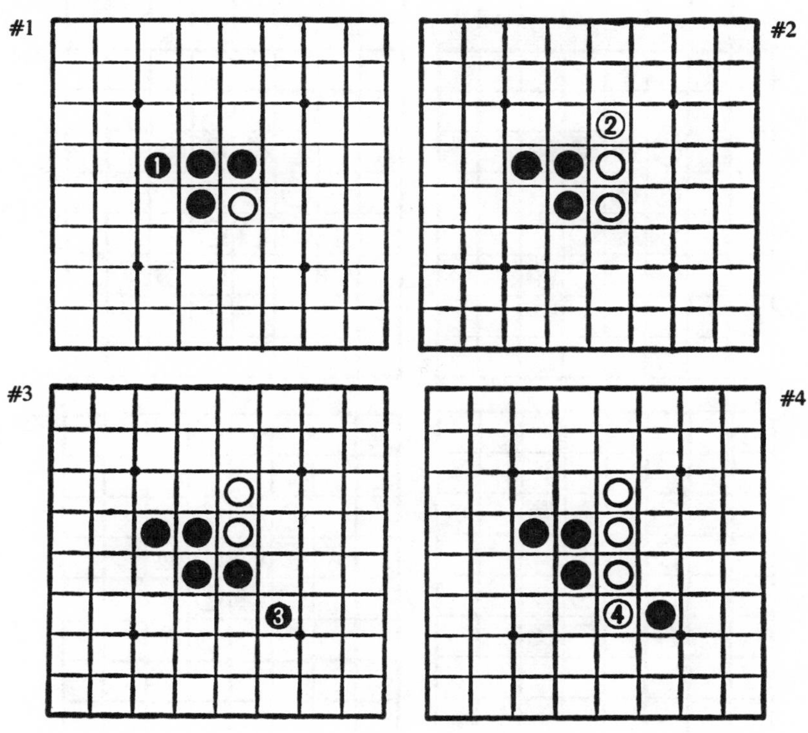

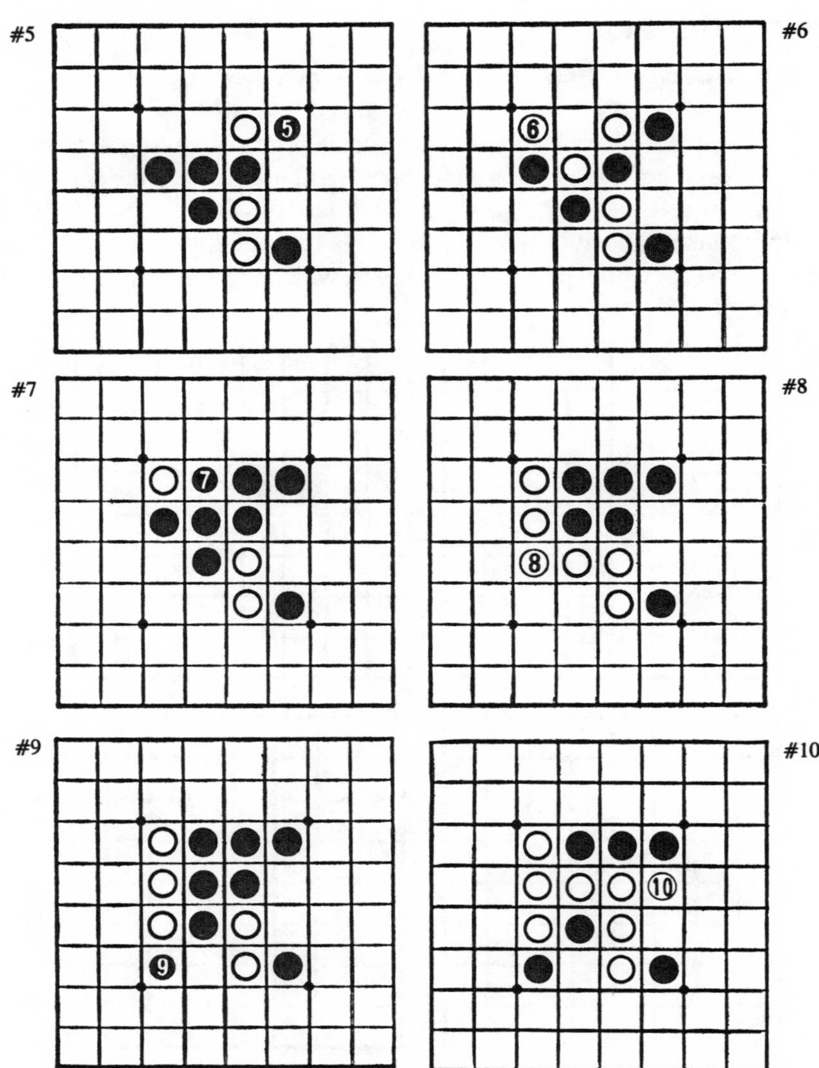
#5
#6
#7
#8
#9
#10

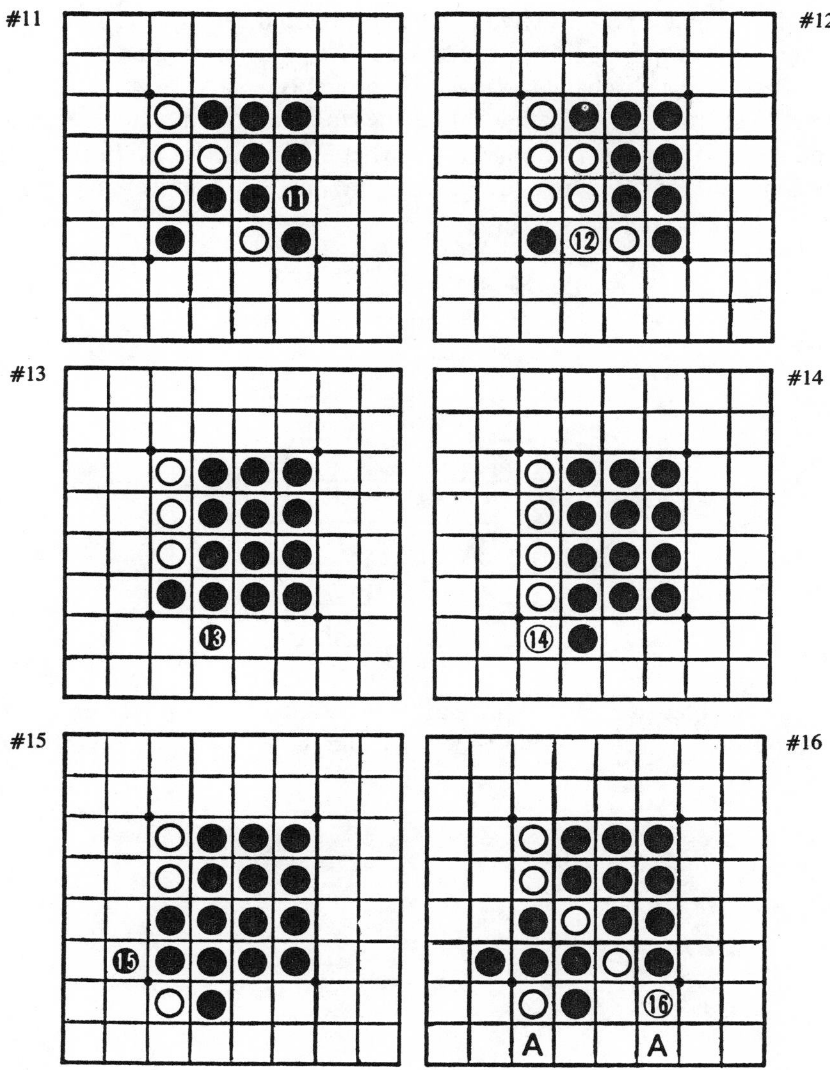
#11
11
#12
12
#13
13
#14
14
#15
15
#16
16
A
A

This is the first time these two players have faced each other. They don't know each other's strengths or tendencies. White starts to play cautiously.

Black's 11 was a debatable move. He probably should have placed it as shown in Diagram 161. Whether White goes to **a1** or **a9**, in either case Black can go to the **b** position and wait to see what White does next. In the actual game Black's 11th move invited White's 12th, and Black himself had to go to an **a** position (#13) before White.

Diagram 161

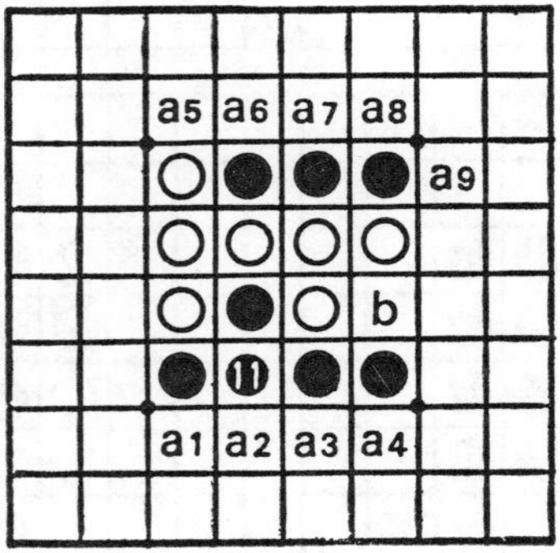

White gambled with her 14th and 16th moves, forceful moves accompanied by risk. White is luring Black into the two **A** positions on the lower edge.

Don't Be Too Cautious!

Suspicious of White's intention, Black moved his 17 to the **B** position, which was a mistake. It would have been better if Black had placed the 17th move in

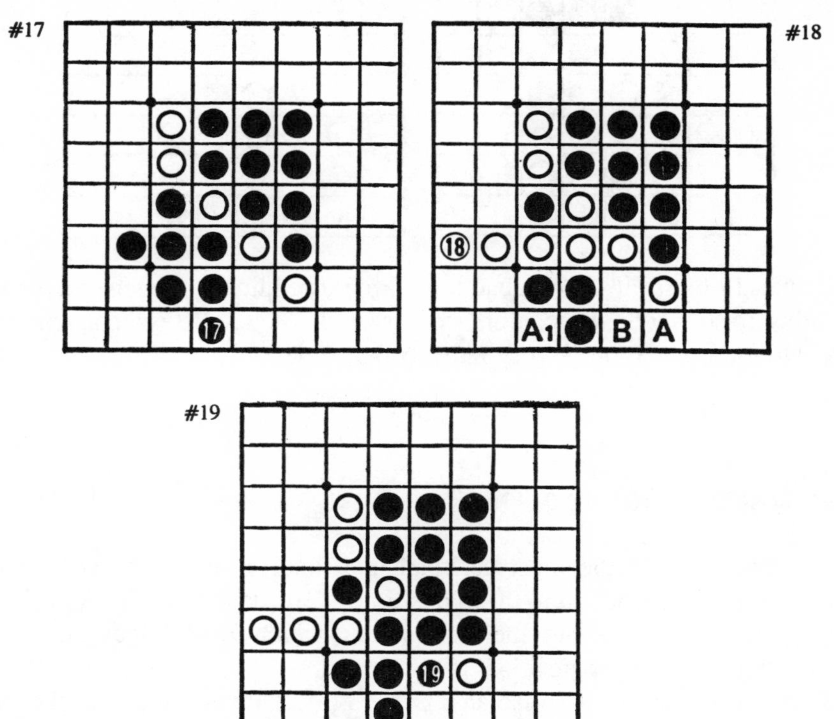

the position shown in Diagram 162. Whichever way White might move, Black could have taken the **a** position, establishing an ideal formation on the lower side of the board.

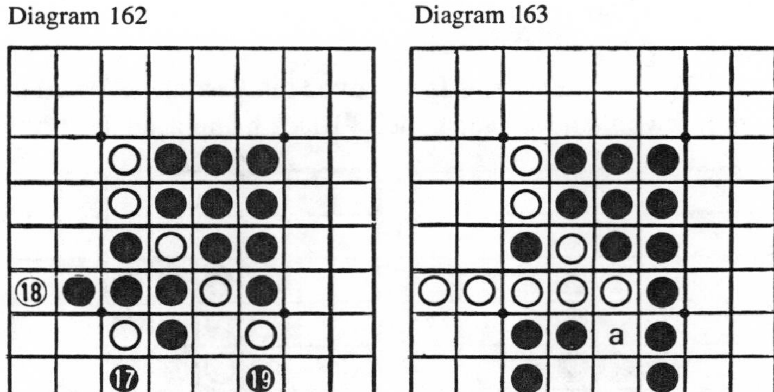

Black's 17 by itself is not a bad move, but it requires an ingenious plan to back this up so that the **B** position is not wasted. White's 18 is a conventional idea. Now the situation is very hard to figure out.

How Did We Get into This?

In play diagram #18 the most desirable position is **B**, but at this point in the game Black still cannot go to the **B** position. If Black went to the **A** position, White would squeeze into the **B** position, which Black does not want. Therefore, Black chose position 19 as shown.

But since Black made an isolated entry into the outer edge with the 17th move, he should have backed this up with the **A** position and strengthened his fort on the lower edge. Moreover, if he had read the board a little more carefully, he would have realized that he did not have to be afraid of White's entry into the **B** position. At his 23rd move, Black would still have the **a** position in reserve.

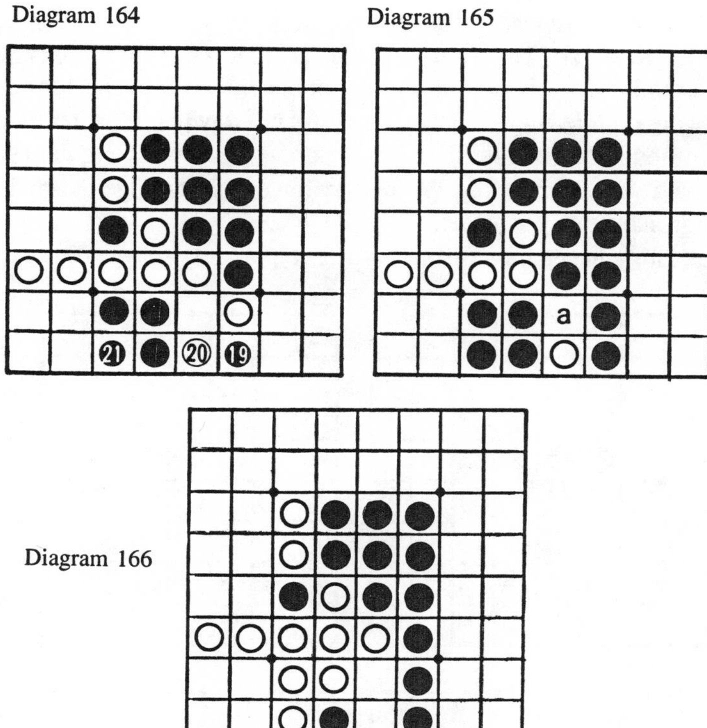

Diagram 164

Diagram 165

Diagram 166

Black's fear that White's 20 might squeeze into a space between two black discs, as in Diagram 164, shows his lack of ability to assess the situation accurately. Suppose Black had moved as in the diagram; would the game really have turned out as in Diagram 165? Actually it would not have. The picture looks too good for Black. White had an entirely different blueprint in her head.

"Look at the eighteenth play," White commented. "If Black's nineteen had been moved to the **A** position, I would have gone to the **A1** position, creating the situation of Diagram 166. This is not too bad for an opening-stage play, but I really did not want this situation because it suggests a tremendous struggle in the middle stage. At the time I did not have any further plan. If the situation turned into this, I felt I could think up some strategy to deal with it."

As she said, in Diagram 166 White may have a slight edge over Black, but the situation is entirely unclear.

It is interesting to see how different the two players' views are. At the point

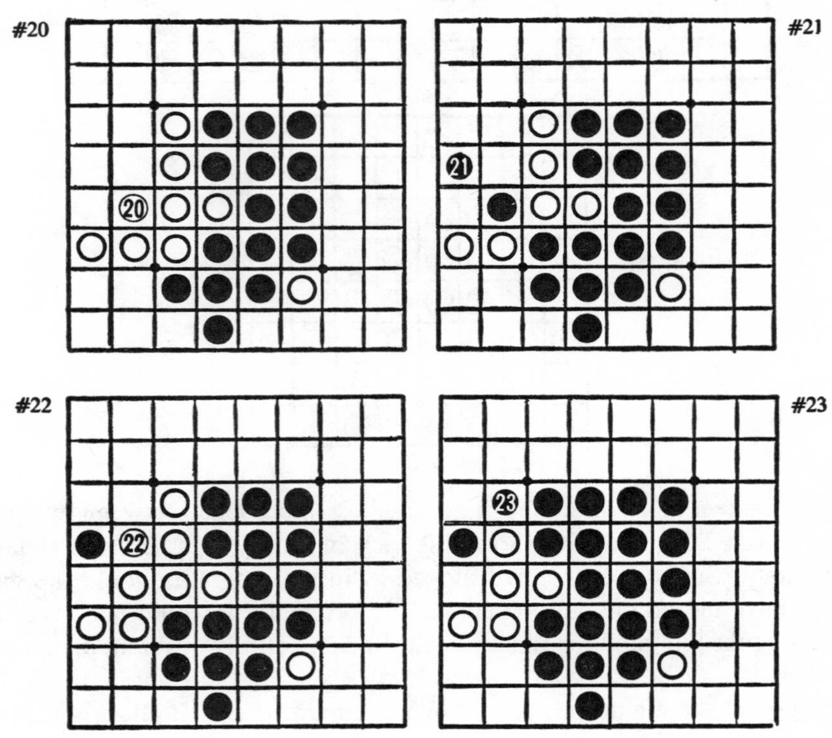

of the 18th play Black pictured the situation shown in Diagram 164, judged he was at a disadvantage, and chose his position 19 on that assumption. White, on the other hand, judged the situation in Diagram 164 favorable to Black and planned to bring about the situation in Diagram 166 instead.

Black's 23 was a very bad move which led him to a stalemate. He had forgotten one of the basic principles of Othello—that you must keep a balanced number of both disc colors on the board in order to avoid forced moves. Black should have moved his 23 as in Diagram 167. This move would have enabled Black to engage White in an exciting battle.

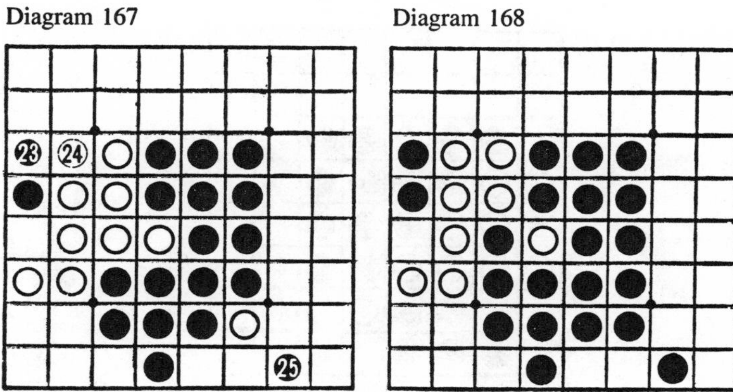

Diagram 167

Diagram 168

Good Save

Possibly dazzled by Black's outrageous 23rd move, White made an uncharacteristically bad move (24). She later said, "As soon as I made the twenty-fourth move, my heart froze with the thought that Black might go to the **A** position [see #24] I was relieved when Black went along with my bad move. Quickly I went to the position of twenty-six and saved myself!

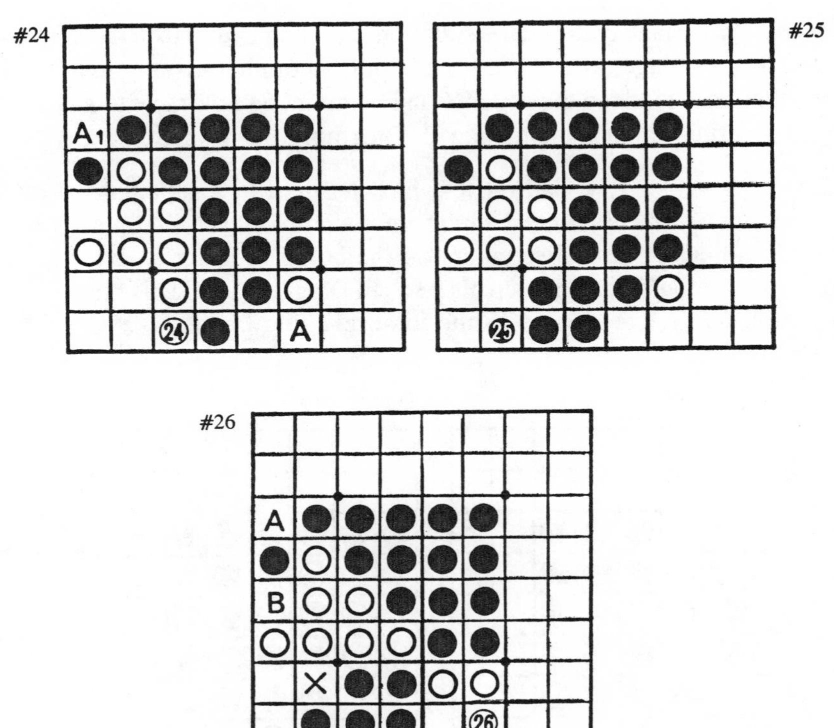

"My twenty-four should have been placed as Diagram 169 shows. It would have been a winning move. I don't know why I didn't go this way."

As White said, if Black had taken the **A** position in #24, it would have confused the situation for White, clouding her foresight. Black really missed a big opportunity with his 25th move. White's 26 led Black to forced moves.

After the game Black admitted that he had not thought of going to the **A** position. What would have happened if he had gone to the **A1** position?

Diagram 169

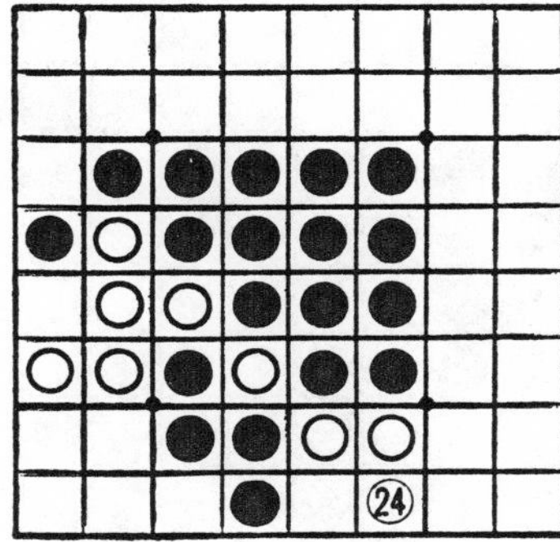

The situation would have developed as Diagrams 170 and 171 show. In this case White's best move would have been the **a** position. Then Black would have had to go to the **C** position and White would have gone to the **B** spot, forcing moves on Black as in Diagram 172. In play diagram 24 the **A** position is the only move left for Black's survival.

Diagram 170

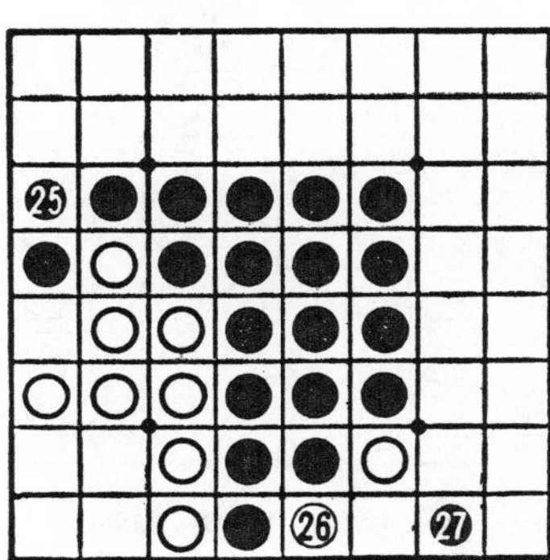

Diagram 171

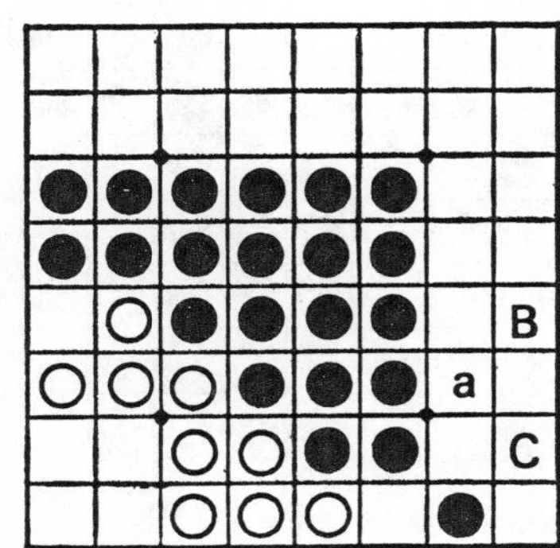

Diagram 172

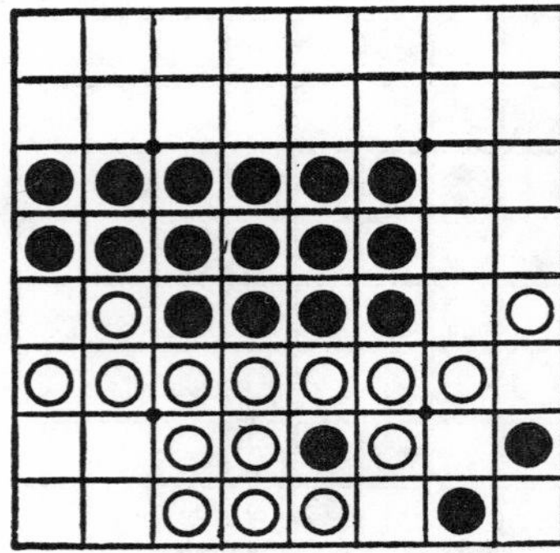

In play diagram 26 Black has six positions to move to, although four of them are forced moves. The others are the **B** and **X** positions. If Black had gone to the **B** position, White would have moved to the **A** position, finishing him off. White's 26 definitely defeated Black. Diagrams 173 and 174 show how the rest of the game was fought.

Diagram 173

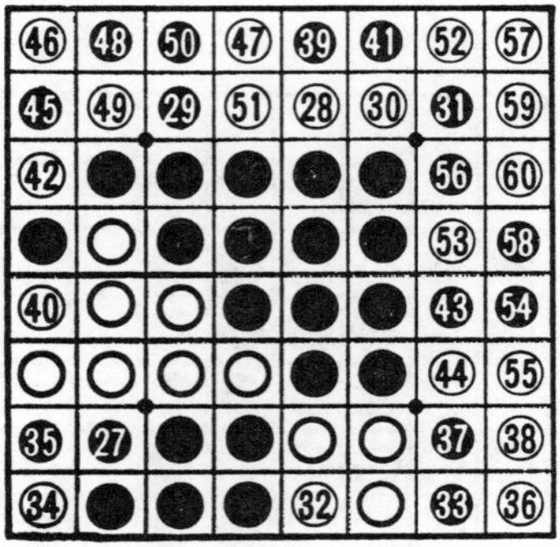

Diagram 174

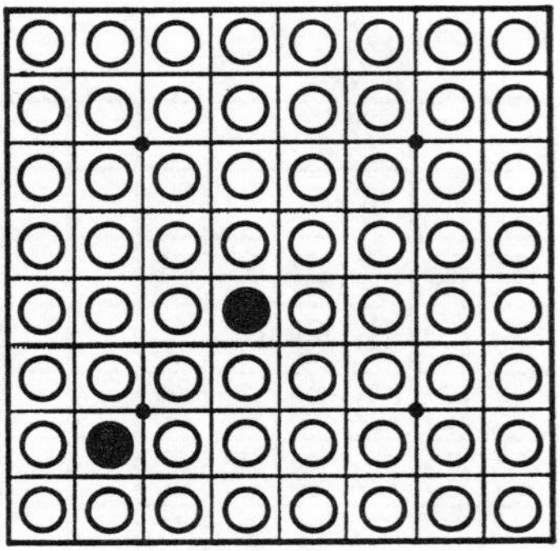

(White's win, 60 points)

The b1 Bomb

The thing to do in the opening stage is to take **b1** positions, in order to push your opponent to **a** positions, so that you can establish outer-edge bases. Well, isn't it? In this game Black thinks so—and keeps trying. And trying!

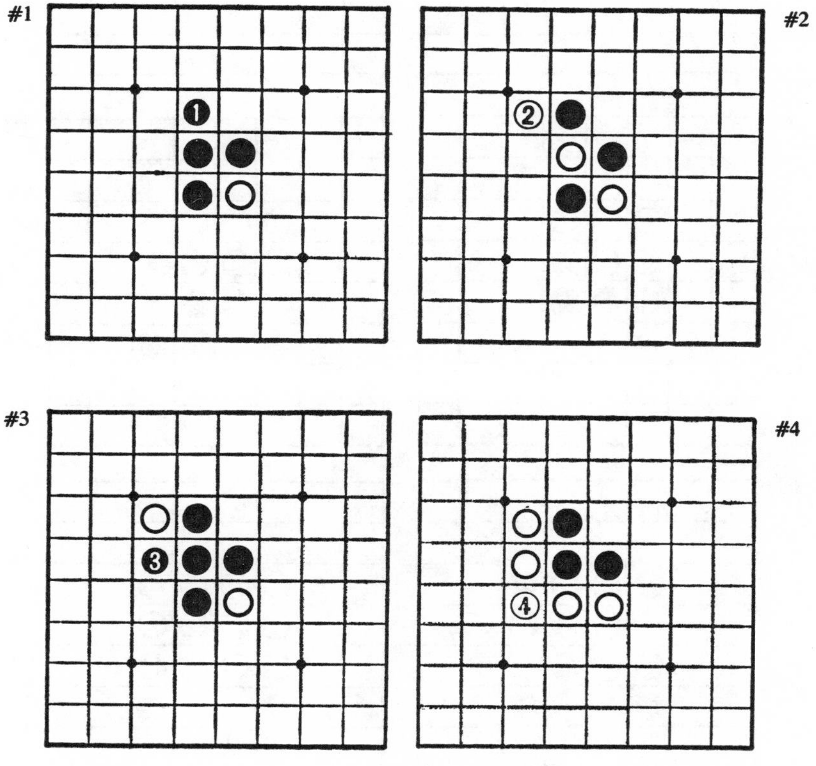

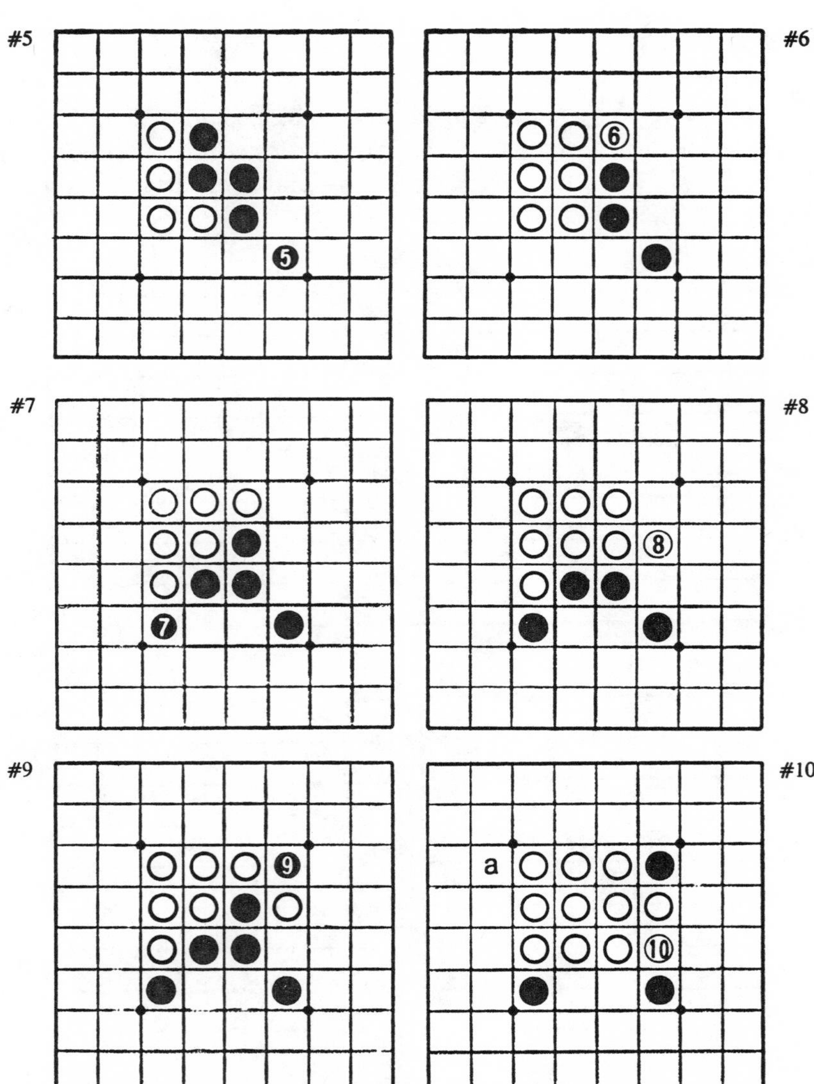
#5
5
#6
6
#7
7
#8
8
#9
9
#10
a
10

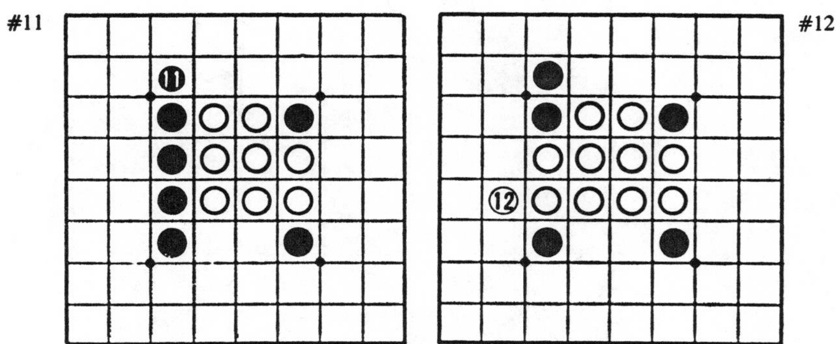

Black moved to **b1** positions with his 5, 7, and 9. White cleverly squeezed his 10th move into a space between two discs. Black, despite his three **b1** positions, was at a loss. Black's 11th move could go to the **a** position (#10), but at this stage it is hard to determine the best move for Black. White's 12 is an excellent trap. The following, Black's 13, is valid.

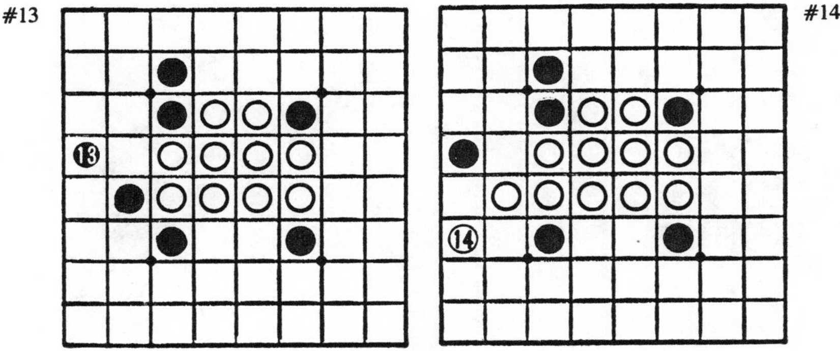

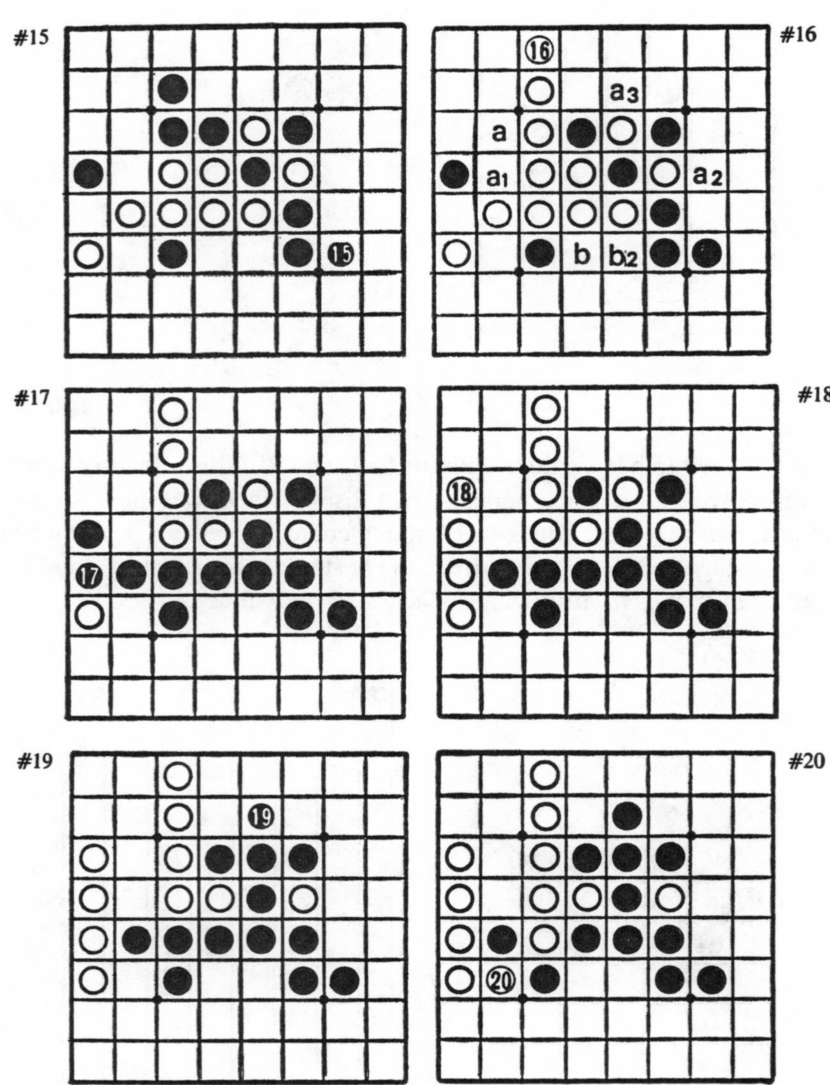
#15
15
#16
16
a3
a
a1
a2
b
b2
#17
17
#18
18
#19
19
#20
20

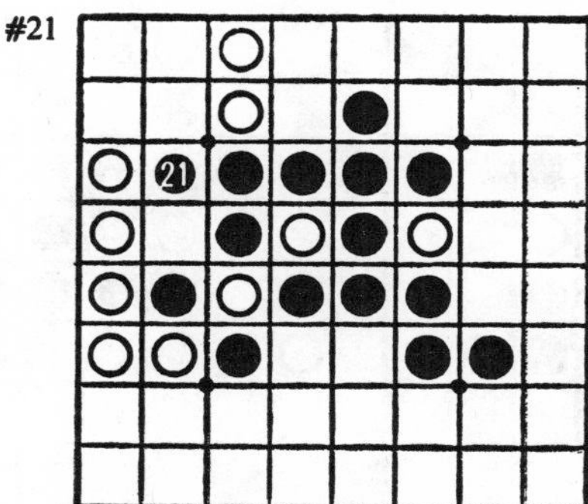

White's 14 goes to the **A** position, confronting Black's 13 in the **B** position. In #14 notice that Black has only one position to go to, despite his four **b1** positions. White's 16th move, to another **A** position, may have upset Black. He made a bad mistake with his 17th move. This gave away the third **A** position to White (#18). Now Black is in bad shape.

An Error in Judgment

Black's 17 could go to any of six **a** and **b** positions to produce a much better situation. Realizing his mistake, Black made the 19th move as shown. He probably chose the move in order to capture as few white discs as possible and keep a balance, but this again was a poor move. White's masterful 20th move almost put an end to Black's game.

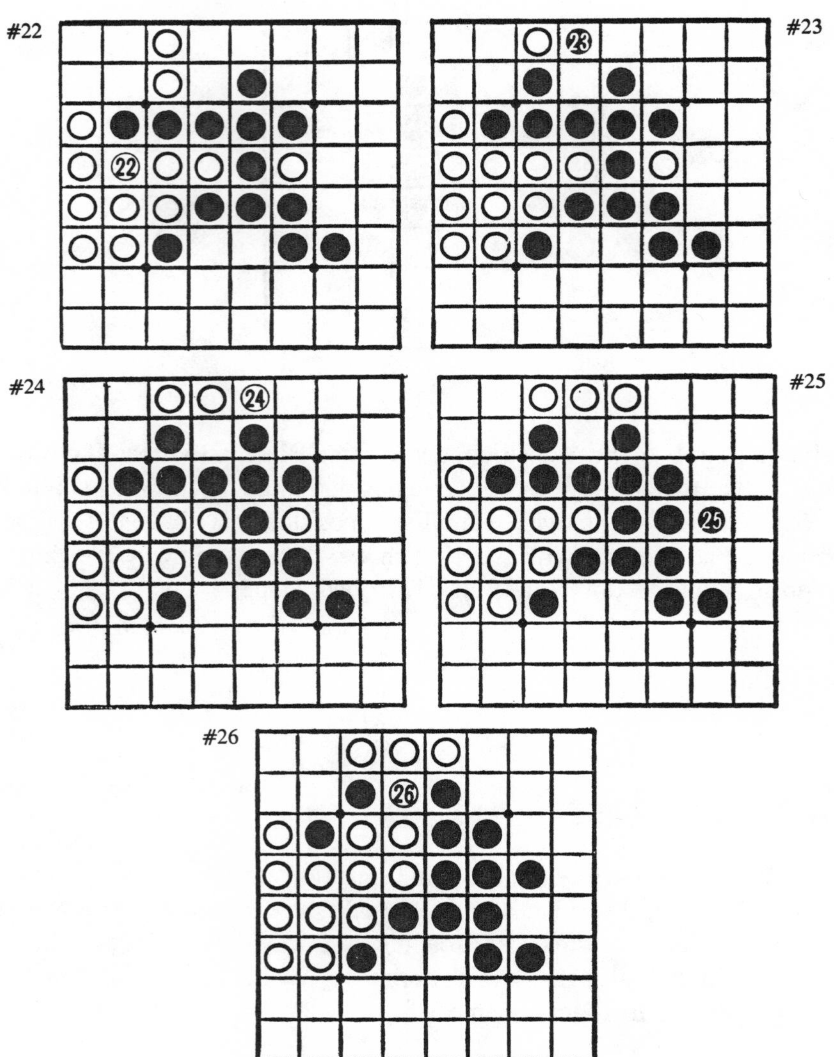
#22
22
#23
23
#24
24
#25
25
#26
26

Black's 21, 23, and 25 are desperate struggles to save himself. White returned rather ordinary 22nd and 24th moves, and with his 26th move he finished off Black.

The direct cause of Black's defeat was his 19th move. It should have been played as Diagram 175 shows. In Diagram 176 Black has a workable formation. Compare this diagram with #21. You can see the difference clearly. In the actual game White's 22 was a fatal shot. In Diagram 176 the situation is only three moves different from #21, but White can by no means deal a fatal blow to Black.

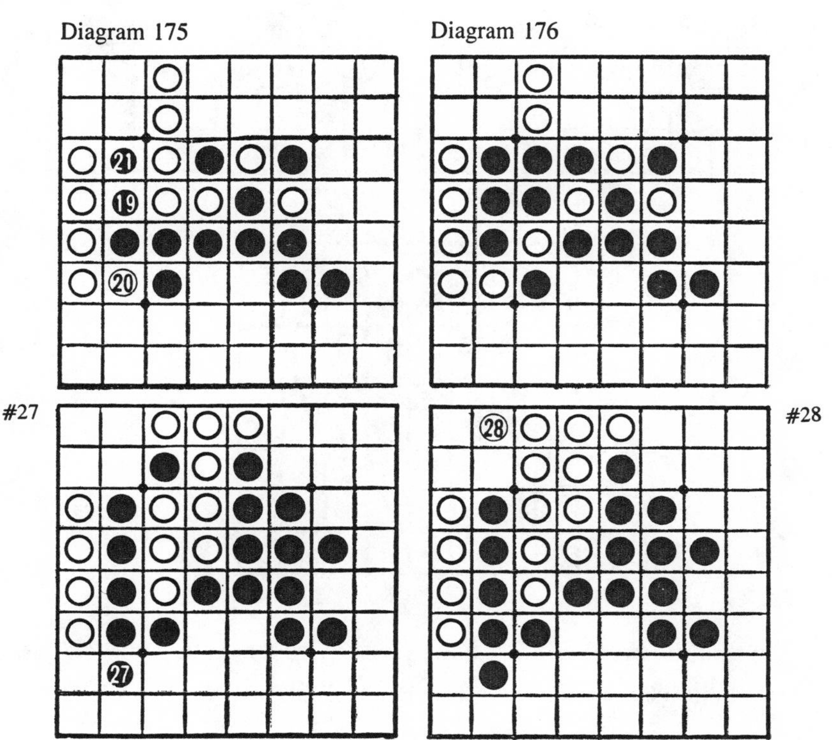

Black's 27 is a forced move. He tried last-minute resistance with his 29th move—in vain. White's 30 left Black with only one forced move to make.

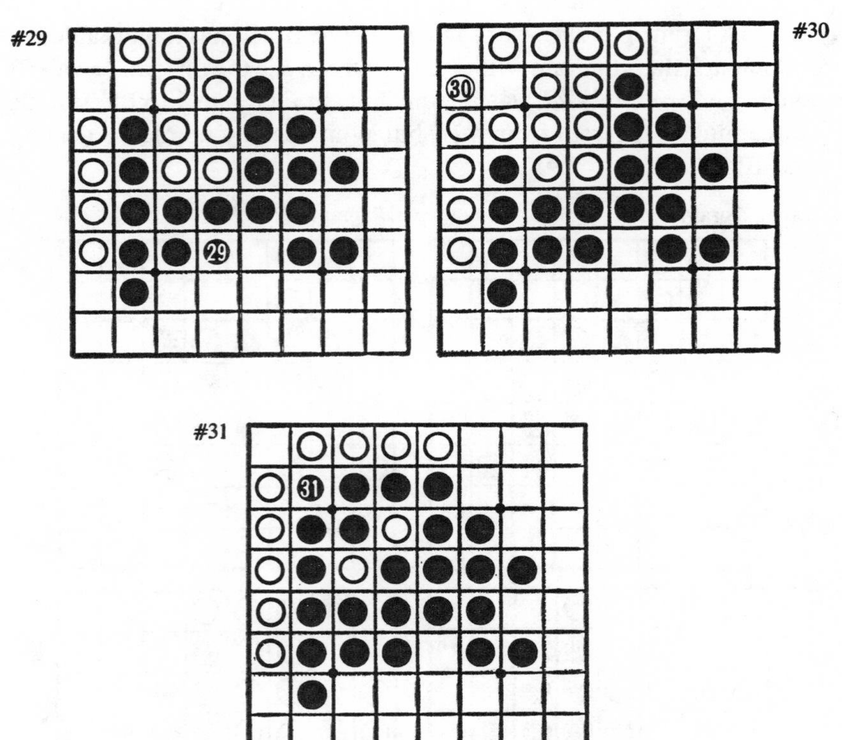

Led to this situation, Black cannot possibly reverse the game. White won an overwhelming victory as Diagrams 177 and 178 show.

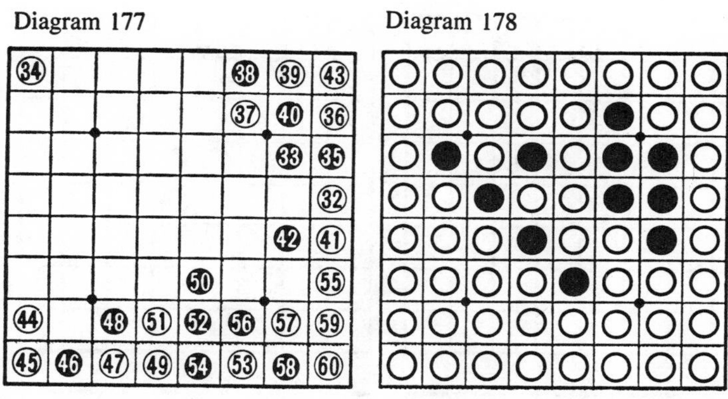

(White's win, 53 points)

Dr. Kitamura's Ingenious B Position Strategy

This game was played in one of the preliminaries for the All-Japan Women's Title Match. Black was played by Dr. Kitamura, the first runner-up. Up to the 12th move Black and White are confronting each other squarely.

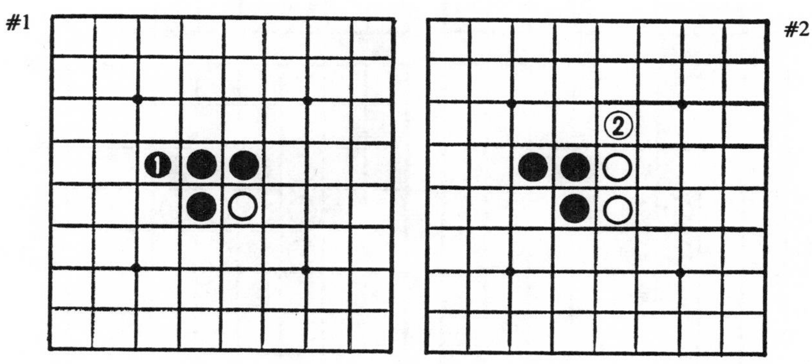

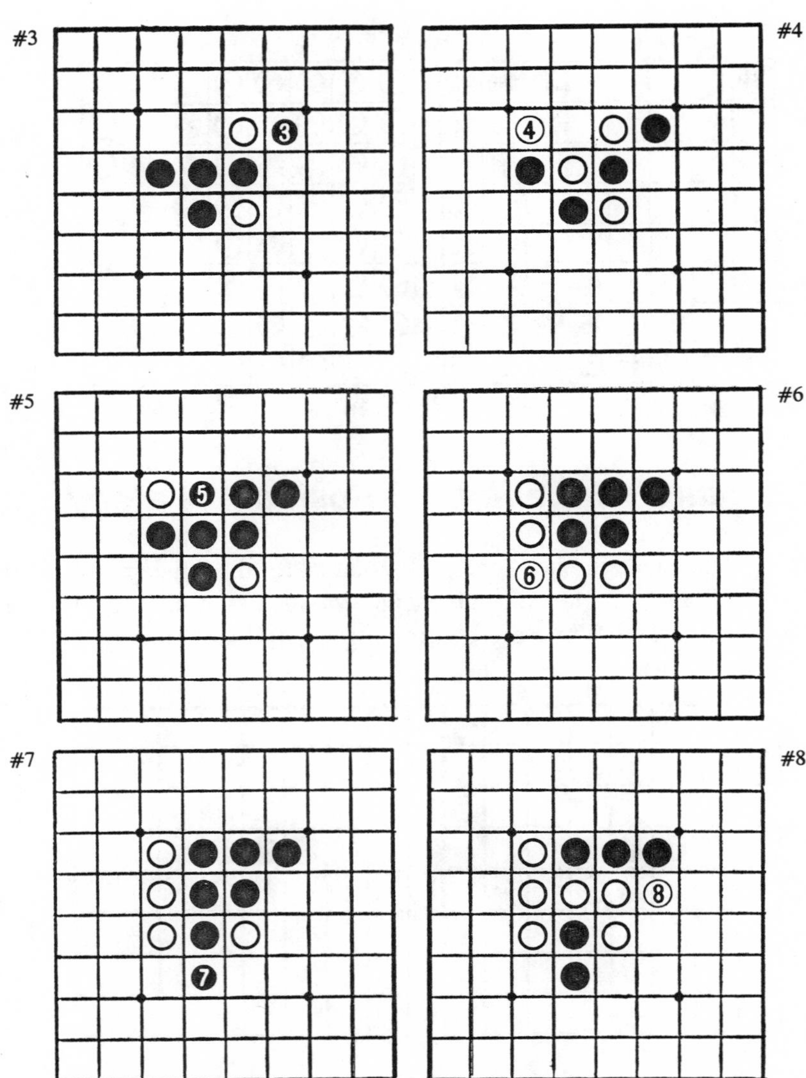
#3
3
#4
4
#5
5
#6
6
#7
7
#8
8

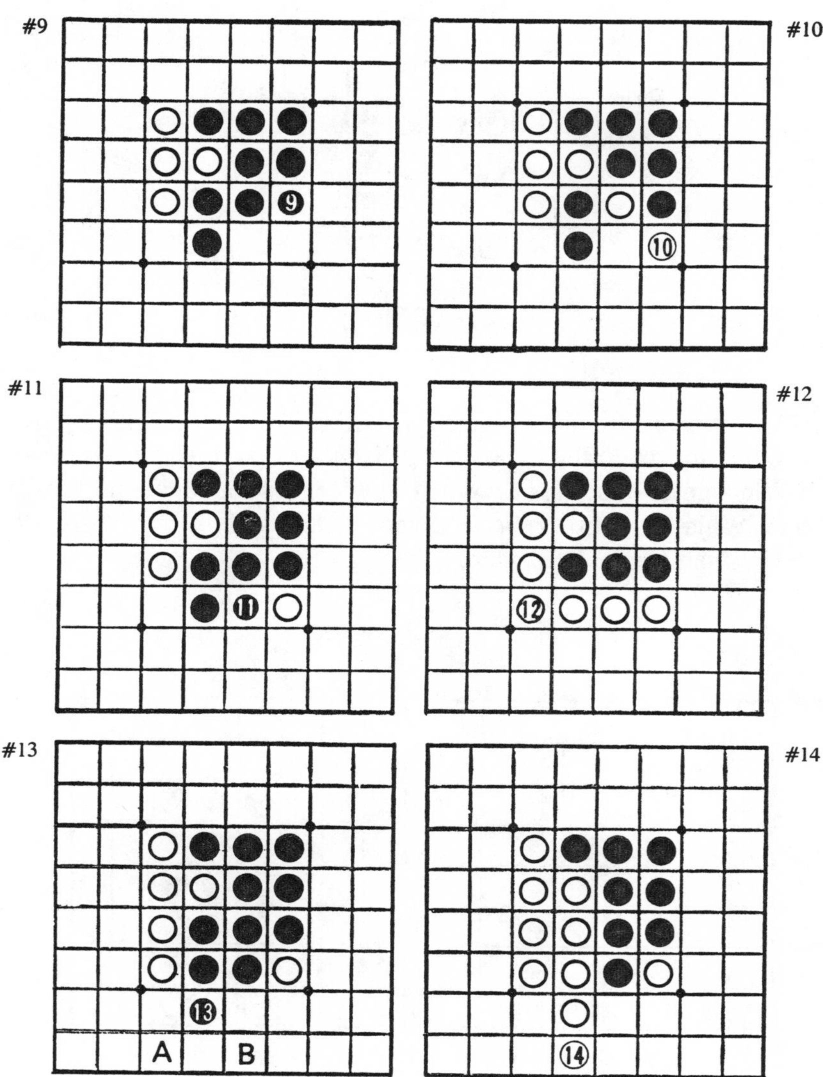
#9
9
#10
10
#11
11
#12
12
#13
13
A
B
#14
14

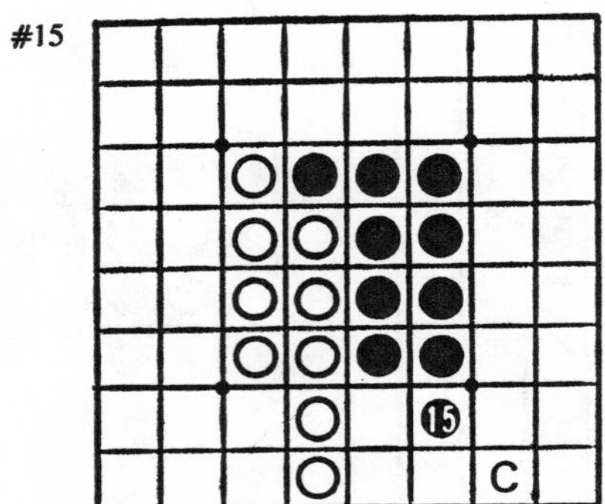

Black's 13th and 15th moves initiate Dr. Kitamura's far-reaching plot. In #13, if White moves to the **B** position, Black will go to the **A** position. In #15, if White goes to the **C** position, Black will play her hand as in Diagram 179, to let White line up her discs (Diagram 180), only to turn them all to black in the final stage of the game.

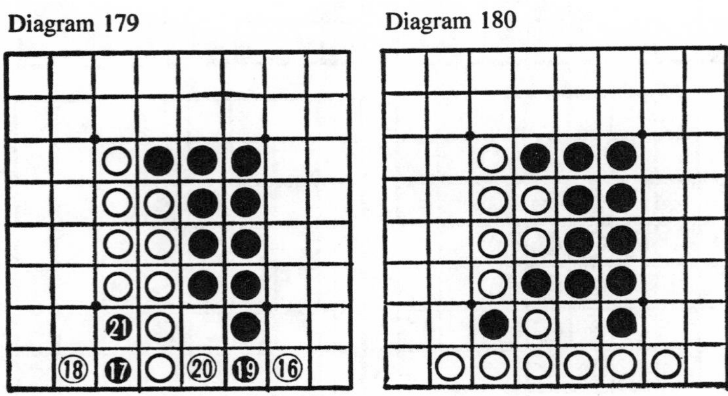

The 17-Disc Strategy

Dr. Kitamura is trying for an advanced tactic called the *17-disc strategy* (so called because if it works, you leave your opponent with only seventeen discs on the board). This strategy is very risky and depends on a well-trained ability to judge each situation accurately in the middle stage. It's for top players who are looking for some adventure.

The logic here is to let your opponent occupy all the outer-edge positions except the four corners (see Diagram 181). In the final stage of the game, if you get to the first of the four corners, you can capture every one of your opponent's discs around the outer edges.

Diagram 181

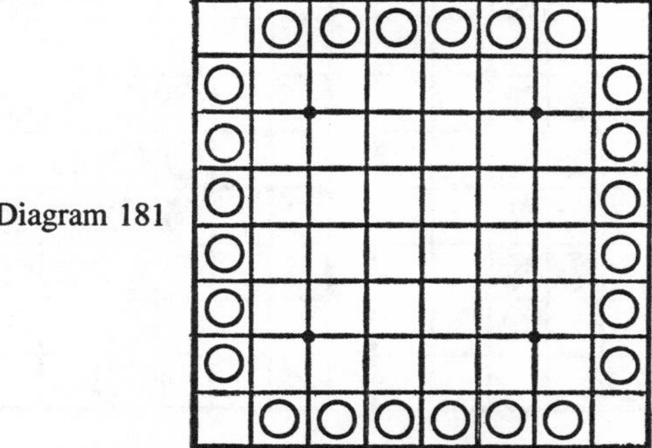

Even if your opponent takes the first corner, if you manage to take one of the other three corners, you can capture half of your opponent's discs. Moreover, once you take one corner, the rest of the empty corner positions are yours. Your opponent cannot take them since he has no enemy discs to flank. While your opponent has to pass, you have two moves which may bring about a big reversal on the board. If this strategy is carried out successfully, your opponent will have 17 discs left on the board. Hence the name—the 17-disc strategy.

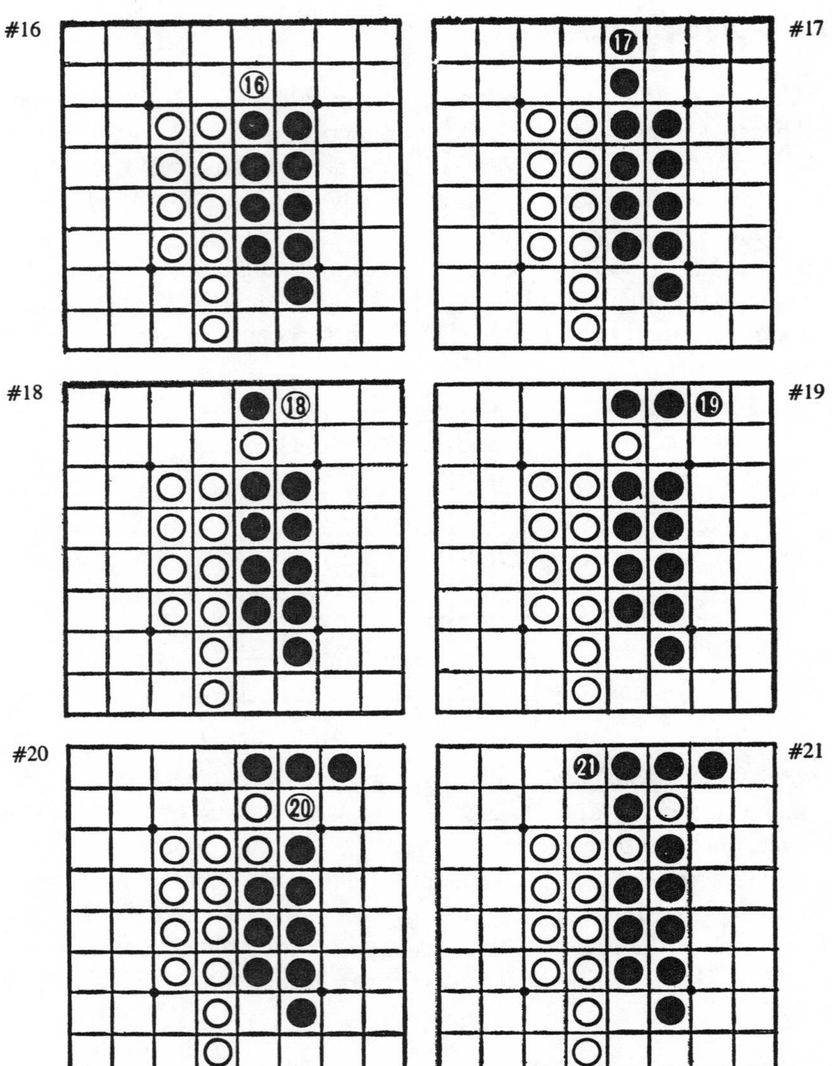
#16
16
#17
17
#18
18
#19
19
#20
20
#21
21

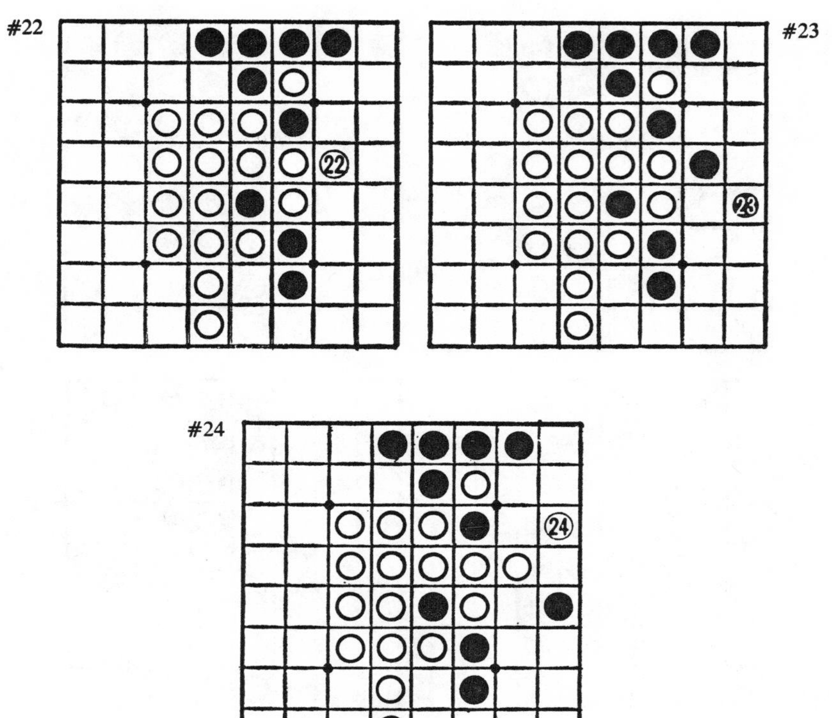

Forewarned Is Forearmed

White figured out what Black was aiming at, so she tried to carry out the same strategy with her 18th and 20th moves.

Black followed White's 22 with a relevant 23rd move. Black could not have moved to any other position without confusing the situation needlessly. White's 22 was a good move, establishing a useful base.

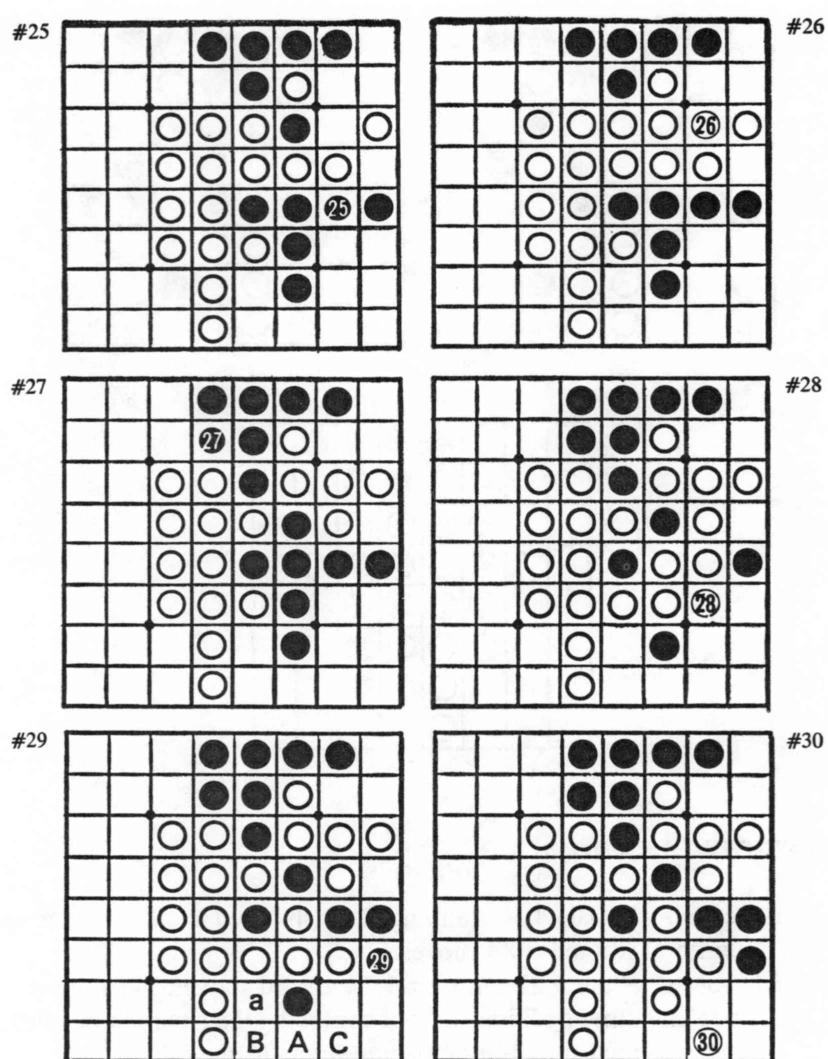
#25
25
#26
26
#27
27
#28
28
#29
29
a
B
A
C
#30
30

White was still going strong with her 26th move. But unfortunately she made a mistake with her 28th. It should have been moved as in Diagram 182. That way Black could not have run White into forced moves as she did with her 29th move in the real game.

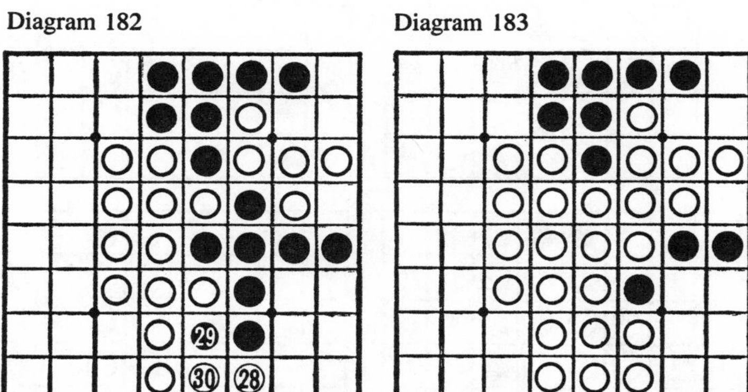

Diagram 182 Diagram 183

Look at play diagram #29. White in the **A** position would invite Black to the **B** position; White in the **B** position would be followed by Black in the **A** position, White in the **C** position, and Black in the **a** position. Either way, White's movement would be blocked. White's 30 is her last resort. Black's 31 is a cool move. White struggled on with her 32nd and 34th moves, but Black's 33 and 35 drove White into the forced move.

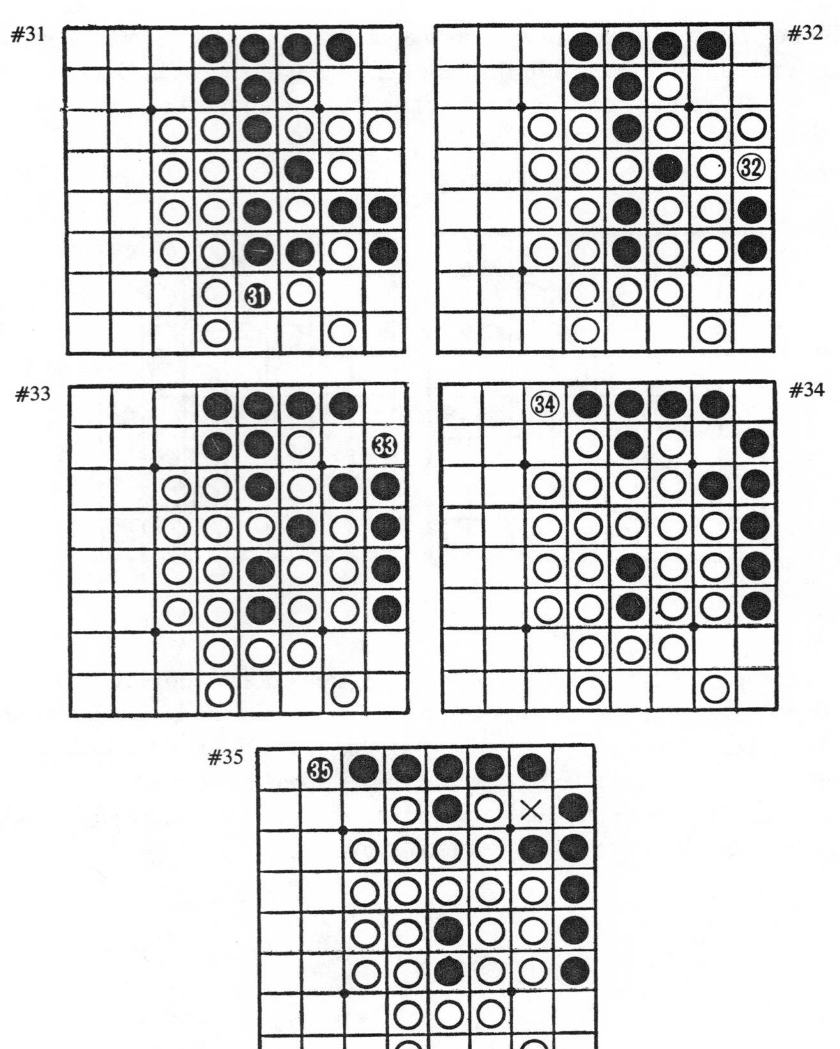
#31
31
#32
32
#33
33
#34
34
#35
35

In Diagram 184 Black's 37 and 41 represent Dr. Kitamura's unique idea. Black's 43, 44, 45, and 47 steadily attacked White. At the end Black managed two last moves, 59 and 60, in succession. It was indeed an ingenious operation.

Diagram 184

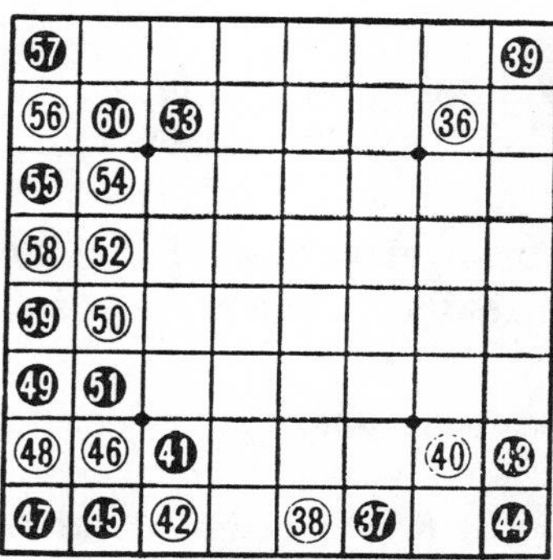

Diagram 185

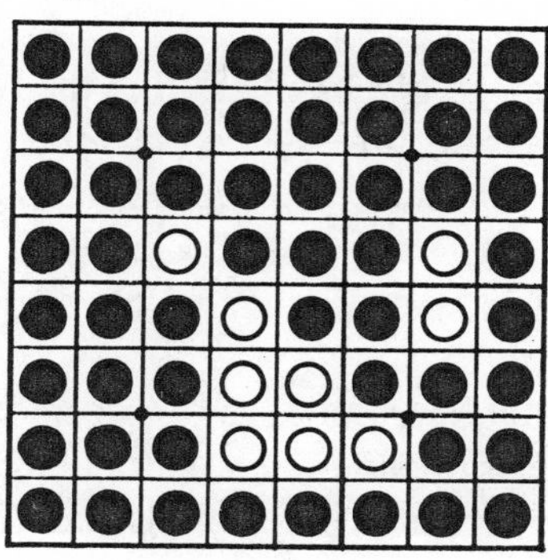

(Black's win, 46 points)

THE FINAL STAGE: THE 41ST MOVE TO THE 60TH MOVE

The final stage of Othello is like the last chapter of a complicated detective story. This is the time all the loose threads come together, all the missing facts suddenly fall into place—all those isolated discs get outflanked!

And not just the isolated ones. Here in the final stage whole fields of black turn white and then flip over to black again, as the control of the board wavers back and forth.

Most Othello games are not decided until the final stage. Weaknesses in each player's opening- and, particularly, middle-stage strategy become disastrously evident, as a player finds that a large section of the board, now covered with discs of his color, is suddenly open to attack.

This is a time for caution. Don't move too quickly; each move affects many discs now. Try to

- connect and protect your forces
- position new discs around the board to protect large areas (for example, if your opponent is about to outflank your discs, get some discs positioned so that you'll be able to win them all back)
- attack your opponent's filled areas—whittle away at them
- think ahead as many moves as you can.

Here are some final-stage plays that illustrate the excitement of this part of the game.

The 17-Disc Strategy Revisited

This is a way to dramatically reverse the outcome of a game in its final stage. The 17-disc strategy is based on the theory that a balanced number of discs is more important than the **A** and **B** positions.

In Diagram 186 White's 6th and 12th moves show unique skill. His 16, 18, 20, and 22 are contrary to the conventional **A** position strategy (trying to take an **A** position as a base of operation). A conventional player would have made

Diagram 186

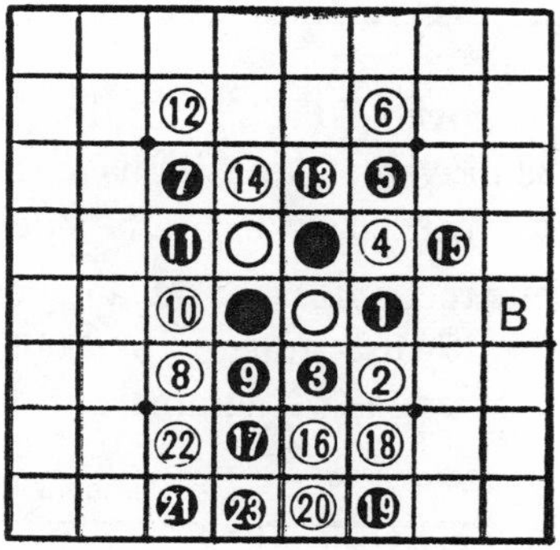

the 16th move to the **B** position, the 18th move to the position of 23, the 20th to the position of 21, and the 22nd to another **B** position.

But look at Diagram 186. Notice that White's moves have a certain consistency. White is deliberately making Black go to outer-edge positions. His aim is the 17-disc strategy, shown in Diagram 188.

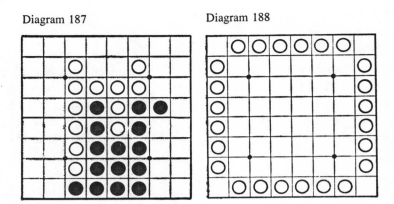

Diagram 187

Diagram 188

After Black's 25th move to the **A** position, White changed his tactics entirely. His 26 and 28 moved to **A** positions in succession. In a brief time an ideal white formation emerged on the right side (Diagrams 189 and 190).

This shows that White recognizes the advantages of the **A** position strategy. But he goes back to the 17-disc strategy, and both black and white discs are lined up along the outer edges (Diagrams 191 and 192).

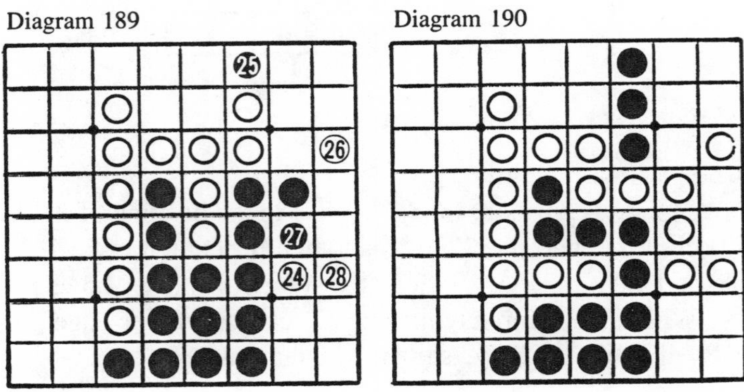

Diagram 189

Diagram 190

Diagram 191

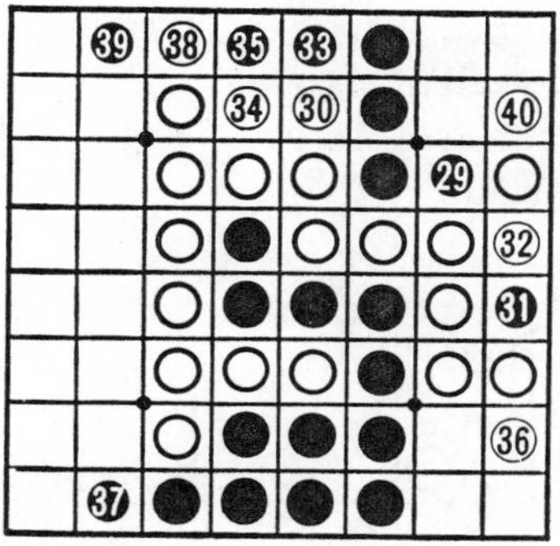

Diagram 192

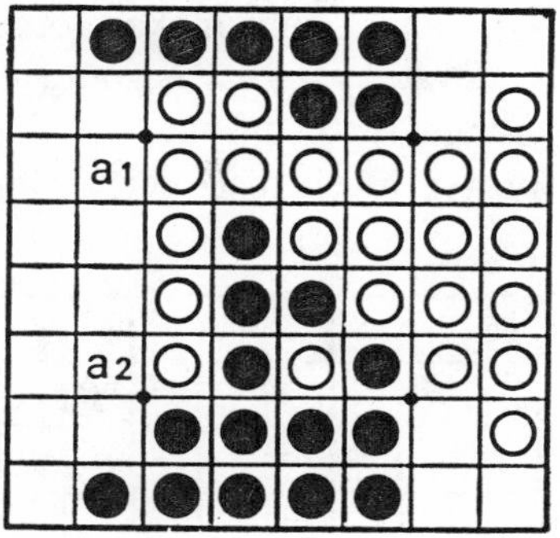

The Final Duel

From Diagram 192 on, the game enters the final stage. Black and White have equal chances. Will White succeed in carrying out the 17-disc strategy? Or will Black be able to knock White out by using White's strategy in his own favor?

Diagram 193

Diagram 194

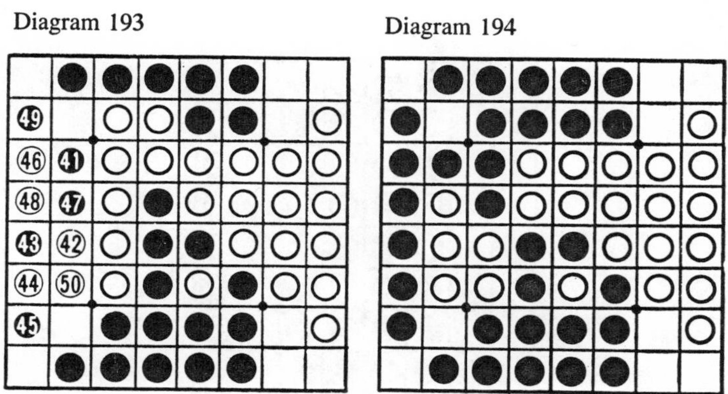

The actual game progressed as shown in Diagrams 193 and 194. In Diagram 194 Black must make a forced move. This is exactly the formation of the 17-disc strategy. Black is going to lose all of his outer-edge positions. The game continued as Diagram 195 shows, and at the end (Diagram 196) there were only five black discs left on the board.

Diagram 195

55						54	52
	57					51	
	53					58	
56						59	60

Diagram 196

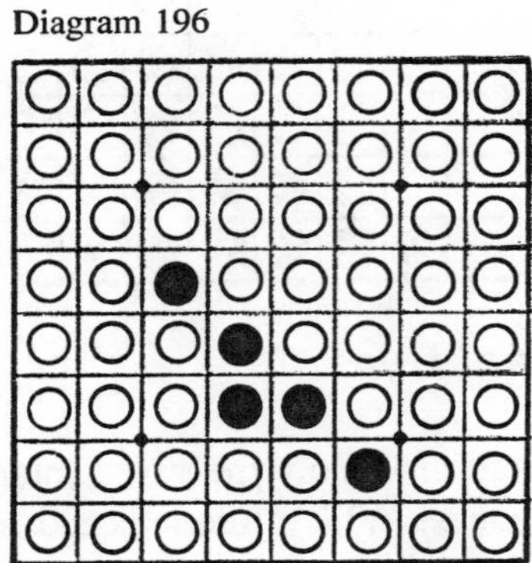

Diagram 197

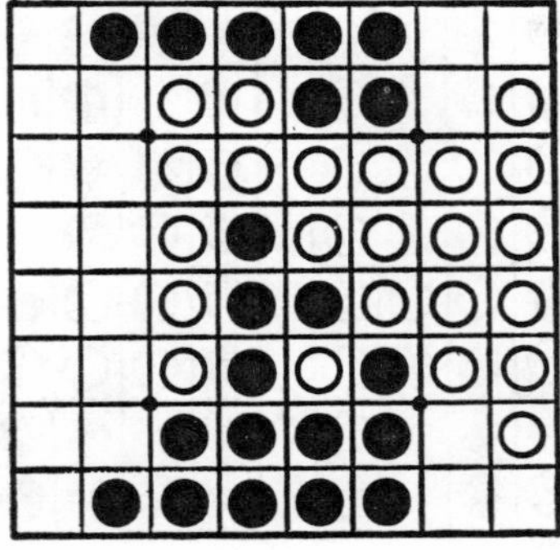

Was White at advantage in Diagram 192?

We asked six members of the Japanese Othello Association to play the same game, starting with the situation of Diagram 197 (the same as Diagram 192). Black won two games, and White one. (See Diagrams 198 and 203.) Note that in all three games Black made 41st moves to positions different from those taken in the actual game.

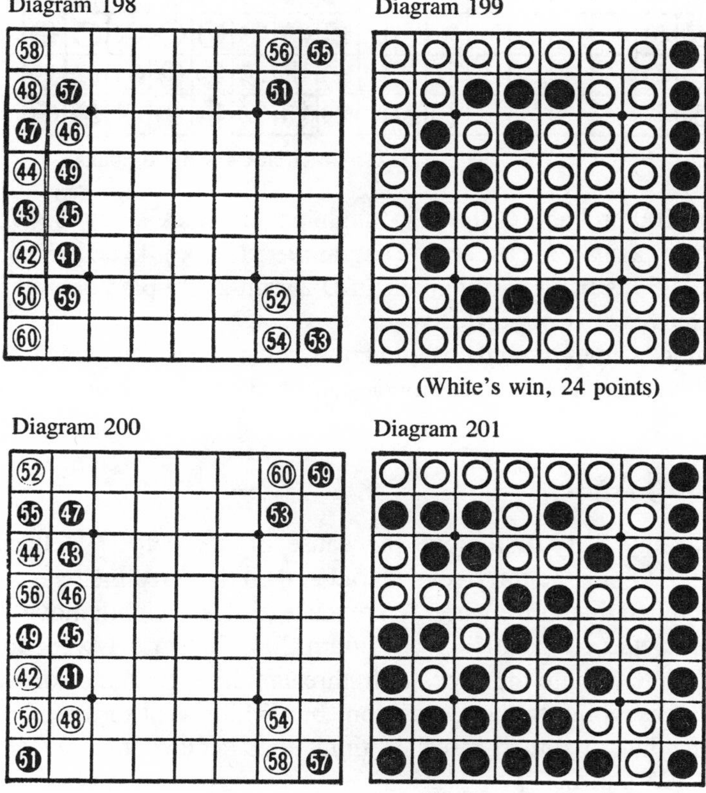

(White's win, 24 points)

(Black's win, 6 points)

Diagram 202

58						54	55
50	46					51	
49	59						
48	45						
47	43						
42	41						
52	53					44	
60						56	57

Diagram 203

●	●	●	●	●	●	●	●
●	●	○	●	●	○	●	●
●	○	○	○	○	●	○	●
●	●	○	●	●	○	○	●
●	●	○	●	●	○	○	●
●	●	●	○	○	●	○	●
●	●	●	●	●	○	●	●
●	●	●	●	●	●	●	●

(Black's win, 30 points)

Diagram 200 probably is the best-fought game. Black's 43, 45, 47, and 53 are good moves in a good order. In Diagram 198 Black's 43 is noticeably bad, and White's 50 is particularly good. In Diagram 202 a plan behind the 44th and 46th moves was not effective.

These mock games proved one thing: If Black in the actual game had moved his 41 to the position of 41 in the mock games, Black would have done a little better.

Conflicting Analyses

"Then was my forty-first move the cause of my defeat?" Black asked doubtfully. "I think the forty-seventh rather than the forty-first was to blame. I really regretted that move when White made his forty-eighth move. I should have gone to the **a2** position in Diagram 204. Because I went to the **a1** position, White went to the **B** position, threatening to go to the corner next. I prevented it by going to the **C** position, but White went to the **a2** position, pushing me into a forced move. I think that decided my defeat." (See Diagrams 205 and 206.)

Diagram 204

Diagram 205

Diagram 206

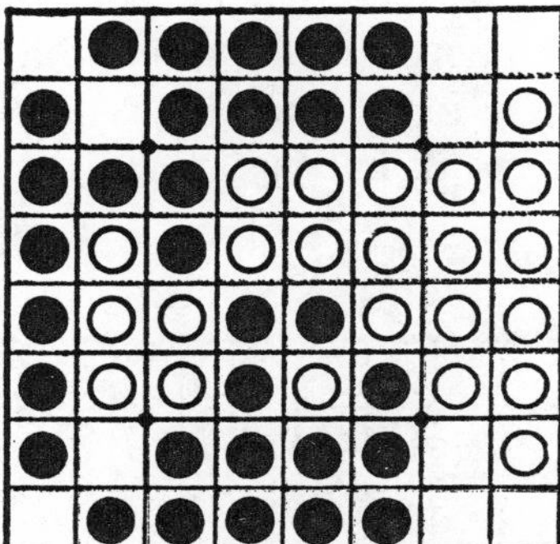

"As I see it now," he continued, "if I had made my forty-seventh move to the **a2** position, I would have won (Diagram 207). My forty-nine is a particularly good move. If the forty-nine had been placed in the **C** position next to it (Diagram 209), I would have lost."

Diagram 207 Diagram 208

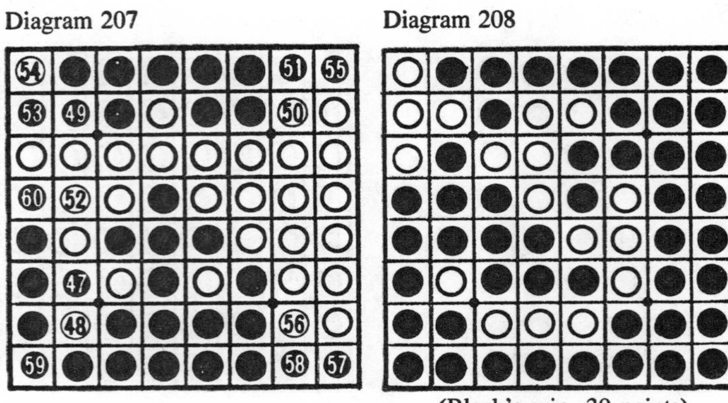

(Black's win, 30 points)

Actually, the 47 in Diagram 207 may be more meaningful than the 47 in Diagram 204. Black might have won the game. But a game in its final stage can change in hundreds of different ways. Black probably could not have won just by changing the 47th move. In Diagram 207 the 50th move is a very bad

Diagram 209 Diagram 210

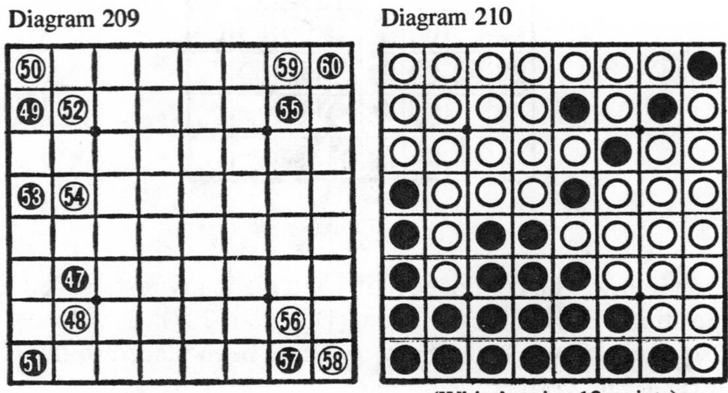

(White's win, 12 points)

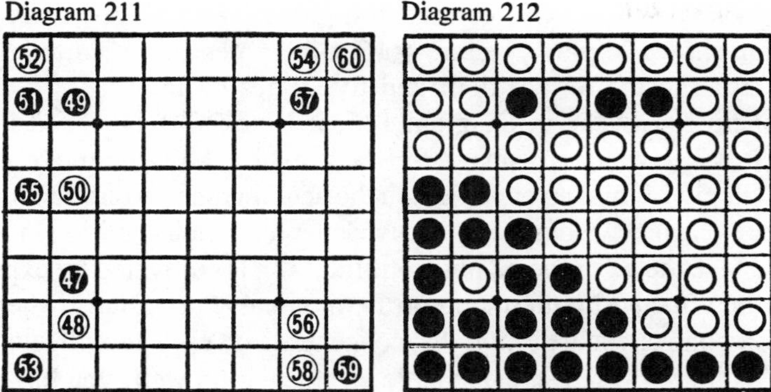

Diagram 211

Diagram 212

(White's win, 16 points)

one, which probably caused White's defeat. But if White had gone to the position of 52 instead of 50, Black could not have won. Diagram 209 proves it.

Go back to the 48th move. It could have been made as in Diagram 213. The move could have led to White's victory (Diagram 214).

Diagram 213

Diagram 214

To see which analysis was correct, test games were played, starting with the position shown in play diagram #46. Five times Black started the game with the move to the **a2** position, and five times he lost.

The conclusion is that in Diagram 186, if Black's 41 is placed in the **a2** position, it will give an advantage to Black, while the same move in the **a1** position will give White an edge. But in the actual game no one can foresee so many future changes. Most players must depend on their intuition in deciding whether to take the **a1** or the **a2** position. Intuition is cultivated by experience, but it can be affected by the mood of the moment. Particularly when you're playing someone of equal ability, just concentrate on each complicated part of the game as it arises. If you can handle each situation well, you have a good chance of winning, even if you haven't plotted your total strategy.

The 17-disc strategy works very well when you play with beginners. Advanced players, like Black in this game, can weaken the strategy

The Effect of One Mistake

Diagram 215

		21		40	38		
		12	25	37	39		31
20	17	4	5	2	3	22	11
	33	1	○	●	9	10	
36	34	6	●	○	8	26	24
35	32	13	16	15	7	18	
		14	23	28	30		27
		19			29		

Diagram 216

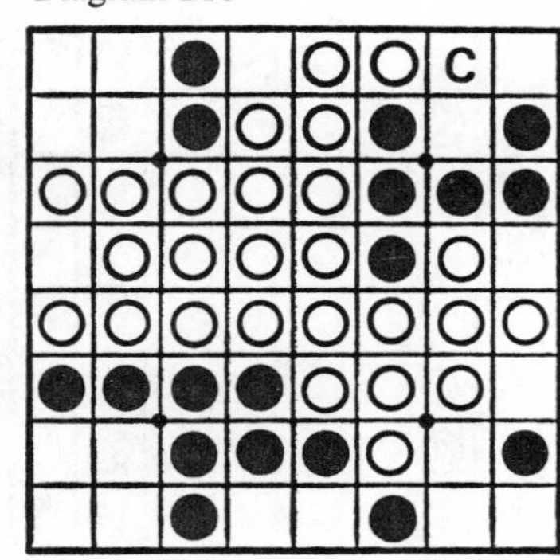

Here, in the final stage of a game, White is in a more favorable position than Black.

If you play the game out on your own board, you'll see that:

Up to Black's 9, Black played well.

Up to Black's 21, both sides tried to take **A** positions, and at the end of the opening stage the game was even.

White's 24 took the first **B** position to challenge Black's **A** position strategy in the right field.

Black's 27 and 31 tried for a risky **C** position strategy.

White's 36 advanced to the **A** position on the left to challenge Black.

In Diagram 216 Black is in a difficult situation, while White still has the **C** position in reserve. On the right, White's **B** position looks more advantageous than Black's **C** positions. Black tried the **C** position tactics without success.

After the game entered the final stage, Black made a series of aimless moves, 41, 43, and 45. White's 46 made the situation worse for Black. In play diagram #47, Black's 47 is a semiforced move. White definitely has an advantage.

#41

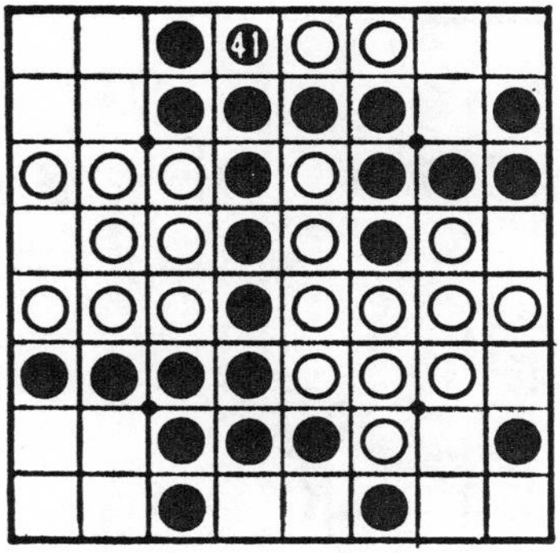

41

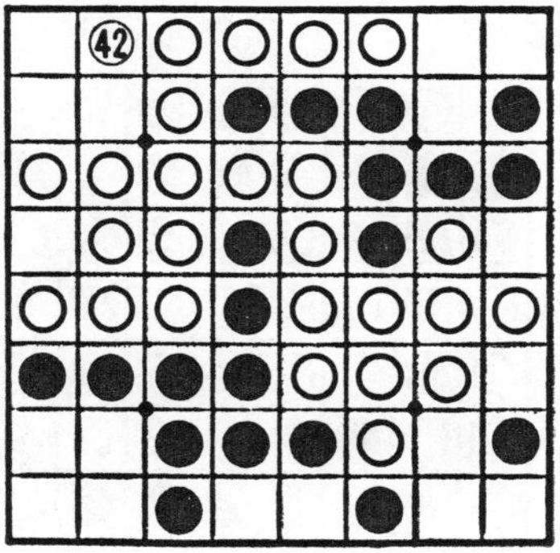

#42

42

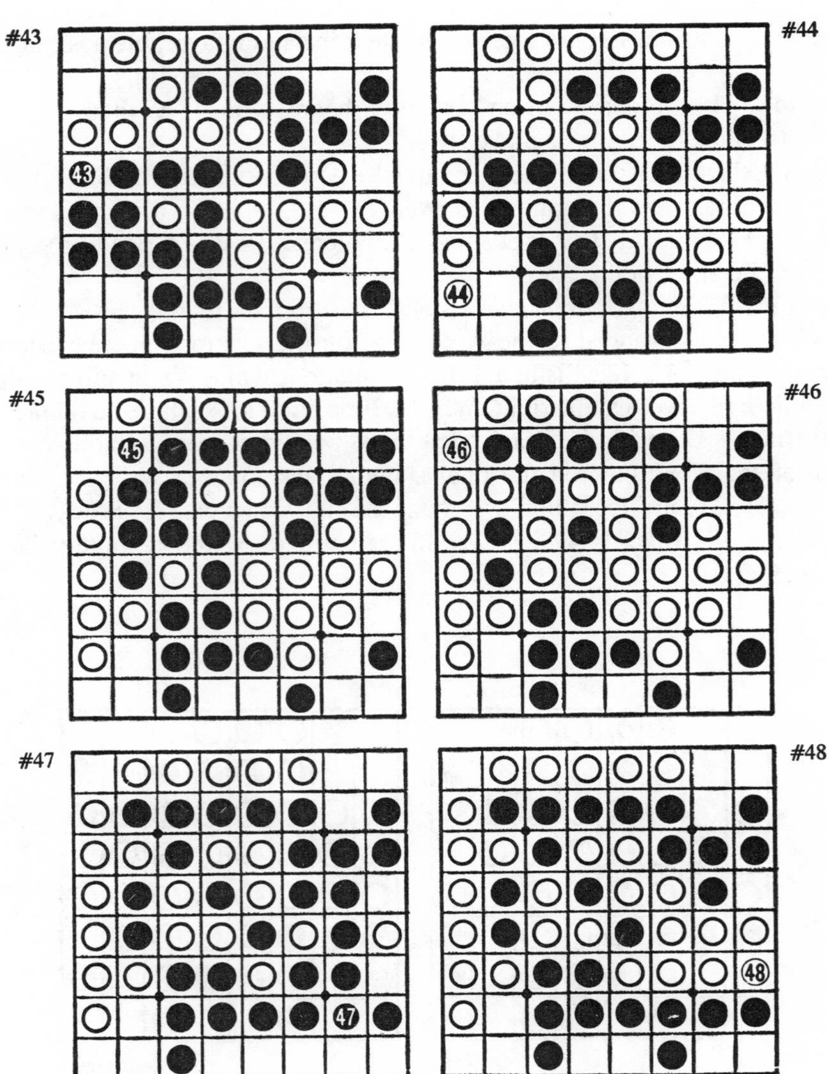
#43
43
#44
44
#45
45
#46
46
#47
47
#48
48

Everyone thought White would win when Black made the 51st move (# 51).

#49

#50

#51

#52

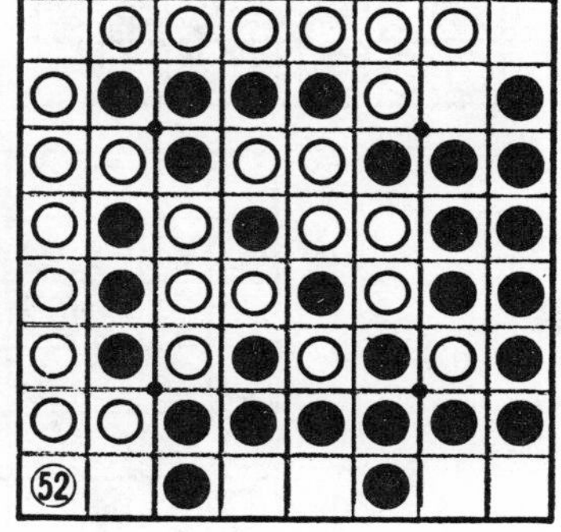

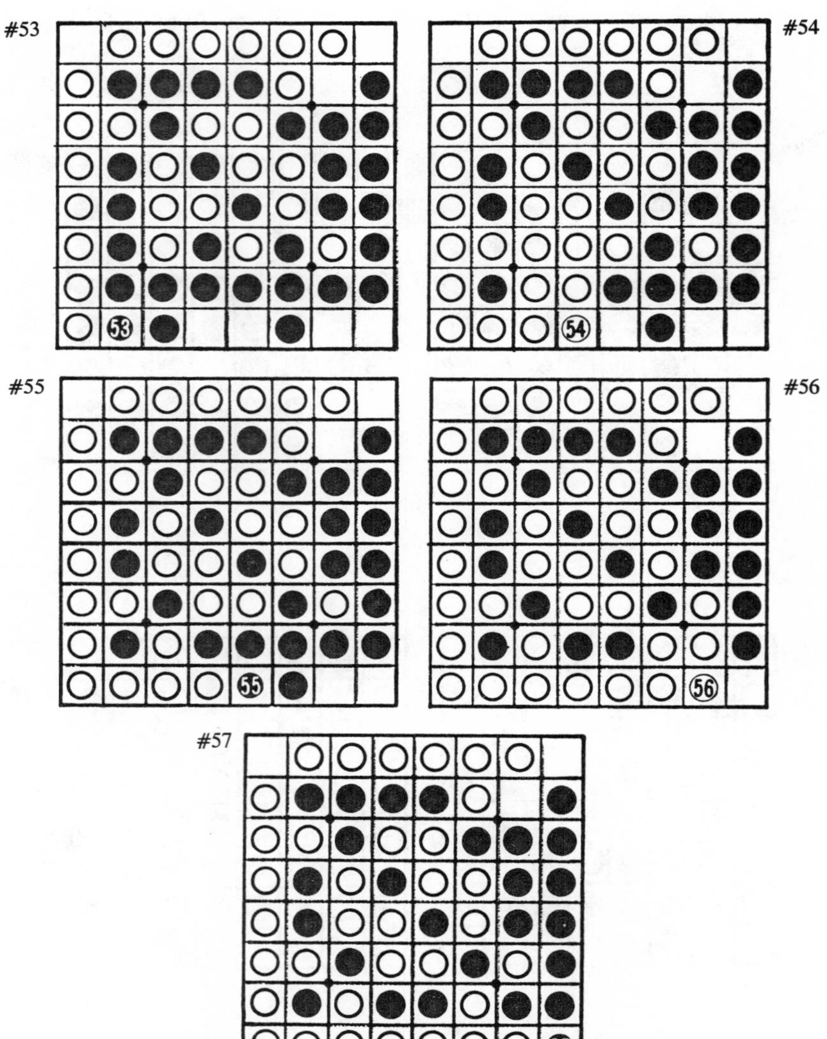
#53
53
#54
54
#55
55
#56
56
#57
57

Don't Look Now, But. . .

But the game progressed as the diagrams show. Black's 55 reversed the situation, causing White to play 56 and 58 as forced moves. Black's last two moves, 59 and 60, brought about a great reversal, making the game Black's victory by four points.

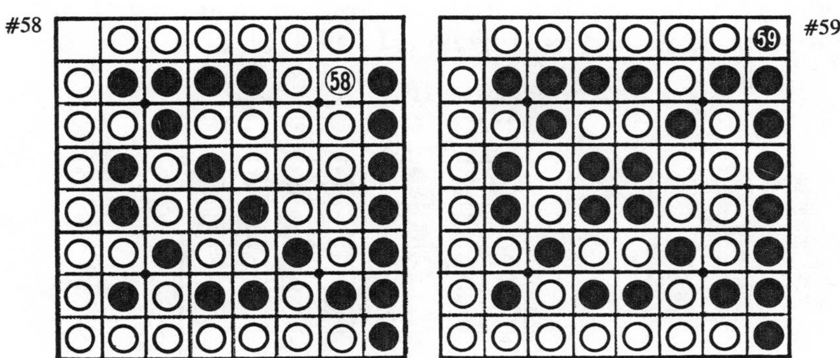

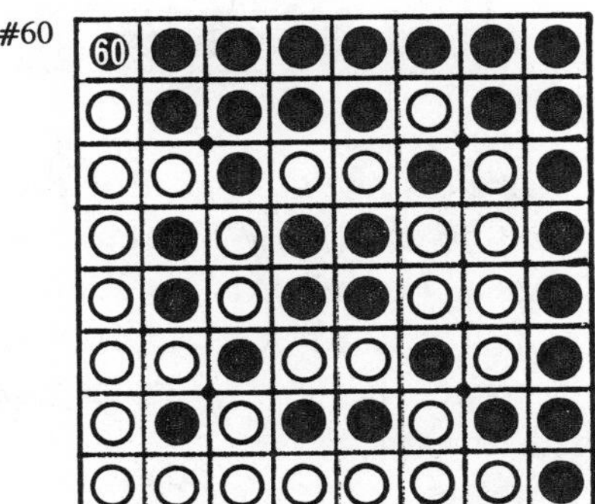

(Black's win, 4 points)

Why did White lose? Let's see.

Look at Diagram 217. In this situation the position White wants most is the upper left corner. To get there White has to capture one of the black discs lined up diagonally from the upper left to the lower right. But right now the situation does not allow him to accomplish this. The most natural course for White to follow is: take the **C** position and push Black into a forced move, either the **X** position at the upper right or the **X** at the lower left, then go to the upper right corner or the lower left corner. If White had followed this course, he would have won a safe victory, as Diagrams 218 and 219 show.

Diagram 217

	○	○	○	○	○	C	
○	●	●	●	●	●	×	●
○	○	●	○	○	●	●	●
○	●	○	●	○	●	●	
○	●	○	○	●	○	●	○
○	○	●	●	○	●	●	B
○	×	●	●	●	●	●	●
		●			●		

In Diagram 217 White has a definite advantage. Nevertheless, he lost the game at the end. There must be a cause; White must have made a mistake which brought about his defeat. He did. Look at White's 48th move (the **B** position in Diagram 211). You must be very careful when you have driven your opponent into a tight corner, because he is desperately looking for an opportunity to get out of the tight spot.

The aim of White's 48 was to capture one of the diagonal row of black discs. White failed to anticipate that Black's 49 would frustrate his plan

Diagram 218

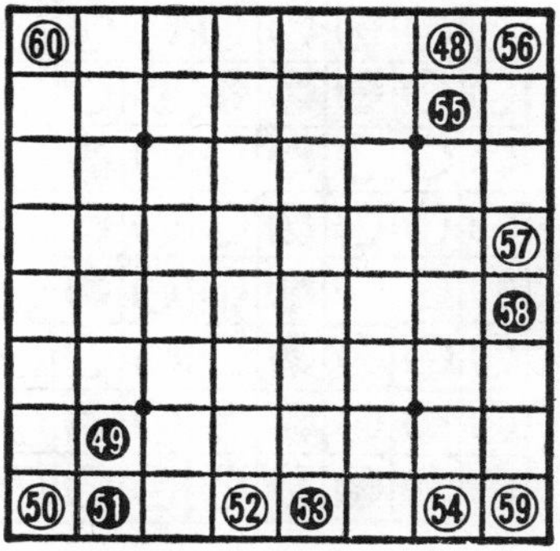

Diagram 219

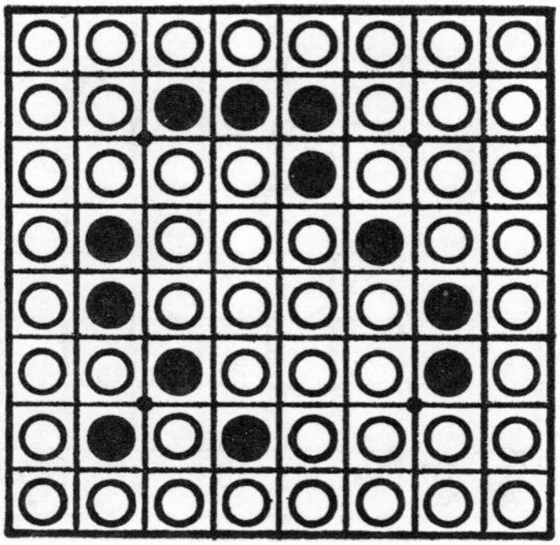

immediately. At a glance it looks like a small mistake, but its effect was great. White's 48 turned a black disc next to it to white. This overturned white disc, together with White's 56, captured a black disc in the **X** position at the lower right. This enabled Black to go to the lower right corner. The same white disc helped force White's last play, 58. The actual reversal of the situation was carried out by Black's 59th and 60th moves, but although it was hard to see at the time, the cause of the upset was White's 48th move.

Yet that blunder wasn't fatal. White still might have saved the game if he hadn't made an even more serious mistake.

Reverse Corner Strategy

The direct cause of White's defeat was the 52nd move to the corner. It is a basic principle of Othello that you must get to the corner ahead of your opponent. But this applies only to the opening stage of the game, *not to the final stage*. Instead of moving the 52 to the corner, if White had placed it as Diagram 220 shows, he could have had a 24-point win.

Diagram 220

54							56
						55	
53	52		60	59		58	57

Diagram 221

○	○	○	○	○	○	○	○
○	○	●	●	●	●	○	○
○	○	○	●	○	○	●	○
○	○	○	●	○	○	●	○
○	○	○	●	○	○	●	○
○	○	○	●	○	●	○	○
○	●	○	●	●	○	●	○
●	●	●	●	○	○	○	○

(White's win, 24 points)

Diagrams 220 and 221 show how White could have won if he had played the game differently after the 48th move.

A hypothetical game starting with Diagram 216 (see Diagram 222 below) presents an entirely different result. In Diagram 222 Black's disadvantage is not as big as in play diagram #46. He made mistakes with his 43 and 45. Suppose he had played his hand differently. The game could have been like Diagrams 223 and 224. Of course this is just one hypothetical game. It could have been played in many different ways.

Diagram 222

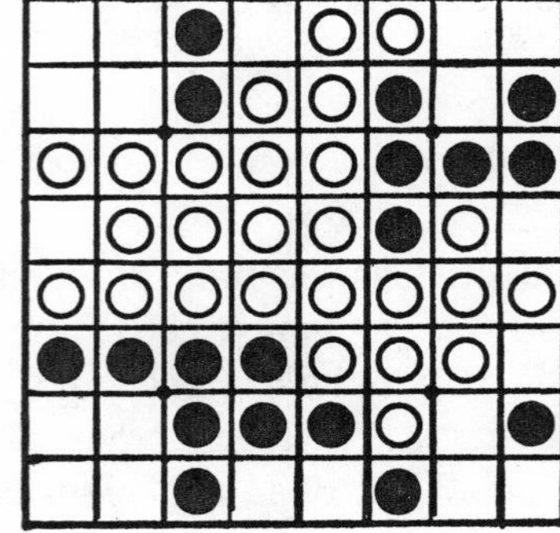

Diagram 223

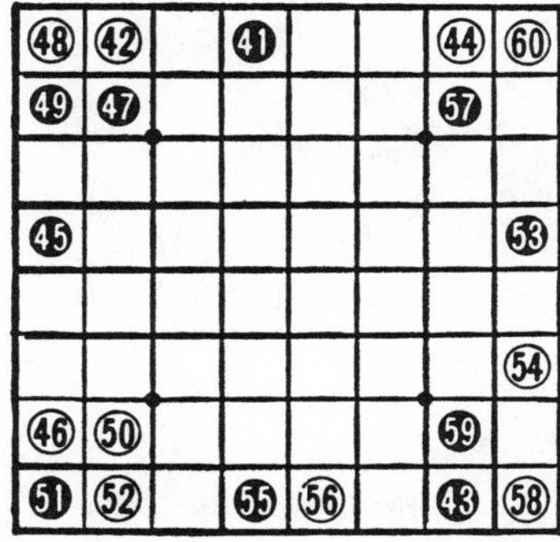

Diagram 224

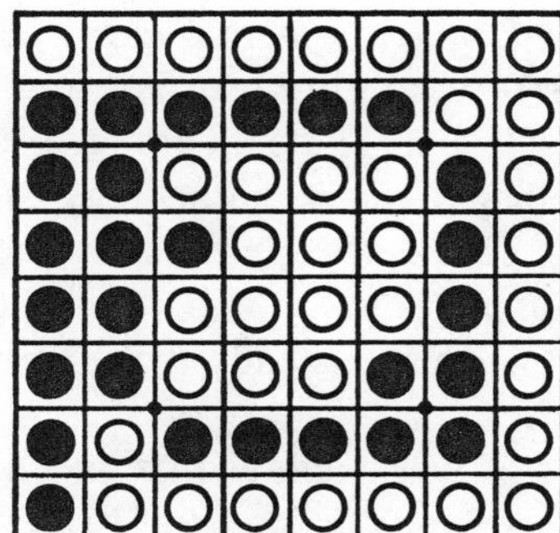

A Great Reversal

We showed Diagram 225 to Othello fans and asked how the situation looked to them. They all answered, "It is very bad for White. There is no question that Black has a big advantage." Is it really so? And if it is, can White possibly recover? Let's see if we can find the answers.

Diagram 225

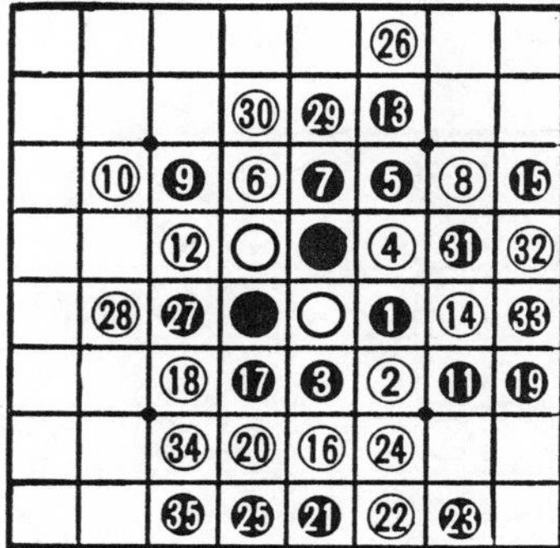

Diagram 226

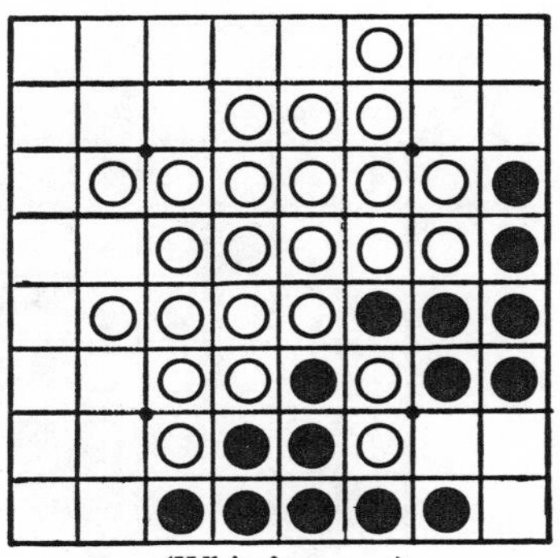

(White's move)

Here is the game so far, as shown in Diagram 225:

White's **8** was a dynamic move.

Black's 9 was faithful to the rule.

White's 10 and 12 made an interesting strategy—hard to tell at this point whether it was good strategy or bad.

White's 16 was an original idea. He could have gone to the **A** position on the upper edge, which would have been the ordinary move.

Black's 19 was a steady move. He completed an ideal formation on the right.

White's 22 was a unique play, not unlike the 17-disc strategy. If Black had not captured this 22, White would have captured the black disc next to it, making a nice formation. So Black had to take it. Black achieved an advantageous basis on the lower edge, a comparable formation to that on the right edge.

White's 26 into the **A** position was made at the right time. This put a stop to Black's filing attack.

Black's 31 completed an ideal formation on the right. White's 32 tried to break the formation, but Black steadily fought back with his 35 and forced White into the **X** position. Black was definitely in a superior position (Diagram 226).

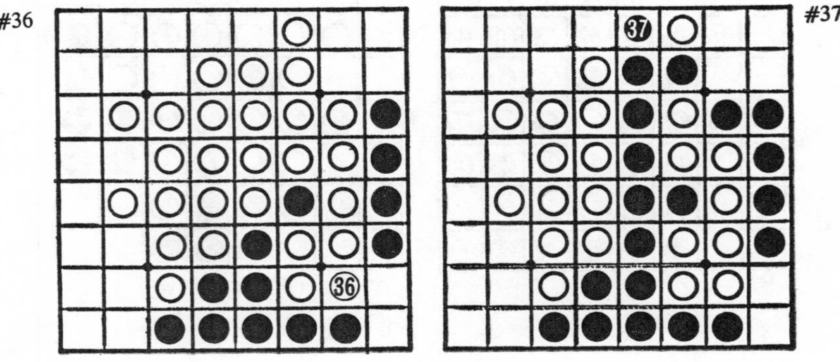

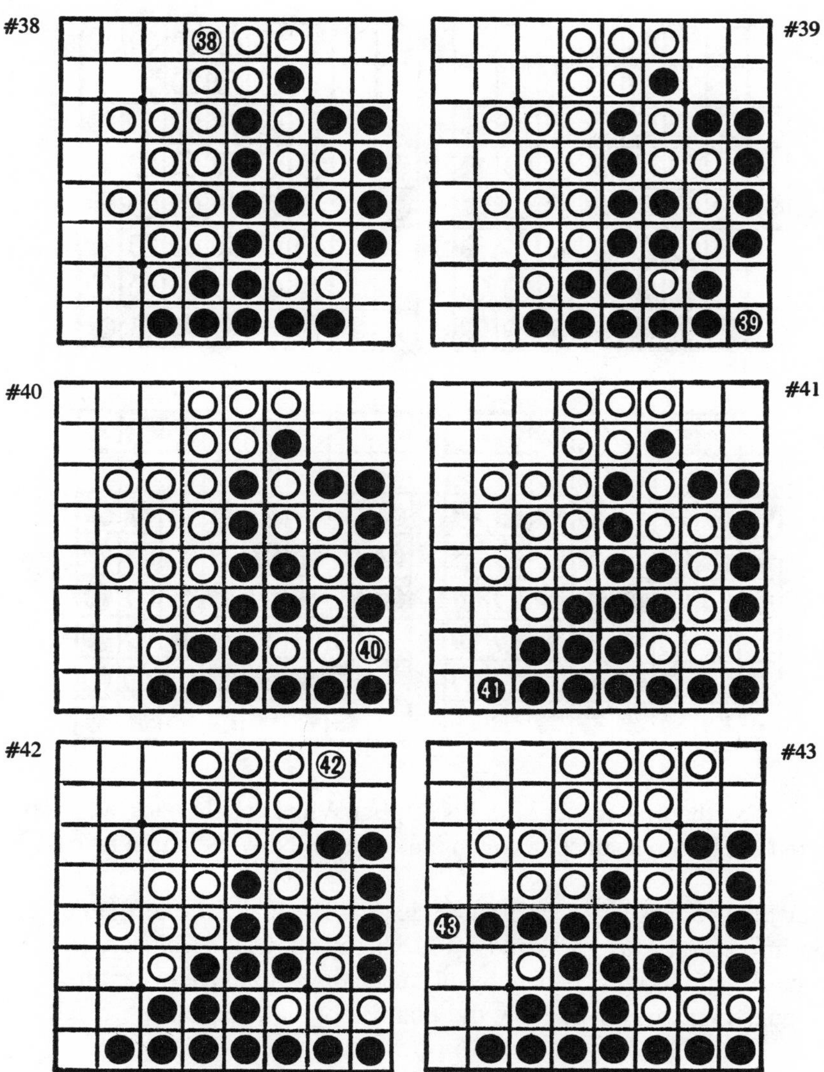
#38
38
#39
39
#40
40
#41
41
#42
42
#43
43

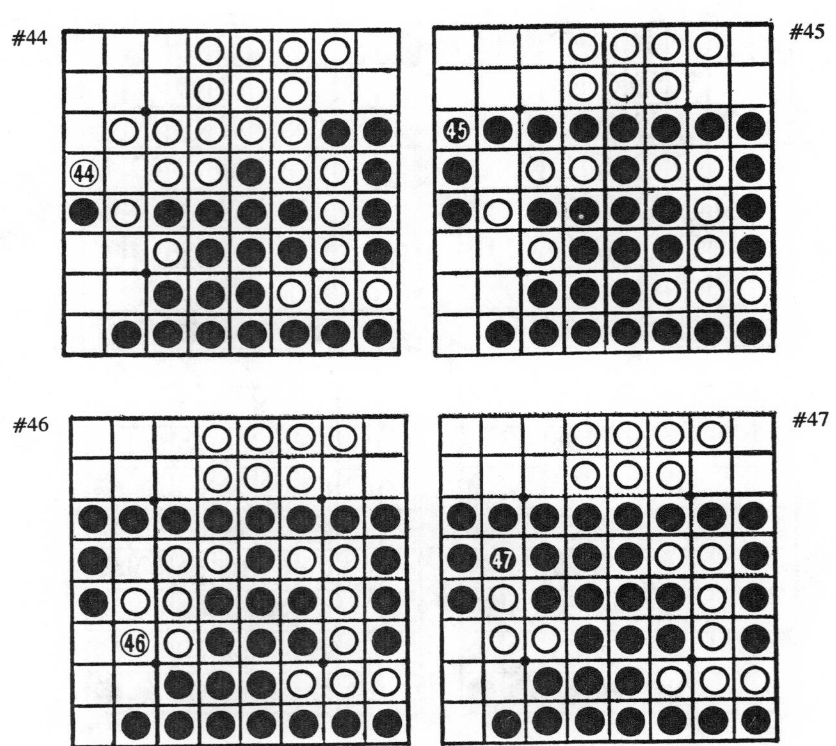

Black took the first corner with his 39, but White fought back well. His 40 squeezed itself into a space between black discs. Now the game is in its final stage.

After the sparring of 41 and 42, Black's 43 reached the left edge. Black should have been wary of White's 44, which followed 43 closely to the left edge, but Black, as if enchanted by 44, made the 45th move to capture it. This was a questionable move. Now the board looks a little bit too black.

Black Ponders

In #46 White's tenacious fight is showing effects. A balanced number of white and black discs can be broken any moment. Where should Black move next? To the position of 47? It looks like a good move, but the 47th move was the cause of Black's surprising defeat. White's 48 was an ingenious move.

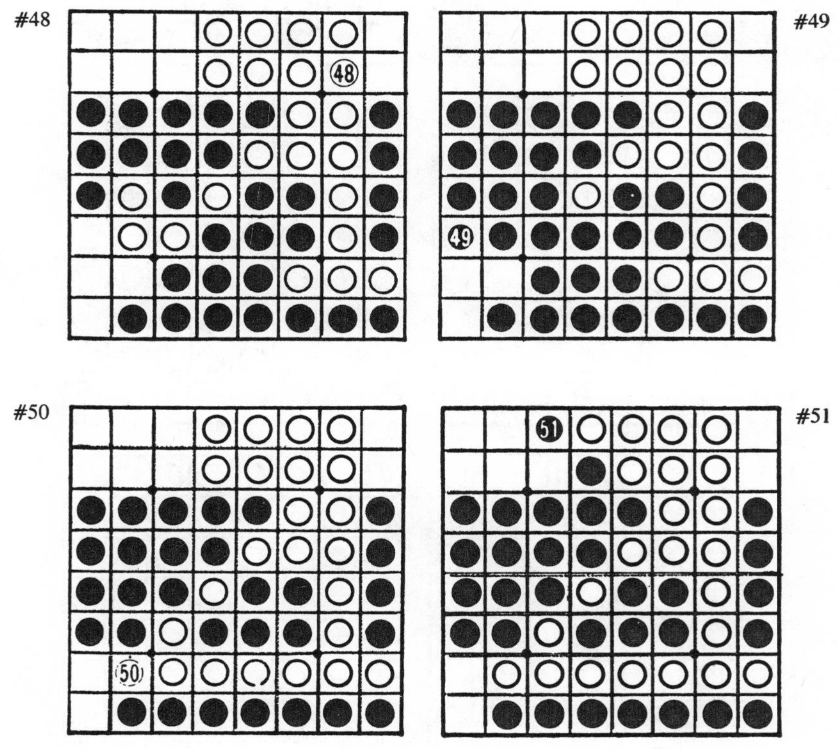

#52

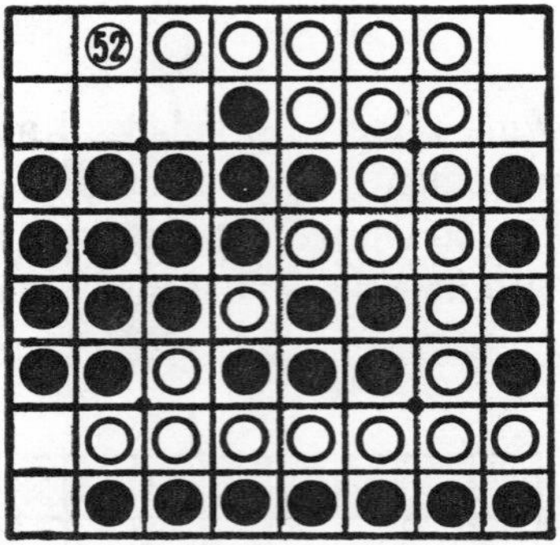

52

#53

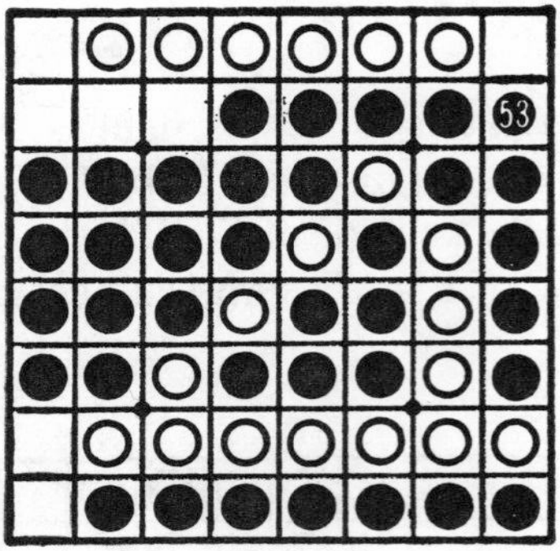

53

#54

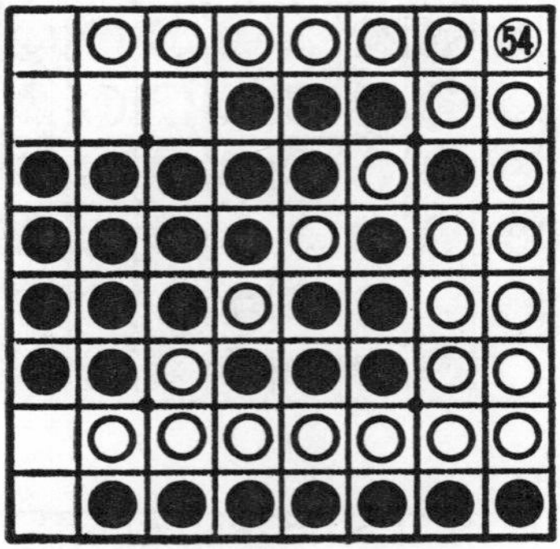

54

#55

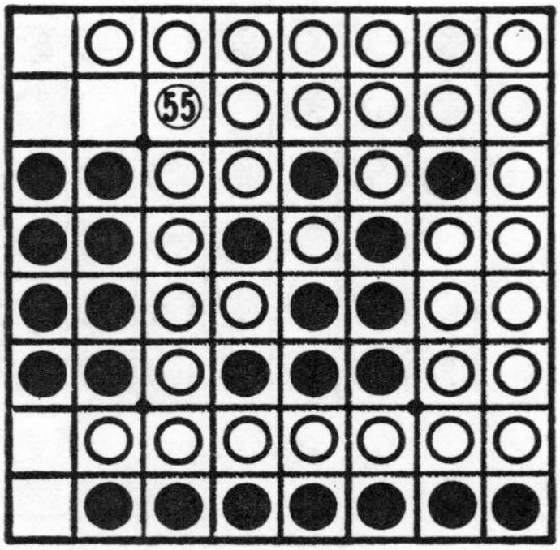

55

#56

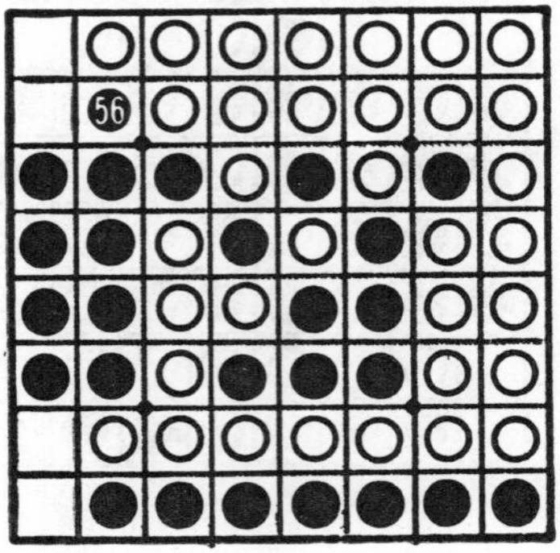

56

#57

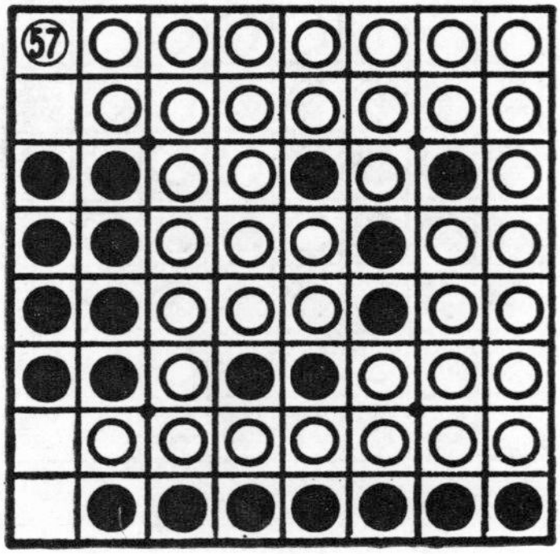

57

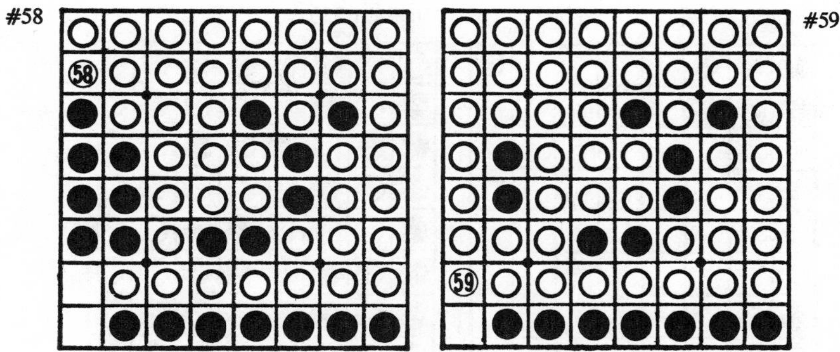

(White's win, 33 points)

Taken aback by this, Black thought for a long time and made the 49th move, a sound move. White's 50 in the **X** position was an exquisite move. It reversed the situation completely.

Black's 53 was a forced move, the only one he could make. Black's 56 was another forced move. After this Black could not make any move. White's 57, 58, and 59 finished off Black, whose formation in the middle stage looked so promising.

Diagram 227

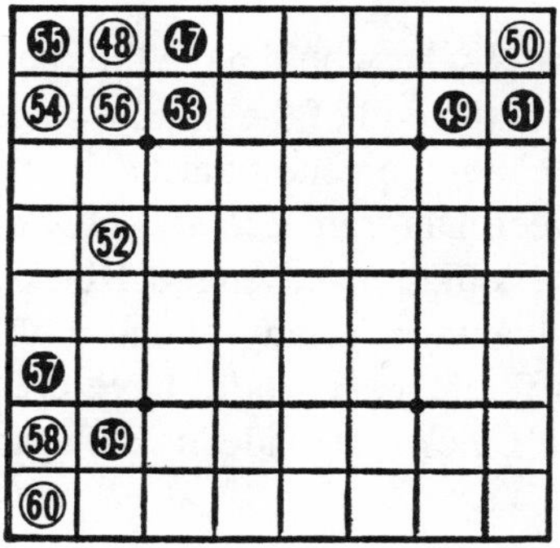

55	48	47					50
54	56	53				49	51
	52						
57							
58	59						
60							

Diagram 228

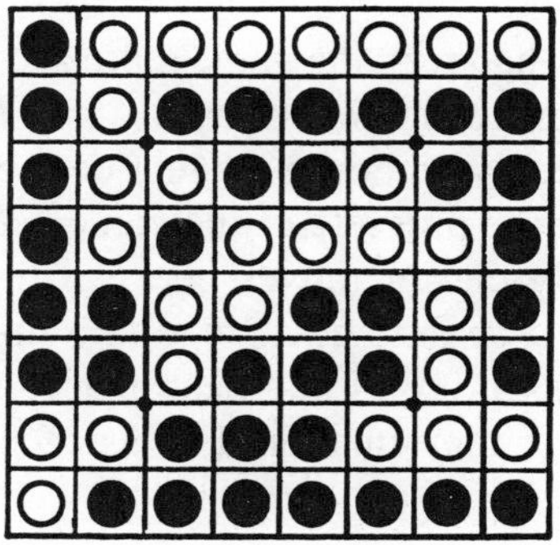

●	○	○	○	○	○	○	○
●	○	●	●	●	●	●	●
●	○	○	●	●	○	●	●
●	○	●	○	○	○	○	●
●	●	○	○	●	●	○	●
●	●	○	●	●	●	○	●
○	○	●	●	●	○	○	○
○	●	●	●	●	●	●	●

Diagram 229

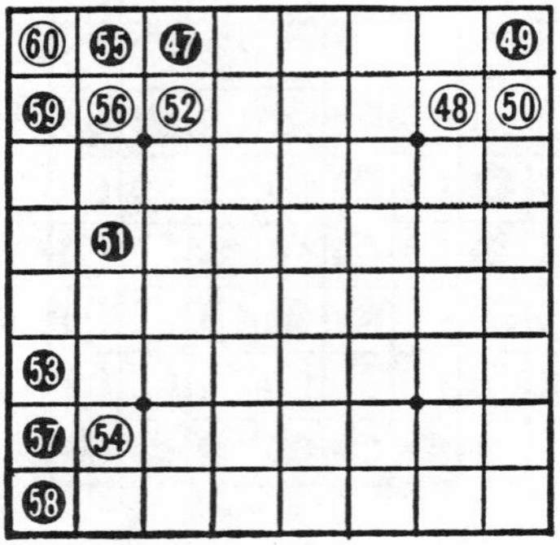

Diagram 230

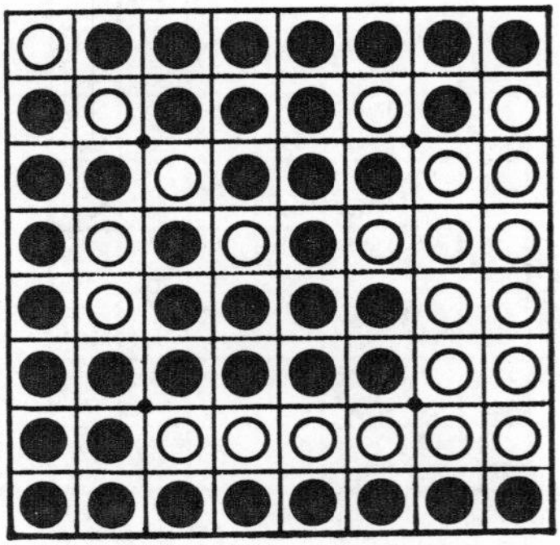

(Black's win, 23 points)

This ending is hard to imagine in Diagram 226. Let's go back to #46. How should Black have played the game? Diagrams 227 and 228 and Diagrams 229 and 230 represent two hypothetical games. In both games Black does well. Of course, these hypotheses are based on Black's viewpoint. If they had been real games, White would have had other ideas and played differently. In any case the best move for Black's 47 was the **A** position as shown in these diagrams. With his 47 in this position Black would be hard to beat.

If Black had read the game more accurately, he would have thought of this move. A move in Othello, particularly from the end of the middle stage to the final stage, can produce a great deal of change on the board.

Look at the progress of the game between Diagram 226 and play diagram #46. Only eleven moves between these situations changed Black's position from a definite advantage to a disadvantage. If any of the 37th, 43rd, 45th, or 46th moves had been placed differently, it would have created an entirely different situation. For instance, if Black had made his 37th move to a better position, he would have won a solid victory. Diagrams 231 and 232 show an example of alternative plays.

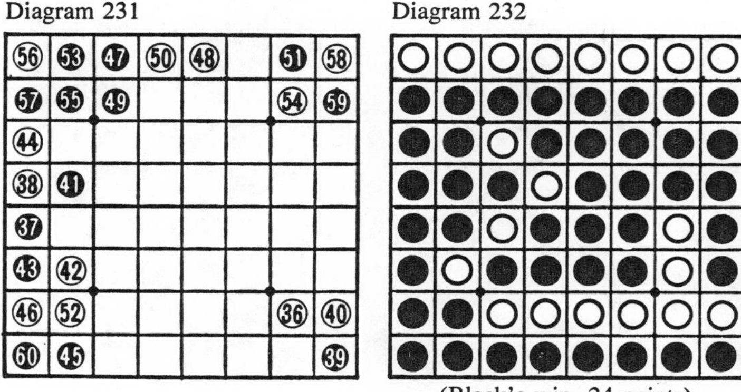

(Black's win, 24 points)

The Importance of the Final Stage

In summation, remember that the final stage is the time to use the greatest caution. Each move can have an enormous effect on the board, so don't move too quickly. Stop and think first, to see what effect each move will have.

Consider your alternatives, and consider where your opponent will move after you've made your play. Try to plan each move.

Watch out for the corners. Now, as in the opening stage, they're great—if *you* can get them. They can lose the game for you if your opponent gets them. So try to avoid placing your discs in **C** or **X** positions, which are stepping stones to controlling the corners. Remember, though, that the corners will fill up now. So take a good look at each empty one. What are *your* chances of getting that corner? Good? Then try to force your opponent to move to an **X** or **C** position, so that you can get the corner.

But if you don't think you can manage to win a corner position, try to minimize the damage if your opponent gets in by breaking up large, solid blocks of your discs. Take an **A** or **B** square if that would protect some of your discs. Then if your opponent finally gets the corner, he can flip only a small number of your discs.

Keep calm. Use your head. And if you lose a game, challenge your opponent to another. After all, by now you've learned a lot about his playing style. Next game you can use that knowledge to your advantage.

Happy playing!

APPENDIX A
SCORING

There are two ways to score Othello. The first way simply tells you who is the winner of a game and by how many points. The second way tells you who is the winner of a match, which consists of more than one game.

1. If you simply want to find out who won a game of Othello:
    a. count the number of white discs left on the board at the end of the game (for example, suppose White has 38 discs).
    b. count the number of black discs left on the board at the end of the game (suppose Black has 26 discs left).
    c. White is the winner because he has more discs, but by how many points?
    d. subtract the smaller number from the larger number:

        White—38 discs
        Black—26 discs
        White—12 points

    e. so White wins this game by 12 points.
2 Othello is often played as a two-game match between the same two players. The winner of the match is the person who has the greatest number of *points*, not discs. Remember to switch colors after each game. The player who is Black in the first game becomes White in the second game, and vice versa. To find the winner of a match:
    a. Find out who won each game and by how many points (use the procedure shown above).
    b. Subtract the smaller number of points from the larger number.
    c. The result tells you who won the match and by how many points.

Scoreboard for a Two-Game Match

The example below shows how to keep score for a two-game match.

Player	First Game	Second Game	Total Score
Jerry	Black: 44 discs	White: 54 discs	White: 44 points Black: 24 points White: 20 points
Warren	White: 20 discs	Black: 10 discs	
Winner's Points	Black: 24 points	White: 44 points	

This chart shows the score of a two-game match between Jerry and Warren. In their first game Jerry had Black, and at the end of that game he had 44 discs on the board. Warren, as White, was left with 20 discs. Obviously, Black won, but by how many points?

Black—44 discs
White—20 discs
Black—24-point win

Game 1

In the second game of their match the colors were reversed. Jerry played White and ended the game with 54 discs. Warren, playing Black, had only 10 discs.

White—54 discs
Black—10 discs
White—44-point win

Game 2

Each player won one game. But who won the match? Simply take the number of winning points each player had and subtract:

Winner of Game 2—White: 44 points
Winner of Game 1—Black: 24 points
Winner of Match—White: 20 points

APPENDIX B
HANDICAPPING

In Othello the stronger player usually gives an advantage to the weaker according to the differences in their skills. For instance, if A is stronger than B, then A is handicapped by a certain number of discs, which will be subtracted from his total and added to B's total at the end of the game.

The purpose of handicapping is to equalize the two players. When one player consistently beats another player by a certain point range (for example, Steve usually beats Bill by 20 to 25 points), the better player should be handicapped by that number of points.

Try out the handicap by playing a few games, to be sure it's correct. (For example, start out by giving Steve a 20-point handicap whenever he plays Bill.) If the game scores are now pretty even, and each player has an equal chance to win, the stronger player is correctly handicapped against that particular weaker player.

Remember to change handicaps or eliminate them when the players change. Steve is stronger than Bill, but about the same strength as Carol. And Ed is stronger than all of them. So Steve's handicap might look like this:

Player	Opponent	Amount of Handicap
Steve	Bill	-20 points
Steve	Carol	0
Steve	Ed	+30 points

Another method of handicapping is to give a corner position, as shown in Diagram 233.

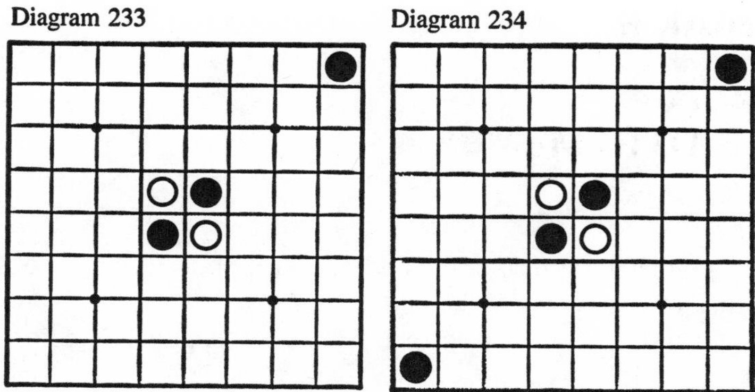

Diagrams 234, 235, and 236 show two-corner, three-corner, and four-corner handicaps, respectively. The corner position handicap can be combined with an advantage of points.

Handicapping is a way to make Othello more interesting and challenging for players of very different strengths. Experiment with handicapping variations to spice up your games.

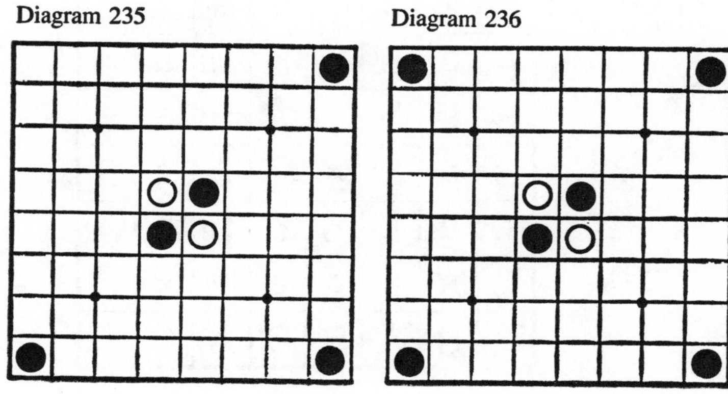

APPENDIX C
POINTS TO REMEMBER

Outflanking—placing a disc at the end of your opponent's row so that you have a disc of each color at the end of that row.

Flipping—turning the outflanked disc from your opponent's color to your color.

Forced move—the only legal move a player can make, when no alternative moves are possible.

Opening stage—the first to the 20th moves.

Middle stage—the 21st to the 40th moves.

Final stage—the 41st to the 60th moves.

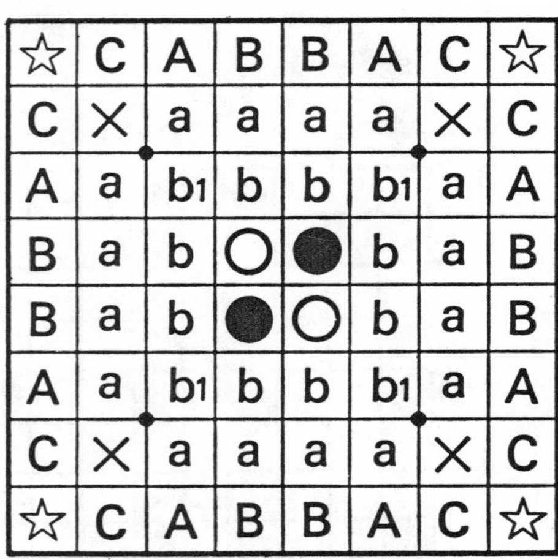

Basic Diagram